CABANOCEY — THE HISTORY, CUSTOMS AND
FOLKLORE OF ST. JAMES PARISH

# Cabanocey

THE HISTORY, CUSTOMS and FOLKLORE

OF ST. JAMES PARISH

by

LILLIAN C. BOURGEOIS

A FIREBIRD PRESS BOOK

PELICAN PUBLISHING COMPANY
Gretna 1998

Copyright © 1957
By Laura B. Bossier
All rights reserved
**ISBN: 1-56554-518-4**
LCN: 58-1769

First printing, February 1957
Second printing, January 1976
Third printing, March 1987

Manufactured in the United States of America

Published by Pelican Publishing Company, Inc.
1000 Burmaster Street, Gretna, Louisiana 70053

*DEDICATION*

*To them, who told the story best
With sorrowed mien or laughing jest,
My five old aunts, some still today
Relate the tales in wondrous way,
Clara, Clothilde, Louloute, Minime,
And Mat, who wove for me this theme.*

*PUBLISHER'S NOTE*

*The author, Miss Lillian C. Bourgeois, died just after she turned over the manuscript for this book to us for publication. We have, therefore, not had her help in reading proofs and making last-minute corrections and revisions. But Miss Bourgeois herself was careful and exact in her work and her manuscript was excellently typed. The numerous lists of names have been carefully checked, however, and it is believed that the number of errors in names and dates is practically nil.*

## PREFACE

I am not a writer, much less an historian, but through the years I have heard the fascinating tales of St. James Parish, the First Acadian Coast. Since no scribe, native or transient, has done us the honor of recording our story, I have dipped into the inkpot and I shall tell, as best I may, something of them who came before us! From Cabanocey on.

My deep gratitude to the following persons who have in some way contributed to this story:

For the use of authentic church and state records: Mr. Lawrence J. Babin, Clerk of Court, Parish of St. James; Rev. Constantin M. Chauve, S.M., Pastor of St. Michael's Church, Convent; Mr. V. L. Bedsole, Head of the Department of Archives, Louisiana State University, Baton Rouge; Mr. Henry A. Dugas, former Clerk of Court, Recorder, Parish of Ascension, Donaldsonville; Rev. B. P. Herrmann, O. M. I., St. Louis Cathedral Archives, New Orleans; Mr. George L. Sioussat, former Chief Division of Manuscripts, the Library of Congress, Washington, D.C.; Mrs. Viola Andersen Perotti and Miss Marguerite D. Renshaw, Reference Librarians, Howard-Tilton Memorial Library, New Orleans; Mr. Roger Rome, former Clerk of Court, Parish of St. James; Mr. José de la Peña, Director, Archives of the Indies, Seville, Spain.

My five aunts: Clara, Clothilde, Louloute, Minime, and Mat, all neé Bourgeois, for innumerable reminiscences; Mr. Louis S. Bourgeois for the story of Nita's Crevasse; Mr. Gaston Brignac for valuable help in the use of the court records; Mr. Charles Chauvin for an account of Le Pape Vert; Messrs. Joseph B. and Jules Dornier for general information; Mrs. Alphonse J. Gaudet for assistance in the use of French expressions; Miss Aline Cantrelle Himel for material on the Cantrelle and Roman families; Mr. George Huguet for the story of the story of the charivari; Mrs. Francis Parkinson Keyes for obtaining copies of records in Seville, Spain; Mr. Ludger Peytavin for the use of his father's unpublished memoirs; Messrs. Aristeé and Mark Poché for items concerning Périque tobacco; Mrs. Eugene Poché for the legend of Marie Lagraine; Mr. Marcel Part for the tale of Mr. Gentil's picture; Dr. William A. Read for interpreting old Acadian French and data on place names; the late Mr. Victor Reulet for the stories of Vacherie; Miss Jacinta Sobral for information on Oak Alley; Mr. Alvyn Woods for facts about the moss industry; Mr. Duralde Woods for data on the parish lands; and in fine to that large number of persons, whose names are too numerous to mention, for little details, specific help, and other miscellany.

An appreciative thank you is due to the librarians and archivists of many of the out-of-state libraries and depositaries, who have generously contributed their time and information to my research.

Last, but not least, I want to thank in an especial manner Miss Essae Martha Culver, Librarian of the Louisiana State Library, and Miss Lucille Mae Grace, Register, State Land Office, for their untiring effort in supplying me with books, pamphlets, records, maps, etc.

The incidents related in this story are the actual happenings of a people who left us the heritage of a glorious yesterday upon which we must build today for those who will come tomorrow.

## La Paroisse St. Jacques

La Paroisse[1] St. Jacques! It is just a little corner in southeast Louisiana barely twenty-five miles long — neglected by historian, forgotten by tourist, and overlooked by artist — but what a fabulous story lies behind its complacent serenity! It was the Kabahannossé[2] of the earliest settlers, le Comté[3] d'Acadie of the first Acadian exiles, the Gold Coast of the richest sugar barons, the educational center of yesterday, the romantic land of far-famed Périque tobacco.

It has known plagues and pleasures, floods and festivities, wars and wakes and weddings. It has entertained princes. It has sheltered paupers. It has welcomed expatriates. It is the land where le garde-soleil[4] de Madame Quarante-Poules and le carrosse[5] de Madame Roman — each played its part. Now - - - - - on with the story!

L. C. B.

### Footnotes

1. paroisse — parish or county.
2. Kabahannossé — the name of the first settlement of St. James, is a Choctaw Indian word meaning mallard's roost. Hakhoba—mallards — anosi — to sleep there — roost. The first settlers spelled it Cabahannocer. At present it is spelled Cabanocey.
3. le Comté d'Acadie — County of Acadia.
4. le garde-soleil — the sun bonnet.
5. le carrosse — the coach.

## TABLE OF CONTENTS

|      |                                           | Page |
|------|-------------------------------------------|------|
| Preface |                                        | VII  |
| I    | The First St. Jamesians: Indians          | 1    |
| II   | The Coming of the Cantrelles              | 6    |
| III  | The Acadians Arrive                       | 11   |
| IV   | St. Jacques de Cabahannocer               | 16   |
| V    | Land Grants                               | 18   |
| VI   | Swapped and Sold                          | 21   |
| VII  | St. James, Mother of Exiles               | 23   |
| VIII | The Great Plantations                     | 26   |
| IX   | Slavery in St. James                      | 38   |
| X    | St. Michel de Cantrelle                   | 41   |
| XI   | Through the Wars                          | 46   |
| XII  | Just People                               | 53   |
| XIII | Içi, On Parle le Français                 | 62   |
| XIV  | La Vacherie                               | 67   |
| XV   | Names: People and Places                  | 69   |
| XVI  | Education                                 | 78   |
| XVII | Government                                | 88   |
| XVIII| The River                                 | 95   |
| XIX  | Curious Customs                           | 99   |
| XX   | Strange Plants                            | 113  |
| XXI  | The Fourth Estate                         | 119  |
| XXII | Folklore                                  | 123  |
| XXIII| Cuisine for Connoisseurs                  | 129  |
| XXIV | Social Life in St. James                  | 139  |
| XXV  | Odd Bits from Here and There              | 145  |
| XXVI | In Conclusion                             | 159  |
| Appendix |                                       | 161  |
|      | Militia Company of 1766                   | 161  |
|      |     "        "       " 1770               | 180  |
|      | Census of 1766                            | 162  |
|      |    "    "  1769                           | 173  |
|      |    "    "  1777                           | 183  |
|      | Marriages, 1766-1768                      | 171  |
|      | First Grand Jury, 1805                    | 193  |
|      | List of Families in St. James, 1807       | 194  |
|      | Officers of Militia                       | 195  |
|      | Taxpayers of St. James                    | 194  |
|      | Plantation Owners, 1845-1856              | 197  |
|      | St. James Soldiers in Civil War           | 199  |
|      |   "     "       "        " Spanish-Am. War | 200 |
|      | Executive Officers of St. James Parish    | 200  |
|      | Judges of the District Court              | 202  |
|      | Pastors of St. Michel de Cantrelle        | 201  |
|      | Population Enumerations                   | 203  |
|      | Directory of Officers, 1957               | 204  |
| Bibliography |                                     | 205  |
| Index |                                          | 209  |

## ILLUSTRATIONS

| | |
|---|---|
| Uncle Sam Plantation | Frontispiece |
| Map of St. James Parish | Op. Page 1 |
| Map of Acadian and German Coasts, about 1790 | Page 10 |
| Map showing Cabonocey Plantation | Page 12 |

| | Opposite Page |
|---|---|
| Oak Alley | 20 |
| Avenue of Oaks at Oak Alley | 21 |
| Uncle Sam Plantation Scenes | 28 |
| White Hall, Home of the Bringiers | 29 |
| Nancy, Daughter of Dr. and Mrs. Potts at Tezcuco | 37 |
| Bocage Plantation House | 37 |
| Act of Sale, Ex-Slave Mimi Zelia to St. Michael's Church | 43 |
| Tezcuco Plantation House | 44 |
| Tezcuco House, Interior and Rear View | 45 |
| The Mississippi River near Brilliant Point | 52 |
| Land Grant to Nicholas Verret | 53 |
| Residence of Valcour Aime | 60 |
| Grounds and Garden of Valcour Aime | 60 |
| Portrait of Valcour Aime and his Wife | 61 |
| "Fort" in Valcour Aime's Garden | 61 |
| Site of Valcour Aime's Garden Today | 61 |
| Tomb of Valcour Aime | 61 |
| Colomb Park House | 76 |
| Armant Plantation House | 76 |
| St. Joseph Plantation House | 76 |
| Old Trepagnier House | 76 |
| Charles Chauvin of Union Plantation | 77 |
| Pape Vert | 77 |
| Welham Plantation House, Today | 77 |

| | |
|---|---|
| Rapidan Plantation House | 77 |
| St. Michael's Church Today | 84 |
| St. Michel de Cantrelle and Interior | 85 |
| St. James Church | 92 |
| St. Michael's Church Sanctuary | 92 |
| St. Michael's Church Grotto | 93 |
| St. Mary's Chapel at Union | 93 |
| First Well Dug for the Ladies of the Sacred Heart — Father Robert Morin, S.M. with his Pitcher at the Well | 108 |
| St. Joseph's School for Colored Children | 108 |
| Flags Flown Over St. James Parish | 109 |
| Marriage Records, St. Michael's Church | 116 |
| Succession of Pierre Hebert, First Page of, 1782 | 116 |
| Pew Rentals and First Page of Burial Record, St. Michael's Church | 117 |
| Lieut.-Gov. Lambremont and his Family | 124 |
| Swamp Scene drawn by the Author | 124 |
| Tante Tinia | 124 |
| Old Slave Cabin | 124 |
| Nita Crevasse | 125 |
| Court House of St. James Parish | 125 |
| Old Acadian House | 140 |
| Trees with Moss | 140 |
| Ruins of an Old Acadian House | 141 |
| Field of Perique Tobacco | 141 |
| Sacred Heart Convent | 148 |
| Jefferson College Scenes | 149 |
| Sugar Harvest in 1875 | 180 |
| Christmas Bonfire | 180 |
| Acadians Coming from Church | 180 |
| Signatures of some of the Prominent Men of St. James | 181 |

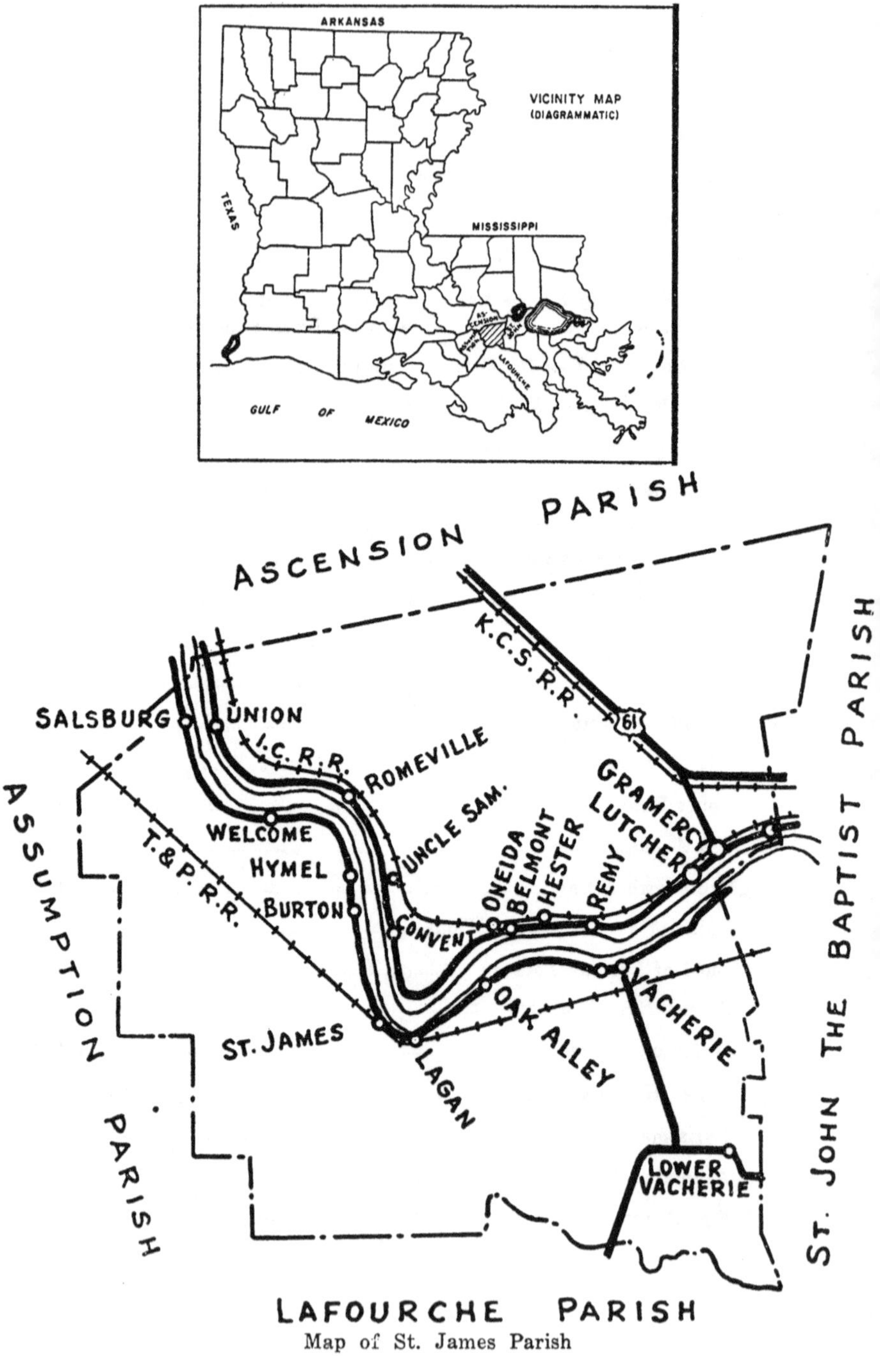

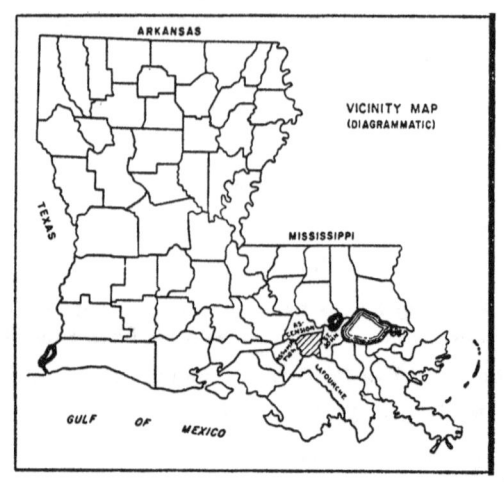

Map of St. James Parish

I

## THE FIRST ST. JAMESIANS: THE INDIANS

It is rather difficult to establish the exact location of the Indians who lived originally in St. James Parish as various tribes lived here at various times. Indians were a wandering people. Floods, wars, game, pestilence, and their white enemy made frequent changes in their abode necessary. But since the Houma and the Chitimacha lived in Ascension, the Mugulasha in St. Charles, the Bayogoula in Iberville, the Washa in Assumption, and the Acolapissa in St. John, it is to be assumed that parts of these tribes were frequently in St. James, which was the center of all these Indian lands. All these tribes were part of the Muskhogean group, except the Chitimacha, and they were often at war with each other. Yet by strange quirk of fate, the Houma, the Bayogoula, and the Acolapissa eventually merged into one group. Wars and the white man's civilization proved to be their undoing and they fused for protection and survival.

When the first white settlers came to St. James, there were few resident Indians left. In the French census of September 1769[1] the following tribes, mostly migrants were listed on the Acadian Coast: The Taensa, the Chitimacha, the Pakana, the Alibamu, and the Houma. Old records show that for short periods several groups of Indians lived in upper St. James during the late 1700's. These were part of small tribes who moved to Louisiana about 1764 because of the cession of Mobile to England. Among them, the Alibamu, crossed to the right bank of the river about 1775 and later left the parish.

According to *D'Abbadie's Journal* an entry, dated April 6, 1764, states that eighty Pacana and Tunica Indians arrived in New Orleans from Mobile and asked for lands. He did not know where to place them so he sent them to camp with the Acolapissa above New Orleans until autumn. However, on the fifteenth the Tunica and the Pacana departed in two boats and established themselves on the west bank of the river near Bayou Lafourche. The Tunica were gentle but the Pacana caused much trouble and embarrassment by their drunkeness. In 1770 the Pacana were still in St. James but on the east bank of the river just below the Houma.

The largest group of Indians found here when the parish was settled by white men was a tribe of the Houma in the vicinity of the St. James-Ascension boundary. It is said that old Jacques Cantrelle[2] and *le gros mico des Oumas*[3] visited each other in most friendly fashion. And since the Houma are so often mentioned in the early history of this parish, I shall tell their story.[4]

The Houma once lived in West Feliciana Parish near the shores of the Mississippi River. The Tunica moved in with the Houma about 1706 and massacred many of them. The remaining Houma fled and for a short time found refuge near Bayou St. John in what is now part of City Park in New Orleans. In 1709 the Houma moved to Ascension-St. James. The main body of the tribe lived in a large village over one mile from the river near the present site of Burnside in Ascension, but there were smaller villages scattered in that area and well within St. James.

Houma is a Choctaw word which means red and surely this color played its part in their lives. They painted their bodies red — their war emblem was a red crawfish — and it was their red pole marking the boundary of their hunting grounds which provoked the French into giving Baton Rouge its name. Perhaps a few characteristics and practices of the Houma people would be in order.

Their reed-palmetto cabins were arranged in double rows encircling a large open space where their ceremonies and games were held. At night this area was illuminated by a torch of long canes planted in the center. In their ceremonial dances the girls wore breech cloths and their bodies were brightly painted. Their hair was plaited and adorned with feathers. To keep time they rattled little dried gourds or waved feather fans. When an Indian was ill, at least two medicine men attended. One chanted while the other beat a drum which was made of an alligator skin tightly drawn over the end of a hollow log. When given a present a Houma would extend his arms and cry, "Hou! Hou! Hou!" These Indians cultivated tobacco, corn, squash, melons, beans, and pumpkins. Although they raised many chickens, they never used them for food. The chickens had been obtained originally from a shipwreck at the mouth of the Mississippi River. The Houma looked upon them as objects of superstition and curiosity and allowed them to stay in their huts.

Many of the Houma tattooed their faces, blackened their teeth, and painted their bodies. This gave them a hideous and ferocious appearance. In winter the women wore fringed skirts and muskrat robes. On very cold mornings, when there was frost or ice, the Houma would bathe in the river and from this strange practice, many became ill and died.

In 1776 the Houma sold part of their land to Maurice Conway, O'Reilly's Irish nephew, and Alexander Latil and subsequently left, some going to Manchac, but the greater number drifting into Terrebonne Parish where their descendants still live. As late as 1784 there were twenty-five warriors under the chief, Natchiabe, still living at little Houma in Ascension Parish. At College Point and other places in the parish there are some Negroes who claim to be part Indian and certainly their features give tacit approval to this claim.

Some Indians, who are said to have lived near Gramercy, are credited with having taught Périque[5] how to cultivate the famous tobacco which now bears his name. There was an Indian village on the Mt. Airy Plantation near Gramercy and legend tells us that they were Choctaws. However, since the Acolapissa were closely related to the Choctaw in language and culture and were a Choctaw-like people and since the Acolapissa had a very large village in neighboring St. John, it is probable that the so-called Choctaws of Mt. Airy were Acolapissa. As a matter of fact the Acolapissa had a small village near the river in the Mt. Airy-Gramercy area as early as 1722.

There is an Indian mound at Belmont. At one time there were three, but two have disappeared through erosion. This mound does not prove that Belmont was the home of the Acolapissa of 1722. As a matter of fact many mounds antedate the discovery of America and the Belmont mound only serves to show that Indians inhabited that section at one time or another. Then too, mounds were not always used for burial purposes as is commonly believed. Instead some were used for signaling, others as bases for temples, or places where sacrifical ceremonies were held. And in this low section mounds were necessary refuge during floods. Nothing is known of the existing mound at Belmont but many spooky stories are woven around it. Some people claim that on dark nights *feu-follets*[6] are seen. Others say that the mound contains a cache of pirate treasure. Still others relate in round-eyed fashion that ghosts prowl there. Perhaps the *feu-follets* are chasing the ghosts who are after the treasure. Who knows?

It is quite possible, too, that Périque tobacco, before mentioned as being of Choctaw or Acolapissa origin, could have been a product of the Houma. The early French explorers described the use of tobacco in the Houma ceremonials, one of which was the throwing of tobacco on a large cross. In 1700, Father Paul du Ru, Jesuit, erected a forty foot cross and a chapel in the Houma village of West Feliciana Parish. Thus some of the Houma were Christianized before their migration into St. James. One of the first Houma baptized was an Indian infant who was named Francis Xavier as was the Houma Chapel.

Another Indian relic found in the parish is a shell mound near the present town of Vacherie. It has become known as Shell Hill as has the plantation there. Originally this mound was approximately thirty feet high and five hundred feet wide at the base. The old residents relate that the mound was built by the Indians who came after the white settlers, and so it is possible that the mound was built by the Pakana or Alibamu. The shells of this mound are being used in road building and in scooping up the shells, the digger frequently finds an Indian skeleton in flexed position. This proves that the mound was not built by the Houma or the Acolapissa as this was not their burial custom. They put their dead on posts.

But no doubt the most curious imprint left on the people of St. James by their Indian predecessors is the use of an Indian stone in the treatment of poisonous snake and insect bites, as well that of mad dogs. It is usually called the mad stone of Vacherie, because it has been in the possession of a Vacherie family for many generations.

This small brownish stone, which is smooth and flat, was formerly about three inches in diameter. It is now worn and broken into two small pieces, each the size of a small coin. An old Indian gave it to an early German settler named Webre.[7] Where the Indian obtained it is another matter, but legend tells us that it originally came from the entrails of a deer. It has been handed down from generation to generation and today it is in the possession of the Gravois family of Vacherie.

But the strange part of this story is that for years on end this stone has been applied to venomous wounds to draw out the poison. When placed upon a wound, the stone sticks and draws the poison out. When saturated it drops off. Then it is washed and readjusted. This procedure continues until the stone no longer clings because all the poison has been extracted. I have never seen this magic stone at work and, frankly, I am quite skeptical, but I do know that every year many people go to Vacherie to have the stone applied and, strangely, do not succumb to snake bite. And since St. James has many species of snakes, four of which are poisonous, the Vacherie stone is in frequent use and there are many who still attest to its enchanted power.

And so from magic stone and mysterious mound to peculiar Périque tobacco, the Indians have left the imprint of their passing on the history of St. James.

### FOOTNOTES

1. Papeles de Cuba, 187 A, Archive General de Indias.
2. Jacques Cantrelle — first French commander of St. James.
3. *Le gros mico des Oumas* — the big chief of the Houma.
4. Facts about the Houma taken from: Swanton, John Reed. *Indian Tribes of the Lower Mississippi Valley and Adjacent Coast.*
5. Périque — One of the earliest settlers whose real name was Pierre Chenet.
6. *Feu follets* — will-o'-the-wisp.
7. Webre — the first Webre who came to Louisiana was Johann Webre of Fort Kehl, Baden. He and his wife, Marie Stadler, were listed in the Louisiana census of 1724. The Webre of this story is no doubt his descendant.

## II

## THE COMING OF THE CANTRELLES

Perhaps if we look back into the era of the founding of St. James Parish, we shall understand better the problems which faced our rugged forbears and we shall appreciate more fully their way of life.

At that time there were but a few thousand persons in and around New Orleans. The sole communication between the city and the river posts was by slow pirogue or canoe. Roads were but dangerous paths through the forests and floods were a common occurrence. Distance was measured by league, money was counted by livre,[1] and land was obtained by grant. Men were minors until twenty-five, yet women were married at fourteen. Alimony was paid in barrels of corn and cords of wood. Indigo, tobacco, and corn were the main products of the Louisiana plantation and the sugar industry was yet unborn.

Although there were settlements in St. John, Ascension, and Pointe Coupeé Parishes, St. James long remained a wilderness untamed. The first attempt to settle this parish was made by the French Duke de Chârost and his son, the Marquis d'Anceny. They obtained a land grant in the Gramercy-Mt. Airy area from the French government and sent large supplies and one hundred persons under the management of Sieur de L'Epinet to establish the settlement in 1720. Seven ships bringing over four thousand colonists arrived in Louisiana in the early part of 1720 and the people of the Chârost-d'Anceny concession were part of that group. However, in March 1722 all the supplies of this concession were stroyed by fire and d'Anceny ordered de L'Epinet to abandon the concession. Thus the attempt to settle St. James by grant to a French nobleman failed.

Some reference is made here and there to the presence of white settlers among the Houma, but little information is available. In the records of the Superior Council of Louisiana dated August 5, 1747, mention is made of Sieur Joseph Blanpin, "settler at the Houma." Since Blanpin was a trader and had a domicile in New Orleans at that time, it is quite possible that he was frequently at the Houma village for purposes of trade but that he was not a permanent settler of Ascension or St. James.

However, according to the American State Papers, Vol. 2, p. 230, one Matthias Frederick inhabited and cultivated a tract of land facing the Mississippi River just below the Vacherie Road in 1756 when an order of survey was given by the French Government. In the earlier official census of 1724 Matthias Frederick was listed as "a good worker, a Catholic, age 29, with wife, one child, an orphan girl, and living on the German Coast." No doubt this was the same Matthias Frederick who had moved from the German Coast into St. James Parish between 1724 and 1756. This proves that there were scattered settlers within the parish before the coming of the Cantrelles.

But it was understandable why St. James was settled later than other river sections. As before mentioned the parish was the center of warlike Indian tribes. In fact Indian raids on some river settlements and lone settlers continued as late as 1748. The land, too, was low and flooded often. But surmounting many of these difficulties, Cantrelle, the adventurer, blazed the trial and came to St. James. And since he was one of the earliest settlers and certainly the first accredited ruler, I shall tell the story of his life. It was a full life . . . that of a pioneer, a builder, and a dreamer . . . a strange life in a strange new world.

In 1720 Jacques Cantrelle came to Louisiana from France on the little braque, *Le Profond*, on a voyage which took three months and seven days. He was a member of the personnel of the Natchez concession. In 1729 almost the entire Natchez colony was wiped out in the Indian massacre and how Jacques Cantrelle escaped is indeed a hair-raising story.

Cantrelle quickly realized that the Indians were attacking. He immediately closed his house, and with his wife hid in his corn-house, scarcely daring to breathe. But fate had set its seal and, miraculously, the Indians did not search there. Mr. and Mrs. Cantrelle remained hidden until darkness set in. Then they gathered together a few light possessions and fled through the woods. But Cantrelle had forgotten some article which he wanted most to save, so he sent his wife on to a designated place to wait for him, while he retraced his steps to his home. Then clutching his valuables he fairly flew to his tryst — but his heart stood still — his wife was not there. He searched everywhere but not finding her, finally came to the river. There was a pirogue and he escaped! Lucky Cantrelle! Of the entire Natchez colony only twenty men survived and he was one of them — but his wife was killed.

He immediately went to New Orleans to obtain help from the Superior Council in the form of a loan — a strange loan: "thirty barrels of rice in straw and a cow." With this and four of his slaves, whom he later recovered, he established himself on land near New Orleans, at Kenner, and began anew to build for the future. And then on April 16, 1730, he took unto himself a second wife: Marguerite Larmusiau LeChoux, a widow, whose first husband, "a Yazoo store keeper and interpreter," had perished in the Natchez massacre also.

The Cantrelle family and fortune grew and in the census of 1731 we learn that Cantrelle had an "habitation sur le long du fleuve,"[2] a wife, a step-daughter, two children, one workman, four slaves, two horses, and "deux hommes d'armes"[3] — no doubt, the latter a protection against the Indians.

In 1735, Cantrelle purchased a lot in New Orleans and not long after, he moved to the city where he became an employee of the Superior Council. In the quaint French city — la Nouvelle Orleans — he took his place as a useful and sociable member of the community. There was seldom a baptism, a wedding, or a funeral — a succession or a sale — a trial or a ball — but that Jacques Cantrelle was there as guest, witness, or official. He gave away brides, christened babies, wrote for the unlettered, witnessed sales, executed wills, appraised crops, sold slaves, loaned money, signed documents, and had a hand in the affairs of church and state.

Early one hot July evening in 1763 as Jacques sat on his porch, he heard loud cries and saw people running into his back yard. Investigating, he learned that a man had just been murdered there, his death caused by a deep sword thrust. Whether this influenced Cantrelle in his decision to leave New Orleans we shall never know, but he moved again: this time to St. James Parish.

Cantrelle and his son-in-law, Nicholas Verret, owned plantations in St. James where slaves were stationed to work prior to 1763, but Cantrelle did not move here until some time between October 7, 1764 and April 4, 1765. His family is not listed in the census of 1766, so apparently, they came later. He settled on land granted to him by French authorities and named his new domicile *Cabahannocer*, the name of a stream in near-by Lafourche Parish. As before mentioned, this is a Choctaw Indian word meaning "mallard's roost," or "duck's hut." No doubt this is why we find the picture of a wild duck hanging across a background of marsh grass on the Cantrelle seal.

St. James was such a forest primeval that Jacques mistakenly built his house on land that had been granted to his son, instead of his own. This is why the Cabahannocer home was near the present site of the St. James Railway station, while the church, for which Jacques Cantrelle had donated part of his own grant, was about two miles above. The error was discovered in time, but Jacques continued to live at the Cabahannocer homestead. At his widow's death, the land reverted to the true owner, his son, Michel Cantrelle.

At Cabahannocer Jacques Cantrelle developed an indigo plantation and prospered. He became commander of the new post under French rule. He made friends of the Indians, welcomed the Acadians, placed new settlers, received the first Spanish officials, originated a landed dynasty, built a church, and ruled the post. And finally he was laid to rest beneath the altar of the little frame church that stood on his own hallowed soil.

At long last the wanderer rested — far from his native Picardie — but under the moss-draped trees of his adopted home. Here he had planted a bit of France that was to retain its mother culture for nearly two hundred years. Here he had founded a little parish, which was finally named after the church of the saint for whom he had been named: St. Jacques!

FOOTNOTES

1. *Livre* — piece of French money in use in Louisiana.
2. *Habitation sur le long du fleuve* — plantation along the river.
3. *Deux hommes d'armes* — two guards or two armed men.

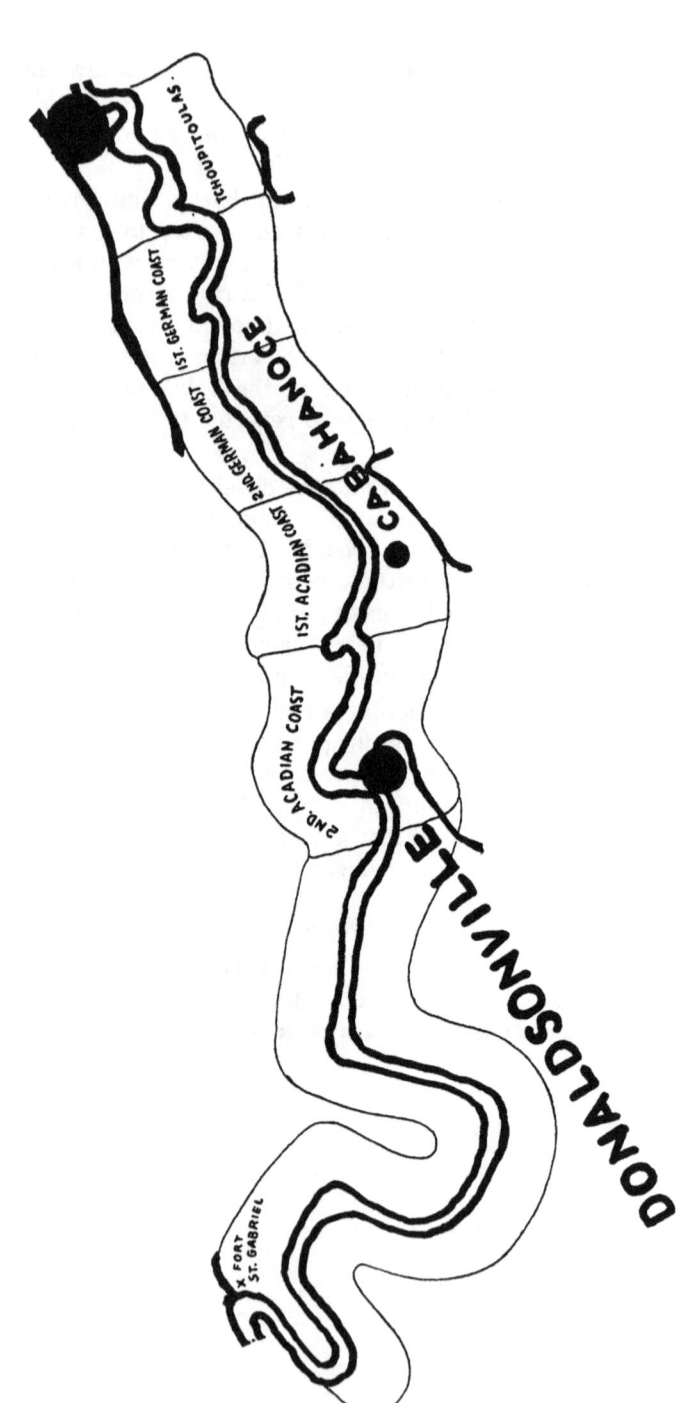

Map of Acadian and German Coasts about 1790. Drawing by Stuart O. Landry (his property).

## III

## THE ACADIANS ARRIVE

Although St. James was founded late in comparison to other river settlements, it grew fast and made up for its laggard start by its quick expansion. This was due in part to the coming of the Acadians in large numbers within a very short time.

The story of the Acadians has been told with many variations by as many people. Actually no one has proved who were the first Acadians to reach Louisiana, where they settled, and whence they came. Some persons claim that the first Acadians who came to St. James comprised a party of twenty who arrived at Cabahannocer in 1755. This can not possibly be true. Cabahannocer had not yet been founded. Then too the distance to be traveled, the rigors of winter, and the poor transportation then available would make the arrival of any deported Acadians before 1756 impossible. Louisiana maps of that time show no settlement in St. James. In Governor Kerlerec's report entitled: "Rapport du chevalier de Kerlerec, gouverneur de la Louisiana Française, sur les peuplades du Mississippi et du Missouri," dated 1758, no mention is made of Cabahannocer. A rough translation of part of that report follows:

"The Houma (Indians) were heretofore very numerous, but like the Tunica, their number has been reduced greatly by the quantity of liquor traded to them. This nation can still furnish about sixty men bearing arms. They are lazy and debased by liquor, but as they are but twenty-two leagues from New Orleans . . . . . they serve as an advance post and barrier against the excursions that our enemies would and could make on our establishments. As a consequence we show them much regard. From time to time they trouble us with some rascality, but they are easy to subdue when we demand satisfaction."

However there is the Mouton legend that the first Acadians to reach Louisiana were the Salvador Moutons and that they settled in St. James Parish in 1756. Now in 1756 St. James was a wilderness and any Acadians who arrived here had, of necessity, to settle near some other settler in order to survive. One of the first, if not the first, settler in St. James was Matthias Frederick who was here as early, or earlier than, 1756. His habitation was near Vacherie about six miles from Cabahannocer. Early records show that the Moutons settled near Matthias Frederick in the environs of Vacherie. Had the Moutons come with the later Acadians in 1765 it is probable that they would have settled nearer Cabahannocer. They are not listed in the census of Cabahannocer of 1766. Yet they were residents of St. James; they are listed in the militia of that year: Salvador, Jean, and Louis Mouton. This suggests that the Moutons may have arrived here before the other Acadians and settled near Matthias Frederick because Cabahannocer had not yet been founded. The Mouton legend could be true.

Certainly some Acadians came here early in 1765. These were part of a group, all of whom are erroneously believed to have settled near Opelousas and St. Martinville. While some of this number were sent to that section, many of them settled in St. James and Ascension Parishes which became known as the Acadian Coast. In a list of thirty-two Acadians furnished by Maxent, "Recapitulation des reçus fournis aux Acadiens refugies

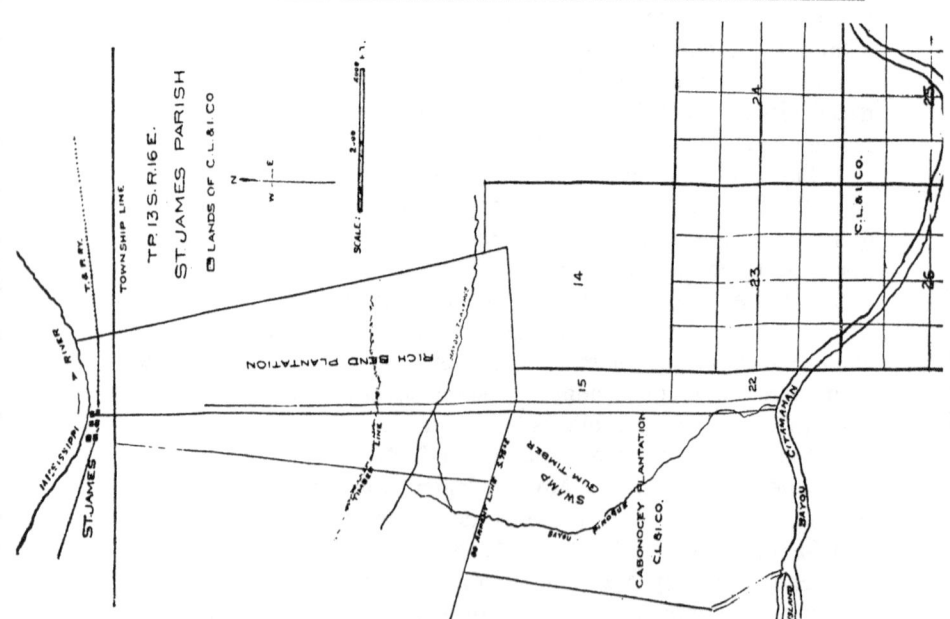

*Map showing location of Cabonocey Plantation — what is left of the original grant to Jacques Cantrelle.*

à la Louisiane..... 1765,"[1] one finds the names of thirteen Acadians who settled in the St. James-Ascension area. They were: Jean Baptiste Bergeron, Jean Saunier, Simon LeBlanc, Joseph Bourgeois, Joseph Guillebeau, Michel Poirier, Abraham Roy, Jean, Pierre, and Joseph Arcenaux, Joseph Guedry, Jean Baptiste Cormier, and Ambroise Martin. The first nine were listed as inhabitants and land owners in the census of 1766. Saunier and Cormier were members of the Militia of 1766. Joseph Arcenaux was listed in the census of 1769. All of them were members of the militia of 1770. Poirier, Guillebeau, LeBlanc, Guedry, and Roy were married at Cabahannocer between 1766 and 1768. Martin, Bourgeois, and leBlanc were wardens of the first church at Cabahannocer in 1770.

The eight Acadian chiefs who signed contracts to raise cattle on a share basis with Antoine Bernard Dauterive are believed also to have settled in the Attakapas region. However, three of these men actually settled here. They were Joseph Guillebeau, Pierre Arcenaux, and Jean Dugas. This contract was signed in New Orleans on April 4, 1765. These men must have arrived here shortly thereafter. Data on Guillebeau and Arcenaux are given above. Dugas is listed in Verrett's Co. of 1766.

According to an item in the St. James Parish Courthouse Archives dated November 9, 1787: Pierre Arcenaux, inhabitant of the parish, left with his family to form his residence at "le Poste des Atacapar ou il a une vacherie considerable" (Post of the Atakapas where he has a large ranch). He left François Croizet in charge of his affairs here. Since he was a member of the Cabahannocer Militia of 1770 and since he and his family still resided here in 1787, he lived here seventeen years before moving to the Atakapas.

Captain Charles Philippe Aubry, acting governor of Louisiana, in a letter dated February 25, 1765 says:[2] "Two hundred Acadian men, women, and children repelled by the climate of Santo Domingo have just disembarked here and will actually die of want if they do not receive succor .... they have been wandering for ten years .... I am going to try to place them on the right bank of the river and as near as possible to the town (New Orleans). One cannot help giving them arms, munitions, tools, and provisions."

Captain Harry Gordon in his Journal, Notes on the Country along the Mississippi from Kaskaskia to New Orleans on October 14, 1766 wrote: "The colony of New Orleans is inhabited twenty leagues above the town on each side of the river..... The upper settlers are just planted, consisting of poor Acadians for the most part..... There are also about 150 Houma and like number of Alibamu .... the last having lately settled here .... withdrawing from the Alibama River when the English took possession of West Florida." This is one of the earliest descriptions of the Acadian Coast given.

Other Acadians to reach St. James of whom there is a definite record were a group of two hundred sixteen, who came directly from Halifax, Nova Scotia and reached New Orleans on November 16, 1766. They were given cattle, tools, and provisions and were located along the banks of the Mississippi River in St. James and Ascension. Others came in quick succession. There were only two small Acadian villages here in 1767, but ten years later the population of the Acadian Coast was nearly a thousand.

There is no doubt that Acadians came to St. James shortly after its founding. On the rosters of the Militia of 1770 are 104 names. All were Acadians except ten. Many of them settled on the west bank of the river between Louis Judice's land grant and Donaldsonville. Judice's grant was just above the Cabahannocer church and was quite extensive. Since much of the land below the church was part of the Cantrelle and Verret grants, there were fewer Acadians there. Early maps show that on the east bank many Acadians settled in the College Point section. However, the Acadian settlers were not confined to one section of the parish. In 1770 the first Acadian Coast (St. James) extended from Sieur Dupart's store and ranch up to Germain Bergeron's property on the east bank and from Sieur Piroteau to Sieur Ducroix on the west bank. This was approximately sixteen miles on each side of the river with the center of the first Acadian Coast at Nicholas Verret's grant (near the present St. James railway station) on the west bank and at Joseph Martin's place (opposite Verret's) on the east bank. This did not include the Acadians of the Second Acadian Coast — now Ascension Parish.

We shall never know how many Acadians came to St. James as they came from various directions. Some came down the Mississippi River via its eastern tributaries. Others came from the West Indies where they had lived for several years before coming to Louisiana. Large numbers of Acadians began arriving in 1765 and the migration continued for twenty years. In checking the early church records of the parish one finds the names of Acadians who were born in Cuba, Maryland, Pennsylvania, and New England, proving that these families had lived in those sections before migrating to St. James.

Among the interesting Acadians who came here was Germain Bergeron. He was affianced to an Acadian girl in Nova Scotia. They were separated during the expulsion and were united and married in St. James.³ They settled on a tract on the upper right bank of the river near Donaldsonville. There are many descendants of the Bergerons in this parish today, but they are not all Acadian, as there was a Bergeron in New Orleans as early as 1726. Many of the French settlers of New Orleans — Cantrelle, Verret, Laprade, etc. — came to St. James just before, or shortly after, the arrival of the Acadians.

The Acadians were an agricultural people and have continued as farmers to this day. Many raised cattle here as they had in Nova Scotia. In older records the allusion is frequently made to "la vacherie de Sieur Tel-et-Tel."⁴ A vacherie was a cow house or ranch.

The Acadians were happy and grateful to find solace and peace at last. Here this wandering legion could look forward to security and contentment, not backward to desolation and want. They were tired of roaming. They established a foothold, took root, and stayed. After nearly 200 years, one finds many of their descendants on the same farms that had been the first refuge of their exiled forbears. No wonder even the ex-St. Jamesians are deeply attached to the old homesteads and one often hears: "Quand j'vais allé coté tantôt, rameme moi à la paroisse St. Jacques."⁵

FOOTNOTES

1. Paris Archives, Nat. Colonies, C 13 A, 45:29.
2. Paris Archives, Nat. Colonies, C 13 A, 45:41.
3. See appendix for list of Acadians who married at Cabahannocer.
4. La Vacherie de Sieur Tel-et-Tel — Ranch of Mr. So-and-So.
5. Quand j'vaid allé coté tantôt, ramene moi à la paroisse St. Jacques — When I die, bring me back to St. James Parish.

See the appendix for detailed information on the Acadians.

## IV

## ST. JACQUE DE CABAHANNOCER

There have been so many contradictory stories about the founding of the first church of St. James that it is a bit puzzling to sift the truth from fact, tradition and fiction. The first settlers were French and Catholic. One of their first concerns in establishing a settlement was the building of a church, to which, believe it or not, the parishoners were bound to contribute by law.

Jacques Cantrelle, owner of Cabahonnocer, gave part of his original land grant for a church site. The records of the state land office show that this land has always been used as a glebe, but strange to say, there is no written legal record of the title to the land claimed.

According to a report to O'Reilly in 1770 a priest was needed at Cabahannocer. Supposedly this post had had a chapel served by a priest from the German Coast before that time, but there is no written proof to substantiate such an assertion. It is much more probable that the priest from the German Coast came here occasionally to perform such rites as were necessary.

Mr. Roger Baudier in his book, "The Catholic Church of Louisiana", on p. 182 says: "In 1770 St. James was organized into a regular independent parish and Father Valentine . . . was appointed first pastor" . . . And on page 192 we find: "The first baptism at St. James was by Father Valentin and was that of Alexandre LeBlanc on June 2, 1770. . . . He also performed the first marriage in the newly established parish, which was that of François Chenette and Marguerite Pankème on December 27, 1770."

An interesting legal side-light in the building of the St. James Church is gathered from the Spanish Judicial Records.[1] It is the story of a carpenter named Étienne Broiard, called St. Quentin, who was engaged in working on the church in 1771. Broiard's home was in New Orleans, or its vicinity, and he owed a sum of money to Dr. Joseph Montégut, who sued Broiard. Broiard had no property, so his wages were garnisheed and he not only had to pay the debt, but he had to bear the expense of a courier sent by boat all the way from New Orleans to Cabahannocer to seize his wages. This was something like adding insult to injury and one can not help but wonder what Broiard thought of it all, as perched on the little church roof in the bright April sun, he nailed together the boards of St. Jacques de Cabahannocer. It certainly shows that legal tangles and human nature were much the same then, as now. And the debt he owed was less than twenty dollars.

René de Senégy de la Peichardierè in his quaint little book of early St. James, "Une Paroisse Louisianaise", tells us that Jacques Cantrelle, Bonaventure Gaudin, Simon LeBlanc, Ambroise Martin, A. Schexnaydre, and Joseph Hubert, called Laprade, were the first wardens. François Landry gave to the church a golden chalice, a censer, a ciborium, and a pair of candle sticks. Joseph Bourgeois donated seven pews, a holy water fount, a dais, and he built a fence around the cemetery. The most important event in the early history of the church was the visit of Bishop Cirillo in 1785. But surely a bit of humor was injected in the annals of St. Jacques in 1792, when Rev. Patrick Mansan, an Irishman, became the pastor in a French community under Spanish domination. That was, indeed, St. James' first league of nations.

In 1840 a second church, whose peculiar Romanesque architecture became a matter of much conjecture, was built and this, in turn, was followed by the present church erected in 1930. Time, the growth of the congregation, and the ever-present encroachment of the river made necessary changes.

But since that early day, before old Jacques Cantrelle was laid to rest beneath the altar of the first church, the Cantrelles have worshipped in the churches built on the land of their ancestors. And until a fairly recent date — the same pews — number one on the left and number four on the right — had always been reserved for the Cantrelle family. Today we find Miss Aline Cantrelle Himel and Mrs. Eugenie Cantrelle Himel Henry members of the congregation. St. Jacques de Cabahannocer has really been the "Cantrelle Church" as it was so often called by the old river pilots.

FOOTNOTES

1. Louisiana Historical Quarterly, Vol. 8, # 2, pp. 322-323.

## V

## LAND GRANTS

Since there was so much land for so few people in the early history of Louisiana, one wonders why so much bother was entailed in procuring legally a tract in this hostile wilderness upon which to build a home and wrestle for an existence. But red tape, money madness, and politics were a part of that era, too, and land was not to be had just for the asking. There were set rules to follow.

St. James was settled just before the advent of Spanish domination, so that land grants in this parish were in the main Spanish patents, although most of them were written in French. After O'Reilly came to Louisiana, he had new regulations as to land grants promulgated. I shall give a few of the requirements to be met in acquiring a tract of land in 1770.

Grants on the lower Mississippi were not to exceed eight arpents[1] fronting the river by the usual depth of forty arpents. It is from this that we, in south Louisiana, speak of "les quarantes,"[2] signifying the customary depth of lands along the river. The land applied for had to be surveyed, approved by the local commandante, and certified by two neighboring witnesses. Only the governor, in the name of the king, could issue a grant and before he did so, the applicant had to build a levee to prevent floods, dig ditches to insure drainage, and lay out and maintain a public road along the river.[3] Within three years, he had to clear and put under cultivation a reasonable part of the concession and during this time he had no right to dispose of any of his holdings. The King reserved certain privileges, such as the use of cypress, and the settler paid various fees. And at long last he received a title to the property. No wonder there were so many claims and counter claims.

An odd story concerning a land grant in St. James is taken from the Index to Spanish Judicial Records.[4] This concession was applied for before 1770, but a title was not issued until 1777. Obviously some of O'Reilly regulations were not employed and certainly a general mix-up ensued.

And so the story goes: There was an Indian village of the Alibamu on the east bank of the river about sixty-six miles above

— 18 —

New Orleans. The Indians, who were always on the move, left and according to law their land reverted to the King and could be reassigned. Now sometime prior to 1770, le Chevalier Le Grand de Bellevue applied for a tract in the deserted Alibamu area. Assisted by Nicholas Verret, Commandante of the Post of the Acadians, Bellevue, himself, surveyed the land. This was, in itself, an unusual procedure, but he managed, somehow, to get a patent for thirteen arpents front. On January 2, 1772, he ceded this land to Marie Jean Gabriel Peyroux de Rochemolive, an apothecary, who was probably St. James' first druggist. Then Bellevue left the province of Louisiana for the very good reason that he was a fugitive from justice.

To complicate matters still more, Peyroux, who lived on the opposite side of the river, did not claim title to this land for two years. In the mean time, Verret promised the land to Miguel Chiason and Francisco Antailla. These two had the land surveyed, built the levee, dug the ditches, laid out the road, gave the required contribution to the church, and paid the necessary fees. Then Verret died, so they applied for the grant through Michel Cantrelle, the new Commandante.

By this time Peyroux woke up. He found out that Chiason and Antailla were settled on his land and he addressed a petition to the governor to recover the property ceded to him by Bellevue. Poor Chiason and Antailla! They had no money to pay the excessive court costs of the complicated Spanish regime, so they simply asked to be reimbursed for the money expended and withdrew their claim. Peyroux paid the cost and in 1777 received the proper title.

Then we have the rather preposterous story of Fillette Laplanche and her daughter, Louise Chapdu. As a special recompense for a favor granted, Fillette gave her daughter a wedding gift of a strip of land thirty-three feet wide but forty arpents deep, right in the middle of Fillette's plantation. Although this deed was duly recorded according to law, it was soon overlooked, or forgotten, and the plantation changed hands through the years with never a bother of selling Louise's narrow land. A century later this slip was discovered and the current owners legally acquired what they thought had been theirs all along.

According to the records of the state land office in Baton Rouge most of the lands first acquired here were held by Cantrelle and his family. A. B. Roman, who became governor of

Louisiana, owned approximately 7300 acres of St. James land, most of which had been a part of a grant issued to the Cantrelles by French and Spanish authorities.

In 1765 Louis Judice, who later became the commandante at the Post of the Acadians at Lafourche, received a grant with a river frontage of thirty arpents. This was just above the present St. James Church. And on June 25, 1765, Nicholas Verret was issued a patent to a concession of twenty arpents front and "all the depth that can be found at Cabahannocer." This was in addition to adjacent lands which he already owned.

Since Michel Cantrelle was Jacques' son and Judice and Verret were his sons-in-law, we see that the Cantrelle family was established on extensive holdings on the environs of Cabahannocer before the Spanish land laws of 1770 went into effect. These grants were all on the right bank of the Mississippi River. One of the earliest grants on the left bank of the river was that given to one Grégoire dated November 3, 1765. It measured twenty arpents front and was twenty-four leagues from New Orleans . . . this was on or near the old White Hall Plantation.

And so from the vast domain of Jacques Cantrelle to the little strip of Louise Chapdu, St. James' land presents a unique story . . . interesting to the last foot of sod!

### FOOTNOTES

1. Arpent — old French measure of land — still used here — a little less than an acre.
2. *Les quarantes* — the forties — land forty arpents in depth.
3. This road was called — *Le Chemin Royale* — meaning the King's Road.
4. Louisiana Historical Quarterly, Vol. 12, # 4, pp. 677-679.

St. James Parish has had the following names
    1. Cabahannocer
    2. Poste de Cabahannocer
    3. La Côte des Accadiens
    4. Le Comte d'Accadie
    5. Poste de Cabahannocer Paroisee St. Jacques aux Accadiens
    6. Paroisse St. Jacques Côte de Cabahannocer aux Acadiens
    7. Acadia
    8. St. Jacques
    9. St. James

*Oak Alley. (Photo by Dan Leyrer)*

Oak Alley  Avenue of oaks leading from the entrance at the River front to the house in the background.
(Photo by Dan Leyrer)

## VI

## SWAPPED AND SOLD

Although a large part of St. James is on the east bank of the Mississippi River, this parish was never included in that region of Louisiana, which was ceded to the English after the French and Indian War. East St. James was in what was then known as the Island of Orleans.

This was an island only by the stretch of the imagination. The island extended along the east shore of the Mississippi River from the Gulf of Mexico to the Iberville River, now called Bayou Manchac. This little stream then forked out from the Mississippi[1] about fifteen miles below Baton Rouge and it was connected to Lakes Maurepas and Pontchartrain, via the Amite River. Thus it was that these connected waterways encircled the Island of Orleans.

France had long found Louisiana a liability rather than an asset and the wily king of France devised a means of getting rid of Louisiana without giving it all to his old enemy, England. So by the secret Treaty of Fontainebleau in 1762, France gave Louisiana, which was the land west of the Mississippi plus the Island of Orleans, to the King of Spain, who was rather loath to accept it. In fact, it was not until 1766 that the first Spanish governor, Ulloa, arrived in Spain's gratuitously acquired territory. And it was still later, in 1769, when O'Reilly, the Spanish Captain-General with an Irish name, took formal possession of Louisiana. Thus St. James actually became a Spanish possession in 1769.

As soon as O'Reilly took charge he had the oath of allegiance to Spain administered to all Louisianians. No doubt, the newly-arrived Acadians, who had so long refused to take the English oath in their old Acadian homeland, must have bitterly resented their quick transfer from French to Spanish authority so soon after setting foot on St. James soil. Like all the French Louisiaians, they were deeply attached to France and naturally suspicious of Spain.

In December 1769 O'Reilly visited St. James and although he was courteously received by the officials at Cabahannocer, he was cooly greeted by the people in general. But O'Reilly sometimes used a certain savoirfaire and he tactfully appointed a Creole member of the settlement, Nicholas Verret, as commandante. And so the Acadians, who had been born of the French, persecuted by the English, now found themselves ruled by the Spanish. But Spanish rule proved more beneficial than the French had been and soon Spanish money began to circulate. The Acadians continued to come in greater numbers and they were supplemented by other settlers.

Then in 1800 came another bolt from the blue, although it was three years in reaching its destination. St. James, as part of Louisiana was once more ceded — this time back to France — by the Treaty of San Ildefonso. But delays always ensued and it was not until November 30, 1803 that France formally received Louisiana. And then before French St. James could properly celebrate its return to *la patrie*,[2] it was within twenty days sold to the United States. But the great day was yet to come. In 1812 Louisiana was admitted into the Union. Little St. James as part of Louisiana had at last become of age.

Soon American planters bought plantations side by side with the Creoles and Acadians. An era of expansion, progress, and good living dawned. Cabahannocer had spread its wings. Valcour Aime in his enchanted garden set the pace and his contemporaries followed. St. James became a byword for wealth, culture, and Creole aristocracy. But pride goeth before a fall . . . and the Civil War was yet to come.

#### FOOTNOTES

1. The junction of Bayou Manchac and the Mississippi River was closed by order of General Andrew Jackson in 1814.

2. *La patrie* — Mother country.

## VII

### ST. JAMES, MOTHER OF EXILES

Truly St. James Parish can be called the mother of exiles. It had just been opened for settlement when in swarmed the countless Acadians . . . penniless and hungry, but welcome. In the slave uprising of Santo Domingo in 1791 and during the various political upheavals in Europe, exiles came to Louisiana and with each exodus some found in St. Jacques de Cabahannocer a temporary asylum or permanent home. Many of these political refugees were among the well-educated men of that time and contributed much to the culture of the parish. Among them were: Christofle Colomb, Augustin Tureaud, J. J. Gentil, Chevalier Marlarcher, and many others.

Among the early exiles who settled here were a group from the Illinois Country. This section had been settled as early as 1703 by French-Canadian traders and merchants. After the French and Indian War, this segment east of the Mississippi River passed under British military rule on October 10, 1765. A few years later came the Revolutionary War and the Illinois Country was snatched from the British by the bold daring of George Rogers Clark. French Illinois then passed into American hands and later became a part of the Virginia Territory, but the Illinois French were never satisfied with British nor American rule. They were far too different in religion, language, customs, ideas of self-government, and freedom of trade. In addition to unsatisfactory government, the Illinois French during the years between 1765 and 1790 were subjected to successive and frequent misfortunes: countless Indian massacres, recurring and disastrous floods, wars, crop failures, lack of coin, trade restraints, and the misunderstood slave provisions of the *Ordinance of* 1787. Although some of the Illinois French had become quite wealthy, many lost all their possessions during this trying period. Others salvaged what they could and left the Illinois Country. Some went to St. Louis, Pierre Laclede's new trading post on the Spanish side of the Mississippi, while others came to south Louisiana where they had friends and relatives.

St. James Parish was in the process of settlement. It was bisected by the Mississippi, the main artery of trade . . . it was in close proximity to New Orleans . . .much good land was available . . . and the people were French. Here the Illinois exiles, like many before and after them, found a safe haven. They settled along the river in St. James, Ascension, and Point Coupeé parishes and laid the foundation of many of these parishes' earliest and well known families: Chauvin, Armant, Blouin, Maurin, Dufresne, Balot, Lambert, Louviere, Beauvais, Peltier, Durand, Pertuis, Loisel, Manuel, Tessier, Mercier, etc. The Beauvais were a segment of the wealthiest family of the Illinois Country . . . the Jean Baptiste St. Gem Beauvais'. The Chauvins were part of the most prominent family of Kaskaskia . . . Joseph Chauvin Charleville, brother of the three Chauvins who settled near New Orleans at Tchoupitoulas in 1727.[1] Daniel Blouin, who had married Helene Chauvin Charleville, had been the leader of the Illinois French in their fight for better civil government. It was he who had been sent to Philadelphia in 1771 to present their petition for self government to the British General Gage. Caught in the maelstrom of the Revolutionary War, several years passed before he saw the Illinois Country again. His son, Daniel II, joined in the exodus and came to this parish some time before 1793. In 1805 he became justice of the peace. Antoine Maurin, too, found refuge here and he, or his son, became the sheriff of the parish in 1815.

Many of the Illinois French were among the better element of pioneers. Some had come originally from the south-western part of France. They were educated business men who had settled in Kaskaskia or its environs. Confronted by the unsurmountable difficulties of the Illinois Country, they came to South Louisiana. The court records show that many were well educated and almost all were literate. They were brave, hardy, and religious, but they loved pleasure too. They brought with them the gaiety of Sunday amusements, the boisterous charivari, the réveillon of the New Year, and the simple childish game of "cache, cache la bague",[2] still a children's favorite here. Many were good artisans and other became merchants and planters. Some were our first church commissioners and were instrumental in building the first church of St. Michel. No doubt St. James was benefited by the addition of the Illinois French.

It is a bit ironic, but none the less true, that some unsuspecting old St. James and Ascension families who pride themselves on being French to their very finger tips unknowingly have

Indian blood in their veins. Many of the early Illinois French had married Indian wives. For instance: Raphael Beauvais married a half Indian Marie Catherine Alarie. She died and on June 4, 1761 he married a full blooded Indian, Marie Françoise of the Illinois tribe. No doubt it was their descendant, Raphael Beauvais, who was district judge here from 1864 to 1872.

Thus St. James became the mother of exiles ... from Acadia, Europe, Canada, the West Indies, the Illinois Country, they poured into St. James from 1765 to the 1800's and blended into the composite whole. Soon they were joined by American newcomers. The Illinois French who had helped the American General Clark in the capture of Vincennes found themselves once more mingling with American neighbors, who in time were all absorbed by Creole St. Jacques de Cabahannocer.

FOOTNOTES

1. There seems to be little doubt that among the Chauvins who settled in St. James-Ascension, some were the New Orleans Chauvins while others were the Illinois Chauvins. However, many of the Chauvin Christian names, handed down almost unbrokenly from one generation to the next on to the present day, are the Christian names of the Illinois Chauvins: Louis, John (Jean), Joseph, Charles, Philip, François, Paul, Jacques, etc. Of the New Orleans Chauvins there was always, and there is still, a Pierre.

One of the first Chauvins which appears in the Acadian Coast records is the birth of Paul François Chauvin, sone of Jean Chauvin, on October 4, 1772. On February 5, 1773 is recorded the marriage of J. B. Chauvin, son of Louis Chauvin and Marguerite Braud — residents of Cabahannocer.

2. Cache, cache, la bague — the St. James version of the game of "Who has the ring?"

## VIII

## THE GREAT PLANTATIONS

The early 1800's was the era of fabulous plantation life in St. James. Acreage was counted by thousands and slaves by hundreds. It was the day of luxurious living, of sumptuous entertainment, of delightful ease. Sugar was gold; the planters were sugar barons; St. James was the Gold Coast. In 1844 the parish had twenty-eight plantations on the right bank of the Mississippi River and thirty-nine on the left bank — and some were large enough to be called agricultural empires. Among the more famous were Uncle Sam, Valcour Aime, White Hall, and Oak Alley. I shall cover only the highlights of the first three, but I shall tell more in detail the story of Oak Alley, because it was a pattern of early plantation life and because it has been restored to its former glory.

### VALCOUR AIME'S

Valcour Aime was one of the first Louisiana planters to make white sugar. He lived in a palatial home which, in time, was known simply as Valcour Aime's. The house was different from other plantation houses in that it had a large patio on one side. The house burned several years ago, but it was then in a sad state of dilapidation.

Valcour Aime seems to have been wealthy from the beginning. In their civil marriage contract in July 1816 Aime brought to the community $75,000 and Josephine Roman, his bride, $19,600, thus giving them a total of $94,600 to set up their housekeeping. This was quite a sum of money for that time. Just a few years later Aime bought a plantation, in this parish, including the slaves, for which he paid $170,000.

The most memorable thing about Valcour Aime's was its beautiful garden — so beautiful, in fact, that the place became known as "Le Petit Versailles." The garden was, indeed, of French origin as Mr. Aime employed a landscape artist, Mr. Despommier, of Dijon, France. There were statues, fountains, streams, even a hill, and ornamental plants were imported from all over the world. This probably accounts for the number of exotic plants seen in St. James today, but not commonly found in other sections. Mr. Aime experimented with all sorts of plants and crops and he took a personal interest in all things that grew. He kept a diary for thirty-one years. He was especially careful in recording the weather and he always checked the temperature at 6:30 A. M.

According to Mr. Aime the weather in St. James could be foretold as follows: The weather for the duration of the moon would be what it was on the fifth day of the new moon if like weather prevailed on the sixth day. Or it would be what it was on the fourth day of the new moon providing the weather on the sixth day was like that of the fourth day. However, the rule did not always apply in the spring and in October. Mr. Aime noted, too, that it rarely rained here on summer nights.

Everything was done at Valcour Aime's in a big way. In one year an immense crop of sugar cane, 5400 barrels of corn, 28 cartloads of pumpkins, rice, tobacco, potatoes, truck, hogs, sheep, cattle, horses, and what not were the products of the plantation. No wonder there were over 200 slaves, twenty of whom were household servants. The slaves cut 1000 cords of wood, 12,000 shingles, 3600 pickets, and 100 fence posts. One hog weighed over 700 pounds, an orange measured nearly fifteen inches around and even the river and the swamp joined hands in making Valcour Aime famous. The river yielded a garfish weighing nearly 150 pounds and the swamp, not to be outdone, produced a six-foot rattle snake. But one slave decided to break all records. He lived to be 107 years old and at 104, he mowed and acre of hay in one day.[1]

The plantation, in addition to its manor, had a hospital, a sugarmill, a store, a church, and a school, plus the slave quarters, barns, outbuildings, and homes for employees and members of the family.

The Aimes gave such stupendous entertainments that after a hundred years, one still hears the story of their daughter's wedding.[2] And no less magnificent is that tale of a banquet, where twelve dozen sets of fine china were bought for the occasion. This is surely a gross exaggeration — but I do know that some of this same china was still in use by Les Dames Trudeau in their old home at College Point in the early 1920's.[3]

Little remains today to mark Valcour Aime's vast estate. There is a cave below his once-famous garden. Mr. Aime had had a great sorrow. His son, who had gone to Paris for his education, returned home to die of yellow fever. Mr. Aime had a cave excavated, a chapel installed, and here he retired daily to pray. Many, many years after Valcour Aime's passing, a Negro caretaker murdered his wife and it was said that he concealed himself in the cave. This was not true. The Negro burned his cabin with his wife in it and skipped. He was never apprehended. Years later a skeleton, thought to be that of the murderer, was found on the batture.

It is practically impossible to enter the cave to-day because of the thick vegetation which surrounds the narrow entrance, but surely one day, some one will restore this cave to its original state and make of it a shrine — a monument to the man who gave Louisiana some of its first white sugar and whose charity and good work have caused him to be remembered as St. James' first and best loved philanthropist.[4]

## UNCLE SAM

Uncle Sam, methodically swallowed by the Mississippi River in 1940, was the last complete plantation unit in the state. It comprised five buildings of Greek revival architecture and two hexagonal pigeonniers. The main building was almost exactly like the Oak Alley house, described elsewhere in this story. On each side were the garçonnières and back of the main building to the left and right were smaller buildings. One was a kitchen and the other was used as laundry and larder. The pigeonniers were far to the left and right.

Uncle Sam was built by Mr. Samuel Fagot in 1836-1840. The complete unit with furnishings cost something under $200,000 — and built with slave labor at that. Until its sale in 1915 Uncle Sam had always been the home of the Fagots and their descendants. Many colorful stories are told about the origin of the plantation's name but the most plausible is that it was named after Mr. Fagot, who was affectionately called "Uncle Sam." However, Uncle Sam was first called Constancia Plantation and appears thus on early maps. This was the name of Daniel Fagot de la Garciniere's second wife: Carlotta Constancia Olivier who was Samuel Fagot's ancestor.

It took four years to build Uncle Sam and litte more than four weeks to destroy it. A new levee was needed. The place was demolished. Not a finger was lifted to save it. Uncle Sam was actually junked — and ironically enough by Uncle Sam. (U. S. Engineers)[5]

Garconiere, Uncle Sam Plantation. (Courtesy Henry A. Gandolfo)

Pigeonaire at Uncle Sam Plantation. (Photo by Dan Leyrer)

Demolition of Uncle Sam Plantation house. Not a hand was lifted to save it. (Photo by Charles O. Subra)

Oak Alley. Looking from the front of the house towards the River. (Photo by Dan Leyrer)

White Hall, first home of the Bringiers. The scene probably shows the boat of Christophe Colomb, the son-in-law of Marius Bringier, being rowed by slaves. His barge with its velvet armchairs and red-fringed canopy rivalled that of Cleopatra. Perspective is slightly wrong as the picture shows the River to be too narrow. (From a painting in possession of Richard Koch, photographed by Dan Leyrer)

## WHITE HALL

White Hall, which extended for a mile along the river, was one of five plantations[6] belonging to Marius Pons Bringier. He came to Louisiana from France, via Martinique, and in 1785 settled in St. James, where his French Gothic home became known as Le White Hall. Nothing stands today to mark the spot where once thrived the agricultural empire of Monsieur Marius, but in its heyday, White Hall equalled, or surpassed, any plantation in Louisiana and the tales which are handed down to us are as fabulous. Among them none is more incredible than the story of Marius' daughter, Betsy Bringier, and Judge Tureaud.

Betsy was a homely, but happy, little girl of thirteen living in the ease and wealth of her father's luxurious plantation. Her father came home one day with a stranger . . . a man who was handsome, courtly, learned, and thirty eight . . . a man of the world, a man of adventure: Augustin Dominique Tureaud.

Augustin had been kicked out of home and country by his wealthy father in France and sent to San Domingo. Shortly after his arrival there the slaves rose in insurrection and Augustin escaped only because his housekeeper warned him of the coming peril and provided a boat for his flight. From an open boat he was picked up at sea more dead then alive and taken to Baltimore where he settled. But Augustin had the wanderlust and one day he came to New Orleans, where he met Marius Bringier who took him to White Hall. Here this charming guest so thoroughly ingratiated himself with Marius that before he left, Marius stunned him with an offer of Betsy's hand in marriage. Augustin's surprise could never equal poor little Betsy's disconsolation, but the marriage was arranged and he came back one year later to claim his child-bride.

But stranger still was the fact that Betsy fell in love with her husband and they lived very happily on Union Plantation — a wedding gift from her father, who named it thus because of this strange union in marriage. And as for Augustin, he dropped all his madcap pranks, used his charm and education to good purpose, and became none other than le Juge Tureaud of St. James Parish, which he so ably served until he died at Union Plantation in 1826.

White Hall was divided and subdivided into many small farms and today White Hall — Union is one of the most thickly populated rural areas in America. It is interesting to know that here dwell many Chauvin families, whose ancestors were among the wealthy and infuential men in early Louisiana history.

The first Chauvin to come to America was Pierre Chauvin, Sieur de Tonnetuit, a Huguenot, friend of the French King. He was born at Dieppe but later moved to Honfleur where he became governor. In 1599 he applied to the French government for a trading monopoly in New France . . . said monopoly to last ten years. This was granted and in the spring of 1600 Chauvin and his partner, François Gravé, Sieur du Pont, arrived in Canada. Here Chauvin became known as Lieutenant of the King in Canada. His feeble efforts to establish a colony failed, but his monopolistic trade operations were apparently very successful. Chauvin died in 1603, but the company which he had begun was reorganized. Samuel de Champlain, the great explorer, became part of the next expedition to Canada. When Champlain returned to France in 1609, he left a Captain Chauvin, Sieur de la Pierre, in charge of the garrison at Quebec. This was the second Chauvin to come to America.

Over a hundred years later three Chauvin brothers . . . Chauvin-Delery, Chauvin-Lafrénière, and Chauvin de Beaulieu with their nephew, Pierre Chauvin, came to Louisiana from Canada. They settled near New Orleans in 1727 where they obtained large land grants at Tchoupitoulas. But since the name and characteristics of Pierre Chauvin, the nephew, still survive in the Union family, a word or two about this Pierre will not be amiss.

In 1723 Pierre Chauvin was a fifer in Commander Loubois' company in Biloxi. He was then eighteen years old. Two hundred years later Pierre Chauvin of Union had inherited the young fifer's musical ability as well as his name. He composed several musical selections. But we still have a Pierre Chauvin with us; he is known locally as Mr. Tit-Pierre, proving in our own inimitable French way that the name has been handed down from generation to generation. And while I do not know if the present Mr. Tit-Pierre is musically inclined like his predecessor and namesake, I do know that he is the manufacturer of the most delicious fig preserves. And so from fife to fig the Chauvins have contributed something sweet to make life more pleasurable. And isn't it strange that the broad fields which once yielded sugar-wealth for the Bringiers now produce preserves for the people?

## OAK ALLEY

Perhaps the story of Oak Alley can best be told by telling the story of the Roman family. Certainly the Romans played an important part in the social, religious, agricultural, military, and political affairs of St. James.

Way back in the early 1720's Jacques Roman came to Louisiana from Grenoble, France as a member of the personnel of the Dubuisson concession. How and why he became an officer in the Louisiana troops we do not know, but it is said that he always wore a silver-hilted sword at his side. His father was wealthy and his mother was related to the Paris Duverneys. And since the so-called Dubuisson concesion really belonged to Joseph Paris Duverney, it is possible that it was through this family connection that Jacques Roman came to Louisiana.

In 1747 Jacques Roman married Marie Josephe Daigle of the German Coast. They had five children, one of whom was Jacques Étienne, who moved to the Attakapas country where he became a rancher. In time Jacques Étienne came to St. James with his wife and nine children. Among the nine we find Josephine Roman, who married Valcour Aime, André Roman, who became the governor of Louisiana, and Jacques Telesphore Roman, the master of the manor: Oak Alley.

And in time Jacques Telesphore, too, took unto himself a wife: Celenia Pilié. And unto them were born: Henry, Louis, Octavie, and Marie. These were the people, direct descendants of the Paris Duverneys and old Jacques Roman of the silver-hilted sword, who owned and loved and lost Oak Alley.

Oak Alley was first called Beau Séjour,[7] but the American Steamboat captains could never remember that French name and called it Oak Alley after the avenue of twenty-eight huge live oak trees, which form a span from the levee to the house. It is said that Valcour Aime first owned Oak Alley and the Romans owned St. James Plantation. When Valcour Aime married Josephine Roman, she did not want to leave her girlhood home, so the Aimes and Romans exchanged plantations. It was after this swap that Valcour Aime planted his famous garden at St. James and Jacques Roman built his beautiful home at Oak Alley.

It is claimed that Oak Alley was planned by Gallier but a better source gives George Swaney as its architect. It was erected about 1837-38 and was built almost entirely by slave labor. Most of the material came from the plantation wood lot, kiln and forge. The architecture is Greek revival and at one time, there was a garçonnière on each side, but these were long ago demolished. There are twenty-eight Doric columns around the house — seven on each side — and there are broad upper and lower galleries all around the house. In the center, upstairs and down, are wide halls flanked on each side by spacious rooms. The house and grounds are a thing of indescribable beauty and the sunrise, seen from the upper front gallery through the long avenue of oaks, is a sight unparalleled anywhere.

The Romans lived in princely style. The house was furnished by Mallard, famous cabinet maker, who came to Louisiana from Scotland in 1829. Mrs. Roman's bedroom suite was of ebony and is said to have cost four thousand dollars. (This furniture is now in the possession of a descendant who lives on the Mississippi Gulf Coast). The mantels were of marble, as was the floor of one room. The walls and ceiling were adorned with delicate plaster hand work and through-out the house were finest objects-d'arts.

The following stories contributed by one of Mr. Roman's grandson, illustrate life at Oak Alley:

The Saturday night boats always landed at Oak Alley to discharge passengers — gay visitors of a perfect host. Mr. Roman had sent his Negro chef, Dérueville, to Paris to learn the culinary art and he boasted that Dérueville could cook anything — even alligator — and that every one would eat it and enjoy it. At this a discussion ensued and wagers were made to the contrary. Several weeks elapsed and the same guests assembled for dinner. They ate copiously and enjoyable of what they believed to be venison, but which was really alligator. After dinner Mr. Roman had his famous chef bring in the alligator heads to the dismay of the guests, who none-the-less, cheerfully paid the bets.

Mr. Roman owned over a hundred slaves. As a matter of fact one hundred eight slaves were sold at his succession. And since slaves were worth from a few hundred to over a thousand dollars, one can understand the wealth of those ante-bellum sugar barons. Mr. Roman rode only pure blooded Arabian steeds and Madame Roman had a luxurious carriage drawn by spirited horses, which kicked up a clatter and a cloud of dust, as her Negro coachman drove her up and down the rough river road.

One night beautiful Louise Roman, while coming down the stairs for a ball, tripped and fell — her heel caught in her skirt. Her knee was so badly injured that she retired from society and after her mother's death, she joined the order of Carmelite nuns in St. Louis, becoming Mother Teresa of Jesus. In 1877, she, with three others nuns, came from St. Louis and founded the Carmelite Convent in New Orleans.

Marie Roman died at sixteen and Octavie Roman became the wife of General Philip Buchanan. Henry Roman married Théresa Bouligny. After Jacques Roman's death Oak Alley was taken over by Henry in 1860. Soon the Civil War came and Oak Alley passed from the hands of the Roman family in 1867. Then came a strange succession of ownership: the English Humphreys, the Italian or Spanish Bozanos, the Portuguese Sobrals, the Jewish Feitels, the French Hotards, and on and on, until it was purchased in 1925 by the Scotch Andrew Stewarts of New Orleans.

The Stewarts restored Oak Alley, modernizing it with the comforts of present day living, but in keeping with its historic and glamorous past. There are lovely gardens with hundreds of trees and shrubs and vines. Mrs. Stewart is a charming hostess and she has captured the spirit of yesterday and blended it with the good life of today.

To illustrate one of her delightful customs: She keeps old-fashioned, frilly organdy frocks of all sizes and colors and before dinner the woman guests don these pretty, bouffant dresses. Dinner is served under soft candle light by Negro mammies in a huge dining room, furnished with antique pieces. This presents a scene so enchanting and so true to yesterday, that one, not familiar with this quaint custom, would halt in the doorway in wondrous surprise at seeing le Beau Séjour of the pleasure loving Creoles came to life again.

## OAK ALLEY

"With magic splendor born within its walls,
The Beau Séjour of olden days,
Oak Alley stands a stately hall,
A lasting theme for tuneful lays.
　　The gnarled oaks and Doric columns keep
Within their understanding hearts,
The secret loves and lives of folk
Long gone to ethereal parts.

> The swaying moss in gentle evening breeze
> Whispers to flowering shrubs and vines,
> Of daring deeds and thoughts of years
> Well spent behind those blue-green blinds.
> Then handsome men would sip French wines,
> well served
> By faithful slaves, in languid ease,
> While pretty girls in ruffled skirts
> Would sweetly laugh and flirt and tease.
> Those vast, dim-lighted halls reverberate
> The mirth of princely beau and belle;
> The charm and grace of long ago
> Resound in the plantation bell."

### Notes On Other Plantations

Bagatelle Plantation was so named by one of Marius Bringier's daughters. The young lady married and the couple went to Europe for their honeymoon. During their absence Monsieur Marius had a home built and furnished for them. Upon the return of the newly-weds, they were presented with the house as a wedding gift.

"What, this bagatelle!" exclaimed the bride. "I won't live in it." And she didn't. But from then on the house became known as Bagatelle. It is in excellent condition having been fully restored a few years ago. Some of the original furniture and a mural, said to have been painted by one of the Tureaud sisters, are still there. The house is presently occupied by its current owner, Mr. Francis H. James. And as for the bride who refused Bagatelle . . . why Marius Bringier simply built her a finer house . . . just as easy as that.

There were two plantations whose names were HOME PLACE . . . one on each side of the river. But there is a unique story about the one on the east bank of the Mississippi. When Técle Nicolle, supposedly a Polish exiled nobleman, built his house on Home Place there were two huge oak trees in perpendicular line from the river road. He placed his house to face the trees and not the highway. The reason: He wanted to see the sunrise between the trees. Whether he was a nobleman, we shall never know, but certainly he was a Pole and an exile, his true name being Louis Lubislavich. The trees were swallowed by the hungry Mississippi when a new levee was built several years ago and when the house was moved, the present owners had it face the highway. It is still Home Place but minus its unusual view ... the rising sun peeping between the giant oaks.

The first plantation in St. James was the indigo plantation of the Cantrelles known as Cabahannocer. This word has the following spelling variants: Kabahannosse, Kabaha-Nossie, Cabahannocer, Cabahannocce, Cabahannose, Cabahanosce, Cabahanocey, Cabahanose, Cabanose, Cabanocy.

Gramercy was formerly the Golden Grove Planation.

Four famous plantation homes were destroyed by fire: Bay Tree, Hester, Belmont, and Sport, better known as Mt. Airy.

Probably the finest avenue of live oaks in America is found on Oak Alley Plantation. They were noted by a traveler passing here nearly ninety years ago.

Among the early owners of Helvetia were Madame Carite, the Tremoulet and Charbonier families, and J. J. Jourdan.

Many plantations changed names when they changed owners. Delogny Plantation is now Bessie K. and Columbia Plantation is now St. Rose.

Famous old homes which are still in good condition and which are now occupied are: Oak Alley, Colomb Park, Welham, and St. Joseph.

The last big plantation home built in St. James was on Sport Plantation at Mount Airy. It was built by Felician Waguespack in 1906 and burned in 1944.

Once both sides of the Mississippi River were lined with plantation manors. Most of them were destroyed by river, fire, or neglectful decay.

There are many very old homes of less imposing architecture in St. James, such as the old Gray and Gentil homes at Convent. There are many smaller crumbling Acadian homesteads, whose moss-and-mud walls are still fighting the ravages of the damp Louisiana climate.

Pape Vert, sometimes called the Thibodeaux house, was never a plantation house. It was built for commercial uses, and, though it was the residence of the Thibodeaux family for many years, its floor plan was never altered.

Rapidan Plantation was named after a river in Virginia. It was once the land of Duncan Kenner who probably named it thus. It was also called Boisjolies.[9]

Jefferson College is built on the lands of the Vavaseur family.

The Dornier brothers . . . Joseph B., Jules, Leo, and Felix . . . became the owners of adjoining tracts of land which had once been the plantation of their ancestor: Jean Baptiste Boucry. The plantation is called Bonne Ésperence.[10]

The Zenon Trudeaux house is of most unique architecture.

The largest plantation ever owned in St. James was that of A. B. Roman, former governor of Louisiana. It comprised 7,300 acres.

Dr. John Sibley, early settler of Natchitoches, who made a voyage up the Mississippi River from New Orleans in 1802, describes life on a St. James Plantation in an entry in his journal dated September 30, 1802.[11]

"Passed a gentleman's house who was sitting with his wife and children under the shade of some orange trees in his courtyard. I stopped, he spoke to me in English asked me to rest myself. I sat down, he ordered some wine and water and invited me to stay all night, being very tired for I never had walked as far in one day before in my life, I consented . . . While I was sitting at the door of this house I saw the most of the barge passing by within fifty yards of the house . . . Just at sundown there came into the gate two young ladies handsomely dressed, a lad and a little miss, the gentlemen presented them to me and told me they were his children who had been to a dancing school. The two young ladies one in particular I thought very pretty, but as they spoke no English and I did not speak French enough to converse with them, could judge of them only by their appearance. Tea was handed about soon but nothing with it. In the evening after sitting in the outer hall an hour or more supper was announced, in a long cool room, open to the back yard, a variety of dishes were on the table, sausages, eggs, meat, salads, etc. After supper was conducted into a cool room on the ground floor, a neat bed with a pavillion round it, I went directly to bed and slept till day light. I got up and went away without disturbing the family. The name of this gentleman I did not acquaint myself with, which was an omission I very much regretted after."

Since the next day he traveled about seven leagues (approximately nineteen miles), tied up the boat for the night, and early the next morning passed Bayou Lafourche, there is no doubt that the plantation which he described was in St. James Parish and could have been the White Hall of Marius Bringier.

Another old plantation house, still occupied after one hundred thirty-five years, is the St. Joseph Plantation house.[12] Prior to 1820 Dr. Cazimir Bernard Mericq of France came to Louisiana and settled on a narrow strip of land, now a part of that plantation. On December 4, 1820 he married Celeste Palmyre Gauthier of Natchitoches and it is generally believed that he built the St. Joseph Plantation house at that time. The house was a two story building . . . its upper floor consisted of four large rooms and a broad center hall. The doctor never finished the ground floor. It served only as a place to park his horse and buggy between calls. But the good doctor died in 1857 and the plantation was sold to Alexis Ferry who had married one of Valcour Aime's daughters. The Ferrys enlarged the house, adding two rooms on each side and they finished the ground floor, separating it into various rooms. The house changed hands in the course of years, but nothing else was altered. And today it is still occupied . . . now by the Simon family.

### FOOTNOTES

1. Figures taken from *The Diary of Mr. Valcour Aime*.
2. For description of life at Valcour Aime's read: Ripley, Eliza Moore. *Life in Old New Orleans*.
3. Les Dames Trudeau . . . Descendants of Zenon Trudeau, territorial governor of upper Louisiana.
4. The chapel at Jefferson College (now Manresa House) was a gift of Valcour Aime.
5. Minute drawings, plans, specifications, etc. were made in a government survey during the demolition. These papers are said to be in the archives of a government bureau in St. Louis.
6. The White Hall Plantation extended approximately from Ben Bourg's property to the George Cox home. It was sub-divided into small tracts by the Wade Hampton heirs.
7. Beau Séjour — Beautiful Sojourn.
8. The early settlers built mud-daubed walls strengthened with dry moss.
9. Boisjolies — beautiful woods.
10. Bonne Ésperence — Good Hope.
11. The Journal of Dr. John Sibley, July-October, 1802. The Louisiana Historical Quarterly, Vol. 10, # 4, pp. 489-490.
12. Information given by Mr. Stanislaus Waguespack. (p. 37)

## IX

## SLAVERY IN ST. JAMES

St. James was founded and settled by farmers and planters and slavery flourished from its inception. Indeed one of Jacques Cantrelle's first gifts to the old church of St. Jacques de Cabahannocer was a slave woman, Marie Louise, to cook for the newly-arrived curé. The first census of 1766 lists 16 slaves and among the documents in the archives of Seville, Spain is a "Census of Slaves at Cabahannocer" dated December 4, 1775. And in the carefully enumerated duties of the first commanders of the post of Cabahannocer, we note that of returning runaway slaves. In the baptismal records of St. Michel there are several books for the separate registry of the slaves baptized.

In the court records of 1796 one finds that in settling the succession of the recently deceased Father Azuquequa the sale of the slave belonging to the parsonage of St. Jacques de Cabahannocer became a controversial issue. This so annoyed the members of the congregation that they petitioned the governor to set aside the judgment of the court so as to keep the slave there. One wonders if this was the same Marie Louise. The petition was signed by Cantrelle, Brau, LeBlanc, Bergeron, Gaudin, Poirier, Bourgeois, Arcenaux, Gauthro, and Armant, thus proving that the earliest St. Jamesians were interested in slavery and approved of it.

As early as 1782, slaves sold here brought as much as $300.00 and one little three year old girl was sold in 1784 to Marguerite Verret for $150.00. He name was Zoer. No doubt the item which appears most frequently in the old court records is the sale of slaves, singly and in lots. Just nine years before the Civil War on a plantation just above the St. James Church, 282 slaves were sold. But the prices paid were more fabulous than the number sold. There are endless entries of sales of slaves at more than $1,500. One slave was sold at a record price of $2,405.00. The successions are filled with pages listing slaves only . . . name, age, aptitude, price, purchaser. The descriptions follow a pattern: "Negro . . . Senegal . . . named Omnia . . . about 26 years

... speaks English and French ... laborious ... good farm hand ... fair carpenter ... estimated value ... $1,100 ... sold to."

Slave names were curious, sometimes amusing. Many had nicknames which were characteristic of their traits or peculiarities. One reads of San Souçi (without worry), Nez Coupé (cut nose), Labelle (the beautiful), Loucki (lucky), La Providence (providence), etc. And in Marius Bringier's succession a slave was sold whose name was Vendredi (Friday) ... perhaps a namesake of Robinson Crusoe's good man, Friday.

Most of the wealth of the antebellum planters of St. James was in slaves and land. No wonder that the Civil War brought on such an economic debacle. In 1860 St. James had approximately eight thousand slaves, whose assessed value was four million dollars. As the Yankees approached some owners moved their slaves to other sections for safety, only to bring them back free — and a complete loss. And for many years after that they far outnumbered the whites.

It is said that the greatest worry of the Sacred Heart nuns during the Civil War was the fear of an insurrection among the recently-freed Negroes. Like most worry, it proved useless. The freed men remained faithful — only one left. On New Year's Day in 1864 the Negroes called in a body on the superior of the convent. They demanded higher wages. Otherwise they would leave. Mother Shannon was courageous, but curt. "Better yourselves — it you can!" The next day they went back to work. They knew that here they would not starve. They also knew Mother Shannon.[1]

Slavery here as elsewhere had its attendant evils, but there is little to prove that the slaves were grossly mistreated. Certainy the abundance of the St. James Plantations provided enough food, clothing, and care for all. But the story is told that a certain planter was once enraged because his expert cook had burned a pot of beans. He insisted that she eat the whole pot full — down to the last charred bean. When one recalls the size of a plantation pot, if true, this must have been a cruel and gigantic feat.

But one old freed woman, who remained faithful to her people when want and distress descended upon them, frequently exercised her prerogative of freedom by going into tantrums. One day in the middle of a big *ménage*,[2] she became violently angry, left the house, and defiantly perched herself on the top of the levee with a big pot-de-chambre which she had unconsciously carried off with her to the deep humiliation of *ce grand monde*.[3] They finally coaxed her in — chamber pot and all — but for days the village buzzed with the talk of *le gros pot-de-chambre jaune de Madame Telle-et-Telle*.[4]

The slaves worked at various tasks assigned to them. The house servants were of a separate caste, so to speak, and often looked upon the field hands as inferiors. There were among the slaves many who were good artizans. They made bricks which have weathered time and element for more than a century. The big plantation manors, the college, the church, and the convent were built mostly by slave labor. And each planation had its kiln, its forge, and its carpenter shop.

In a place where four thousand whites owned eight thousand blacks, emancipation brought many problems: financial, social, and agricultural. The millions of dollars invested in slaves were a total and immediate loss. Worse yet, there were no hands to till the soil to recover the losses. Fortunes were swept away, plantations changed hands, and weeds grew where sugar once thrived.

The readjustment was slow. Nearly a century passed in the process. Then science and invention came to the rescue. Today the plantations are mechanized. In the broad fields one sees fewer and fewer Negroes. The roaring tractor, the bright flame thrower, the chugging cane cutter, and the avid gang plows have taken their place. Sugar is going forward again and St. James, west bank, has just erected a new million dollar co-operative sugar mill. And strangely it has risen just above the old Cabahannocer homestead where the Cantrelles' first cultivated indigo. A new era has dawned. Pity that a Civil War had to give it birth!

### Footnotes

1. Story taken from: Callan, Louise. The Society of the Sacred Heart in North America.
2. Ménage — Used here to denote housecleaning.
3. Ce grand monde — people of quality.
4. Le gros pot-de-chambre jaune de Madame Telle-et-Telle . . . Mrs. So-and-So's big yellow chamber-pot.

## X

## ST. MICHEL DE CANTRELLE

By 1807 St. James had become a part of United States territory and it was entering an era of development and prosperity. The Acadians had come to the parish in great number and the plantation dynasty of the Creoles was being founded. On the east bank of the river there were over one hundred families and a church was needed. Up to this time the inhabitants had to cross the river to attend church services at Cabahannocer.

In order to erect and establish the first church of St. Michel, thirteen commissioners were selected and entrusted with that undertaking in 1807. They were: Étienne Reine, Daniel Blouin, Jr., Pierre Thériot, Jean Baptiste Picou, Joseph Michel, Paul Bourgeois, Jean Charpentier, Christofle Roussel, Martin Dubourg, François Arcenaux, Silvain LeBlanc, Louis Gauthreaux and Louis Marlarcher. The last named elected president-treasurer. The first meeting was held on Mr. Caillouet's plantation and here it was decided to build a church and name it St. Michel for Michel Cantrelle. Application to build a church was made to the Territorial Legislature and this was granted after some delay.

In 1808 the commissioners selected Benjamin Fulcher as contractor, agreed to pay him $1495 for his work, and gave him one year to construct the building. Thus St. Michel de Cantrelle . . . a small frame building measuring fifty by thirty feet . . . was erected on land donated by the Cantrelles. By this time the commissioners had turned over the affairs of the Church to five duly elected wardens who were: Pierre Michel, Bonnaventure Gaudin, Étienne Melançon, Pierre Chenet and François Duhon. On October 10, 1809 Father Charles Lusson of the Ascension Church of Lafourche blessed the new church with Michel Cantrelle and Mrs. Pierre Michel as sponsors. And to pay for its upkeep each Catholic property holder had to pay a yearly tax of one dollar per acre fronting the river.

For several years St. Michel was only a mission with no resident pastor, but in 1812 Father Gabriel Chambon de la Tour, the new curé, arrived. Already ailing and seventy, he died before the year was out and St. Michel again was pastorless. Jean Baptiste Petrimoult, sexton, read the prayers for the dead and christened the babies. Other pastors came but it was not until 1822 that Father Charles de la Croix, a Belgian who had been an Indian missionary in distant Louisiana outposts, took charge of St. Michel. Better days were now in store. Father de la Croix was an untiring worker and after a few years he decided that a finer temple should be erected. He went to his native land for help and when he returned three years later he had collected $2,000 from the Catholics of Belgium. To this was added the contributions of the Sacred Heart nuns,[1] the bishop of New Orleans, and the parishoners. Father de la Croix had raised the goodly sum of $19,445.

A tract of land just above the frame church was purchased from an ex-slave, Mimi Zélia, and brick by brick St. Michel rose anew. Before the church was dedicated a new bell arrived from Belgium on which was inscribed... "1831 — cast in Louvaine — in the name of the Catholics of Belgium for their Catholic brethern in America." With grand ceremony in 1832 the bell was christened, Eugenie-Louise, with Mother Eugenie Audé, superior of the convent, and Mr. Louis LeBourgeois as sponsors. It is the same bell which calls the faithful to worship today and it has merrily rung the weddings and sadly tolled the funerals since December 11, 1832. Then in resplendent ceremony the new church of St. Michel was solemnly dedicated by Bishop de Neckère on March 9, 1833. The good bishop, by the way, was resting at Convent after a most trying period in New Orleans. News soon reached him that the plague had struck his city again and he returned to New Orleans to minister the sick and bury the dead. Ten days later he, too, lay dead. This greatly saddened the parishoners and their pastor. Bishop de Neckère had spent many of his summer vacations resting at St. Michel and here he was well-known and well-loved. Too, the residents of St. James had frequently paid their toll in death to the monsters of yellow fever and cholera ... only the year before several orphans and eight nuns had died in quick succession at the convent next door to the church. But storms and plagues and wars could not halt those hardy pioneers and soon St. Michel, like all the Acadian Coast, was on its way.

And for those who would like to know what became of the first little church: It stood just the other side of Mye Breaux's

*Act of sale of ex-slave Mimi Zelia on whose land the St. Michel Church was built.*

house for years and years, used for this, that, or the other, until one day what once had been the temple of God housed the lowly forge of a blacksmith's shop. Suddenly a rebellious spark ignited the building, it burst into flames, and burned . . . its smoke curling up to Heaven and its ashes settling back to Mother Earth in silent resignation.

In 1863 the Marist Society was given the curacy of St. Michel. This was their first assignment in the archdiocese of New Orleans and here they have labored long and well. As time passed many improvements were made, especially during the pastorate of Father Henri Belanger. The Church was enlarged, the steeple built, and a new façade added. A painting of St. Michel was given by the LeBourgeois family and the side altars donated . . . that of Mary by Mrs. D. Fagot and that of Joseph by Mrs. J. LeBourgeois. Mrs. Welham and Mrs. Godberry added the stained glass windows. The Society of Mary donated the main altar purchased at the Paris exposition in 1867, but made in Mans, France.

The church feasts were observed with beauty and solemnity and much of the life on the east bank of the river centered around the activities of the church, the convent, and the college. For instance: Concluding a very successful mission at the church in 1873, Rev. Mother Boudreaux of the convent decided to add her bit to the beautification of the church by donating a large mission cross. On Easter Sunday afternoon a procession was formed to transfer this cross from the convent to the church. The church, convent, college, and surrounding plantation bells began to ring at four-thirty. Shortly after, the procession began and two thousand persons took part. First came the church banners with an escort of cavalry. Then the clergy, followed by the young ladies of the parish and the convent all dressed in white. Then came the laity, the college band, and the college students. Last was the mission cross carried by twenty men. As they slowly walked the half mile separating the church and the convent, everybody sang the hymn "Vive Jesu, Vive sa croix" . . . incidently this hymn is still sung at St. Michel . . . and in French.

The Marist Fathers have a great devotion to Mary, the Mother of God, and it was with much zeal that they undertook construction of the Chapel of Lourdes at St. Michel. The work for this, one of the first grottos of Lourdes in America, was placed in the skilled hands of Christophe Colomb, artist and artizan. Mr. Colomb, believed to be a descendant of Christopher Columbus, was surely part French. His father had come to St. James as a political exile from France, via San Domingo, and he had married Françoise, daughter of Marius Bringier. Certainly Christophe Colomb, the son, was possessed of many of the artistic qualities of the Italian and the French and it was he who left the singularly interesting and beautiful grotto of Lourdes at St. Michel.

Tezcuco, a Bringier house. Now owned by Dr. and Mrs. Robert H. Potts. (Photo by Ray Cresson)

*Tezcuco interior. A Bringier house now owned by Dr. and Mrs. R. H. Potts. (Photo by Ray Cresson)*

*Tezcuco—rear view of house showing colunms and three flights of stairs.*

*Nancy, daughter of Dr. and Mr. Potts, at Tezcuco.*

*Bocage. Built in 1801 by Marius Bringier for his daughter, Fanny, and her husband, Christophe Colomb. (Courtesy Mrs. Potts)*

With bagasse clinkers and mortar, Christophe Colomb fashioned the rocks for the niche. He used an inverted iron sugar kettle for the dome and with little shells he built an altar. The effect is beautiful and unusual and people from all over the United States visit the grotto and marvel at its unique construction. A story worth telling is that of Mr. Vasseur Webre.

Mr. Webre and two companions went on a hunt at Nita Plantation. They became lost and for several days wandered aimlessly and hopelessly through the woods and swamps back of Nita. Frantic searching parties looked in vain. Mr. Webre alternately prayed, hoped, and called. He promised our Lady of Lourdes public recognition if they were rescued. At the end of the fourth day, they were found . . . weak and exhausted, scratched by briars, devoured by mosquitoes, and blistered by the sun, but alive and grateful. . . . Mr. Webre's little marble "ex-voto" is perched in a conspicuous place among the rocks of Lourdes to this day. It reads: "Ex-voto — le 25 Juliet 1876. Reconnaissance a N.D de Lourdes."

And before closing our story of St. Michel, perhaps a word about *le bon vieux Pierre*[2] would not be amiss. Pierre, an old Negro who recently died in his eighties, spent his whole life in the service of St. Michel. One might say that he was butler, sexton, gardener, and what-not . . . a real pillar of the church. Priests were changed, new wardens were elected, parishoners died, or moved away, but Pierre like an old land-mark stayed on. All his life he saved the wages paid him by the church and when he died he willed most of that back to the church.

And today St. Michel, nestled close to the banks of the mighty Mississippi, still stands . . . undaunted and unshaken . . . consecrated in the past, blessed by the present, and hopeful of the future.

FOOTNOTES

1. The nuns donated $6,000 and the bishop $2,675.
2. *Le bon vieux Pierre* . . . the good old Pierre. His real name was Pierre Duhon.
3. See index for list of pastors.

## XI

## THROUGH THE WARS

There have been so many wars in which St. Jamesians have participated that a volume would be required to give everything in detail, so I shall confine my remarks to a more general outline.

By 1752 the Indian wars in Louisiana were on the wane, and since St. James was founded after that time, the first St. Jamesians were not troubled by the Indians. In fact, there were few Indians in St. James and these were friendly. No doubt, old Jacques Cantrelle, remembering his own unhappy experience with the Indians in the Natchez massacre, took especial care to cultivate the friendship of the dwindling Houma here.

The French and Indian war did not spread to south Louisiana, but the result of the Secret Treaty of Fontainebleau in 1762 had an important effect on the history of St. James. After this treaty, east St. James, as part of the Island of Orleans, and west St. James, as part of the vast Louisiana domain, were ceded to Spain. Thus we passed under Spanish rule. The St. Jamesians resented this, as did most of the French people of Louisiana. They particularly disliked the trade laws and restrictions imposed by the Spanish government. In 1768 the people of the parish openly sided with the New Orleans patriots in an effort to free Louisiana of Spanish domination. Many Acadians, Creoles, and Germans of the Acadian and German Coasts[1] led by Noyan and Villeré, marched into New Orleans and actively participated in the revolutionary movement there. The Spanish Governor left and, apparently, the revolutionists had won their cause, but O'Reilly arrived with twenty-four ships and a large army and the rebellious Louisianians were subdued. Noyan and Villeré subsequently lost their lives in this coup, but St. James, as part of Louisiana, remained in the Spanish fold.

We know that by 1770 St. James had a well organized militia. It was headed by Nicholas Verret, Jacques Cantrelle, Jr., and Michel Cantrelle. It was known locally as the Cabahonnocer Company, but officially as La Premiere Compagnie des Milices de la Côte des Acadians. A roster of this company is given in the appendix.

Contrary to popular belief St. James played its part in the Revolutionary War. We were under Spanish rule but the vicinity of Baton Rouge was held by the English. In 1779 Spain declared war against England. Don Bernardo de Galvez was then Spanish governor of Louisiana. Although he was a very young man he was a daring and able officer and as soon as news reached him that Spain was at war with England he marched from New Orleans and captured Manchac and Baton Rouge. He personally recruited the Germans and the Acadians along the river and the Cabahannocer Company joined him here. They took part in the engagement at Manchac and Baton Rouge and some followed Galvez to Mobile and Pensacola. Thus many St. Jamesians actually fought in the Revolutionary War. An interesting letter from Jacques Cantrelle to the Governor follows:

I had the honor of receiving your letter dated January 17 (1780), with the royal copy by which His Majesty authorizes all his American colonies to attack and to defend themselves against the colonies of Great Britain. This I had published and posted in our parish as soon as it was received.

Your very humble and very obedient servant,
Jacques Cantrelle[2]

Dated Feb. 14, 1780.

It is interesting to note that the edict from the King of Spain was received in this parish several months after the fighting took place at Baton Rouge.

During the war of 1812 St. Jamesians joined Jackson in the defense of New Orleans. Fortier in his Louisiana, Vol. II, p. 589 says... "three hundred Acadians from the Acadian Coast joined Jackson on December 30, 1814." Early in 1815 word was received in St. James that the British might try to come up the Mississippi River, via Bayou Lafourche. St. James volunteers, among whom were the Webres, Trudeau, Oubres, Romans, Gaudins and Forestalls, rushed to Donaldsonville to help defend it, but Jackson gave Pakenham such a drubbing at the battle of New Orleans that no English ever appeared at Lafourche.

In the Civil War we find a noted St. Jamesian trying to avert the blow. André B. Roman, who had been governor of Louisiana, was sent to Washington in 1861 as one of the representatives of the Confederacy. The object of the mission was to try to arrange a peaceful withdrawal of the southern states from the Union. The committee failed and Mr. Roman returned home to pledge his all to the cause. His son, Alfred Roman, organized a company known as Les Chasseurs de St. Jacques, which later became a part of the eighteenth infantry and served with valor. Among them were six Webre brothers. Adolphe Webre, officer and volunteer, died in action, and four of the other brothers, Charles, Emile, Ernest and Septime were wounded.

When Admiral Farragut captured New Orleans in 1862, the war really came to St. James. General Butler occupied the city and the river section above it. Federal gunboats came up the river shooting at random across the levee, with the people running to the river rather than away from it because the levees afforded the only protection. Unexploded cannon balls are still found on many plantations. The gunboats tied up at the Convent wharf in May and Union troops occupied Jefferson College.

The convent was the property of French nuns and the French flag flew over it. Federal officers from the gunboats called at the convent and Mother Shannon, Irish by blood but Confederate by adoption, received them. They asked her to lower the French flag and to raise the Union flag. She politely agreed to lower the French flag, but she positively refused to raise the Union flag. General Butler gave orders to his troops stationed here to protect the nuns and their property and the convent was not molested. Food became scarce and at the convent, as elsewhere in the parish, corn bread, salted pork, and syrup were the main articles of diet.

Alcée Fortier, grandson of Valcour Aime, describes the events on his grandfather's plantation at that time:[3]

"After the fall of New Orleans, the Federal gunboats ascended the river, and being attacked by Confederate batteries on the banks, bombarded the plantations as they passed. This was natural where there were batteries, but, too often, houses were bombarded in front of which stood no batteries. How well do I remember the flight of our whole family to the river front to seek the protection of the levee, whenever a gunboat was coming. There we stood behind the levee, my sisters and myself, our school mistress and our nurses, while our father stood on the levee to look at the Federal gunboats and at the shells, which generally passed over our heads, but which, occasionally were buried in the levee and covered us with dust. Our house was never touched by the shells, but those of a number of our relatives and friends were considerably damaged, and I remember seeing cart loads of balls strewn in the yards. How dramatic all this was: the huge iron clad *Essex* passing in triumph the river batteries, her shells whizzing like huge meteors over our heads, and we helpless against the invaders! I remember also the holes dug in the ground and covered with thick beams and several feet of earth, the inside arranged like a comfortable room and filled with provisions of all kinds. Then came the Federal soldiers in garrison on the plantation, and well-behaved: then the insolence of some of the liberated slaves, the temporary arrest of my father and my grandfather, the serio-comic scenes at the provost marshal's court, where, too often, favors, or rather rights, had to be bought; then the flight of the family to the Téche and the pillaging by the conquering army; the return home and then complete ruin."

Although little or no fighting took place in St. James proper, money was raised, horses, food, and other supplies were donated and singly or in groups the men went off to war. Madame Boucry's entry in her diary[4] dated September 15, 1861 says simply: "La compagnie de Monsieur Druilhet est partie." (Mr. Druilhet's company left) In private homes and at the convent the woman sewed for the soldiers. The nuns sent clothing, medical supplies, and religious articles to the troops. The enrollment at the convent dropped from 200 in 1860-61 to eighteen in January 1862. While the convent property was guarded and respected by the Union troops, the rest of St. James did not fare so well. There was much raiding, ransacking, and pillaging and Mother Shannon appealed to General Butler to have his troops stop such marauding which he actually did. Clothing became very scarce and the old spinning wheels were taken down and again cottonade was woven by the Acadians. And Valcour Aime, too old to fight, donated $500 to each company which was officially organized. The following military companies were formed:

    Tirailleurs de St. Jacques (Co. K. 30th Regt. La. Infantry)
    Chasseurs de St. Jacques (Co. E. 8th La. Infantry)
    Chasseurs de St. Michel (La. Militia—served in St. James
        Regt. Ind.)
    Valcour Aime's Guards (Co. A. later 30th La. Infantry)
    French Company of St. James (La. Militia Ind. Co.)

National Guard of St. James (La. Militia Ind.—Captain: F. E. Lapaginier)
St. James Guards (30th La. Inf. Lecoul's Co.)
St. James Rifles (Co. A. 18th La. Inf.)

In 1864 the Marist Fathers, known as the Society of Mary, acquired Jefferson College. This, too, was a French order and as France and the United States were on friendly terms, the Union troops were withdrawn from the college to the upper end of the parish where they camped in an old saw mill.

The period of Reconstruction brought with it the same problems here as elsewhere. The Knights of the White Camellia eventually reestablished white supremacy, but this took some time because the Negroes in St. James had the superiority in number. It was at this time that St. James had three Negro sheriffs and that the parish seat was moved to Convent. Prior to this, the courthouse was located near the St. James Church on the west bank of the river. It is said that $90,000 was appropriated to build the new courthouse at Convent, but that only $10,000 was spent on it. The other eighty thousand "went carpetbag."

The Spanish American War was of such short duration that it had little or no effect on St. James, other than the movement of volunteers from here, who went to New Orleans to enlist.[6] World War I is so recent that it will not be necessary to write on that topic except to state that St. James sent its quota, five of whom made the supreme sacrifice. Most of the casualties of World War I were caused by the flu epidemic and the record lists "lobar-pneumonia" or "influenza" more frequently than "killed in action". Four St. Jamesians died on the field of battle and one subsequently died of wounds received thereon. The list follows:

        Octave Baudry, Jr.—Lutcher
        Adrien Kliebert—St. Patrick
        Lazzard L. Landry—Lutcher
        Alcide C. Lasseigne—Welcome
        Walter B. Webre—Union

And here is a little story handed down to us from World War I: St. James sent many men who spoke no English. One of them had a peculiar French name and his top sergeant gave it an English pronounciation. For the first three days the sarge called the roll and marked the soldier absent. A check was then made and the French-speaking soldier had to do a lot of "lingo" to convince his top-kick that he had been there all along — the trouble being that he didn't recognize his Anglicized name and didn't know that he was being called.

And in World War II the young St. Jamesians, like their ancestors of 1779, once more fought for America. And though, like the soldier of World War I, some spoke only French, the cause of freedom is the same in any tongue. And many St. Jamesians were decorated for service beyond the call of duty, one of whom was Henry Ockmann of Merrill's Marauders fame.

Yes, St. Jamesians have done their share through the wars. They have defended well the rights won by their gallant forbears. And on the green isles of the vast Pacific, on the time-worn battlefields of Europe and Asia, and in the deep blue waters of ageless seas, some of the fighting sons of St. James sleep in eternal rest. In this little parish, too, the people have sadly, but bravely, learned the meaning of "blood, sweat, and tears." And deep in the hearts of present St. Jamesians should be forever inscribed the names of them who in World War II gave their all. Let us not forget:

Charles Accardo—Hester
James E. Bourgeois—Convent
Hughes Braud—Gramercy
Odell Breaud—Lutcher
Leroy J. Callaghan—Lutcher
Miller Chauvin—Union
Joseph L. Falgoust—Vacherie
Neil Gaudet—Paulina
Charles A. Granier—St. James
Clarence Green—Gramercy
Wilfred Guidry—Union
Étienna Labat—Lutcher
Gaspard Lassere—Vacherie

Joseph Lassere—Vacherie
Donald Lemoine—Lutcher
Wilton Poirier—Paulina
George Pollet—Paulina
Harry C. Porta—Central
Edmond Peltier—Lutcher
Wilson Reulet—Vacherie
Larry Roussel—Hester
Ray Roussel—Paulina
Ulysse Roussel—Hester
Nelson Savoie, Jr.—Gramercy
Walter Schexnayder—Welcome
Fern J. Trosclair—Lutcher

And though we fought two wars to end all wars, we never won the peace and again we found ourselves engaged in tragic conflict. And while some defined the Korean War as a minor incident, to them who lost a son it was a deep and lasting sorrow which only a permanent peace can assuage. So once again a cross of valor marks the final resting place of some of St. James' sons:

> Joseph Cantrelle, Jr.—Gramercy
> F. J. Gendusa—Convent
> Larry Kinler—Paulina
> Melvin J. Waguespack—Central
> Clifton Watson—Lutcher

### FOOTNOTES

1. Acadian Coast . . . St. James and Ascension Parishes . . . German Coast . . . St. John and St. Charles Parishes.
2. Papeles de Cuba, 193 A, Archivo General de Indias.
3. Fortier, Alceé . . . Louisiana Studies, pp. 221-222.
4. This diary was compiled by Madame Jean Baptiste Boucry. After her death it was continued by her daughter, Madame Jules Dornier, and followed by her grand daughter, Miss Marie Dornier.
5. See the appendix for the list of soldiers of the Civil War.
6. Listed in the appendix.

The Mississippi River near Brilliant Point, so called because of the sparkling, brilliant water there. (Photo by Charles O. Subra)

# TRANSLATION

Cabanoce'

Pursuant to the petition hereto annexed, of Nicholas Verret, and in view to facilitate the establishment which he wishes to form for his seven children, we have granted, and do hereby grant by these presents to him, twenty arpens front with all the depth that may be found, on a tract of land adjoining & below the one he now occupies; situate on the river St. Louis or Mississippi, at the place called Cabanoce, above & on the other side of New Orleans; — so that he, his heirs, or assigns, may hold & possess in fee & usufruct as a property belonging to them, — safe, prior titles on possession contrary to this: under conditions, that within one year of this date he will cause them to be valuable yield; in default of which, & said term having expired, they will be replaced in the domain of the king, who will dispose of them as if this grant had never been made; and also, under condition to pay the *seigneurial rights*; if any were hereafter established in this province. We shall, in the same manner receive in the name of H. Majesty, all & in particular, the necessary timber for the construction of forts, stores, and other works which are, or may hereafter be annexed by H. majesty, & even for repairs of his vessels whenever required, as well as the necessary land for construction & fortifications.

Respecting the courses which must limit said twenty arpens front, they will be established by posts planted to that effect, for which a proces verbal shall be made & annexed to these presents, after they have been dully registered on our register of concessions.

Given at New Orleans, under our seal of arms, & the counter-signatures of our secretaries, this 25th of June 1765 — Signed, Aubry & Foucault

Countersigned: Soubie & Duverge'
Charles Philippe Aubry
Dennis Nicholas Foucault

LAND GRANT TO NICHOLAS VERRET — 1765

## XII

## JUST PEOPLE

I have given so many character sketches in this story, that I presume that only a word or two about the people will suffice. And since St. James is mostly Creole and Acadian, it is best, that this space be devoted to them.

For many years there was a great dividing line between the Creoles and the Acadians. The Creoles here were mostly of French descent, although there were some Spanish. They were a proud lot, these people — sociable, charitable, cultured, but proud. As the big plantations fell into post-bellum decay, many Creoles moved into New Orleans, but among those who stayed, there were many who lost all of their money and none of their pride, and "Catchez les apparences"[1] became the family watchword. No help was given, certainly none was asked, and I doubt if any would have been accepted, as I have heard, at least one say, that between begging and stealing, she'd rather steal. This is, I know, a very isolated instance, but the remark serves to show how deep rooted was their pride.

It is difficult to describe accurately the Creoles as they were so individualistic. Certainly they were people who were easily bored and many were quite temperamental. For instance, when visting in New Orleans one St. James lady refused to ride in a carriage unless it were drawn by two white horses. And in a certain Madame's house in Convent, people who rocked had to place their rocking chairs parallel to the floor boards so as not to mar the floor by cross-wise marks. And even though some of the high-toned ladies were illiterate, or nearly so, this did not prevent them from putting on the grandest airs. One such grande dame upon returning from a visit to New Orleans brought some orange-flower to her daughter-in-law. In presenting it she said: "It is the best — from France." The daughter-in-law, who was highly educated, decided to give the old lady, upon whom she wasted no great affection a poke in the ribs and read from the label that it was a product of Italy. Well, said the old lady drawing herself up proudly: "L'Italie est bien dans la France!"[2]

The Acadians were the small farmers, the artisans, and the traders of that day. They built small houses filled them with big families and gave the parish much of its colour and natural charm. They were a friendly people. They loved gaiety, laughter, music, and bright colors. Their little homes, entirely lacking in luxury, were brimful of life, love, and friendly understanding. The Acadian has an appropriate way of describing his home. "C'est pas grand chose, mais c'est mon nic."[3] Here his friends are welcome. And if there is one thing that an Acadian really enjoys it is meeting an old friend whom he has not seen in a long time. One such Acadian moved away from Convent and though the distance was short, he did not see his old neighbors often. He set himself up in business and prospered. One day two ladies, who had been his close neighbors and whom he had not seen in twenty years, stopped in. He waited upon them with a curious air and then one of the ladies asked him if he did not recognize them and they introduced themselves. Confounded, but with genuine delight he exclaimed: "Oh, non, but dat ain't you all, ein?" And that fifteen cents sale and thirty-minute reminiscing was surely the high point of his day. The Creole ladies enjoyed it too, because one of the first remarks made by the Acadian after his breathless surprise was: "How come you all ain't got ole?" And that is the way to a woman's heart!

In time many barriers were let down. Acadian and Creole intermarried and together they absorbed the German element. Today Creole-Acadian St. James with a sprinkling of les Americains,[4] a large contingent of Italians, and scattering of others, carries on with much of the characteristics of their forbears. How they enjoy *la tite partie*,[5] *un bal*, a pass-the-day, *une causette*, and a *tit-cou*. They love to talk-to each other and about each other — and there's a dash of red pepper in their quick tempers.

It is very difficult to select a few personalities from the long list of St. Jamesians. Like all communities, the parish has had its odd characters, its famous men, its gifted women, its humdrum people, its distinguished persons, and its riff-raff. I shall here describe a few St. Jamesians, not because they have been the most unique or the most influential persons, but rather I shall draw from here and there to give a picture of the people, past and present, of St. James.

## From the Arts

### AN ENGLISHWOMAN, MRS. LILLIE TRUST GRAY THIBODAUX

Mrs. Lillie Trust Gray Thibodaux was a woman of unusual character and charm. Through the long years that she taught music at the Sacred Heart Convent, she, and her adopted daughter, Miss Annie Gray, passed on her way to the convent with such punctilious regularity that people could set their clocks by the rattle of her carriage wheels.

We are told that Lillie Trust was a beautiful young girl, the daughter of a gifted English musician. One day during the Civil War, another Englishman, Dr. Charles Gray, who was stationed with the Union troops at upper White Hall, drove down to Convent in a buggy, quite a trip for that time. Near the Trust home Dr. Gray had a minor accident and through his delay here, he and the Trust family became acquainted. A friendship ensued between the two Englishmen, no doubt encouraged by Dr. Gray's heart interest in beautiful Lillie Trust. And like all good stories, it ended in romance, and Lillie Trust became Mrs. Gray in 1869.

Just five years later Dr. Gray was killed in a duel with Mr. Denis Richard. Mrs. Gray was an accomplished musician. She was playing the organ at St. Michel's when the message came that Dr. Gray was dead, but she did not leave the organ until the service was over.

After eleven years of widowhood Mrs. Gray married Mr. Lucien Thibodaux. She continued to teach music at the convent and to conduct and accompany the choir at St. Michel, where she was organist for forty years. She had a lovely soprano voice and her choir was noted up and down the river for its fine singing.

Lillie Trust had large, sparkling brown eyes, which flashed with interest in all things. She was tall and straight, cultured and friendly. She knew and was known by everyone and her passing in 1919 left a void in musical circles in St. James Parish.

The old Gray homestead here was recently purchased and is being restored by the Frank Vigueries. Mrs. Gray had a fine collection of antiques and an extensive music library. The antiques were sold by Miss Annie Gray to collectors and dealers and the music was purchased by the Louisiana State University School of Music.

And so here we have an English woman, who spent her entire life in a French community and, in passing, contributed much to the culture of St. Jacques de Cabahannocer.

### From the Unique

#### AN OLD NEGRESS, MARY JEFFERSON COLLEGE

I went to see Mary Jefferson College one day. Mary was in her garden and as I stood on the front porch waiting for her to come, I could hear her: "Who dat? What she want?" Yes, Mary had lost none of her pep, her quick fiery talk, her high staccato voice. From a distance, she sounded more like fifteen than the one-hundred-five, which she claimed. Even though she walked with a little difficulty, she wore no glasses, and she had the same animation of a day long past. She greeted me thus: "I can't walk good! I can't walk good! I'm getting old!" *Getting* old at a hundred-five — what a remarkable record!

Mary was a small, bright-colored mulatress, whose real name was Mary Tircuit Jeannine. She was a maid at Jefferson College for fifty years, which accounts for her strange appellation. Often when old Jeffersonians drove through Convent, they stopped to see Mary. The story is told that once an old Jeffersonian, now a prominent man, stopped to chat with her. He gave his name and asked if she remembered him. Came the quick reply: "Yas, indeed, — yas indeed! Gimme that quarter you owes me fer pressin your pants." And with much laughter the longstanding debt was paid with interest.

Mary's children and her husband were long dead and she lived with her granddaughter. Mary used no tobacco, but she enjoyed a tit-cou of wine or beer. She confided that she did not feel up to par that day, because she had not had a "lil drap" of wine for her dinner. She talked of old times and remembered many of the old students and Marist Fathers and her last words as she waved good-bye were: "When you see my old boys, tell em howdy — you hear — tell em howdy." And so, I'm passing Mary's message on — "Howdy boys."[6]

FROM STATESMANSHIP

A CREOLE, GOVERNOR ANDRÉ BIENVENU ROMAN

Governor Roman ranks as one of Louisiana's ablest governors. This was, no doubt, due to his splendid qualifications for high offices: honesty, integrity, modesty, and good judgment, to which we can also add education and refinement. These qualifications are sometimes overlooked by politicians, some of whom have self adulation and personal accumulation as their major objectives.

André Bienvenu Roman was not a native St. Jamesian, but like his name, Bienvenu,[7] he was welcome. He was born in St. Landry Parish and came to St. James after completing his education at St. Mary's College in Maryland. He was a brother of Jacques Telesphore Roman. The story of the Roman family has been covered in the chapter on Oak Alley.

Governor Roman served as governor two terms: 1831-35 and 1838-43. His administrations were confronted with many difficulties. There were floods, cholera, yellow fever, storms, and political unrest. Among his achievements we note progress in the advancement of education, order, finances, and public works. Yet when he left office he said, "I leave the office with which I have been honored, with the painful conviction of having done very little for the good of the state."[8]

Gov. Roman lived on his plantation in St. James in the ease and opulence of that time, but soon the Civil War came and he lost everything. He moved to New Orleans and died suddenly while walking down Dumaine Street on January 26, 1866. He was buried at St. Jacques de Cabahannocer in the dark days of Reconstruction, beloved and mourned by the whole state.

Several years ago the all-powerful Mississippi River decided to disturb again the dead of St. James and the Cabahannocer Cemetery was once more removed. Governor Roman had been dead over fifty years. He had been buried in a heavy steel casket with a thick glass front. When the outer steel cover was pushed back, there was Gov. Roman sleeping peacefully, exactly like the day he had been buried. Apparently, he had loved St. James so well, that he was loath to leave it and though he was quite dead— he was quite himself. Only his spirit had flown to meet the Master he had served so well.

## From A Fortune
### A Portuguese, Antoine J. Sobral

Another St. Jamesian of unique story is Antoine J. Sobral. It begins with the Dalferes family of Donaldsonville — only, then the family was known by its true Portuguese name: De Alfarez.

From Portugal came news that a fortune had been bequeathed to the De Alfarez family and they quickly dispatched a member to claim the inheritance. He was gone a long time and when he returned he brought back bad news and a wide-eyed little boy of ten years — no fortune. The riches could never be found. The De Alfarezes were disappointed and there was much conjecture and dismay along the banks of sleepy Bayou Lafourche. But the little boy's quiet, shy way, and his big brown eyes warmed the hearts of the De Alfarez clan and they began to call their little cousin from Portugal, "la fortune," instead of Antoine. Antoine's visit lengthened into years and when his uncle finally went back to Portugal, Antoine refused to go. He loved Loiuisana and here he stayed.

When the Civil War broke out Antoine Sobral enlisted in Captain Landry's Company of the Donaldsonville Artillery. He fought throughout the four years of the war and although he saw much action, being in Lee's army in Virginia, he was never wounded or imprisoned. Years later Mr. Sobral and his Donaldsonville cronies fought those battles over and over every Sunday afternoon. They told long, tall tales which always ended in explosive laughter and: "We gave those Yankees hell!"

When the war ended Mr. Sobral returned to Donaldsonville where he became an overseer on a plantation nearby. Here he married a Spanish girl, Evalina Gonzales. Later he bought St. Amelia Plantation in St. James and then he became co-owner of Beautiful Oak Alley, where he lived for twenty-three years. The dreamy-eyed little cousin, who had been "la fortune" of the Dalferes family had come into a fortune of his own.

## From the Pioneers
### A Commandante, Michel Cantrelle

No story of St. James could be complete without the story of Michel Cantrelle. His life was synonymous with the growth of the Acadian Coast which he served from 1770 to 1812.

He was born in New Orleans and christened by the Famous Father Dagobert on March 24, 1750. When he was fifteen years old, he moved with his father, Jacques Cantrelle, to Cabahannocer — a plantation in the willderness. At twenty he was a lieutenant in the militia and six years he was commandante of the Acadian Coast.

A Spanish commandante was the most important person in the post. In this capacity, Cantrelle wielded a great influence on the growing Acadian settlements. He could bestow many favors. He awarded contracts for building public works and for furnishing provisions. He issued land grants and he employed many persons. He had the power to make "cadets" of the children of the settlers. This was a privilege that *paid*. A cadet was given pay and provisions and in time could become an officer in the army. Although the salary of the commandante was small, there were many additional fees to gross the income and to boot there was the honor of being: "Don Miguel Cantrelle, Lieutenant in the Armies of His Majesty and Commandante of the Post of Cabahannocer, Parish of St. Jacques of the Acadians."

During the Revolutionary War Cantrelle fought under Galvez at Manchac, Baton Rouge, and Pensacola. When Louisiana was sold to the United States in 1803, Cantrelle was reappointed by Governor Claiborne. Dr. Watkins, who as the Governor's representative, visited the parish in 1804, wrote as follows: "Mr. Cantrelle was and has by reappointment been continued commandante. He has exercised the duties of this office for twenty-eight years to the general satisfaction of all the inhabitants. He is a wealthy and very respectable planter, a man of good sense and great unrightness of character, possessing popular manners and the universal esteem and confidence of his district. He does not, however, speak English."[9]

When the parish government was reorganized by the territorial legislature, Cantrelle became the judge of the parish of Acadia (St. James and Ascension). When Acadia became two separate political units Cantrelle served as parish judge of St. James until 1812.

Under the flags of France, Spain, and the United States Michel Cantrelle spent forty-two years of his life in the service of St. James Parish. He used his might and did his best and died just as the era of fabulous plantation life dawned. A pity!

Somehow Michel Cantrelle would have fitted well into the pattern of that golden age of rich brown sugar.

## From the Military
### Colonel Leopold L. Armant

The well-known St. James name, Armant, first appeared in the early history of the Illinois Country. By 1796 J. B. Armant was established on his own plantation adjoining that of Valcour Aime on the west bank of the river in St. James Parish. Here the Armants lived in the traditional fashion of the fabulous antebellum era. But the Civil War brought fame with sorrow to the Armants.

So Many St. Jamesians joined the renowned Eighteenth Louisiana Regiment that to the people of the parish it was known simply as *Le Dix-Huitieme*.[10] There could be no other. Among them was Leopold L. Armant, who became colonel of the Eighteenth after the battle of Shiloh.

Col. Armant was the son of General Seraphim Armant and Louise Émelie Fusilier de la Clair. At the time of his death he was engaged to marry Valcour Aime's grand-daughter, Anna Fortier. Col. Armant saw action in many sections but it was at the battle of Mansfield that he was killed on April 8, 1864.

Leading his beloved regiment with his father's sword flashing in the sun, he was hit in the arm and unhorsed. Cheering his men on, he was then wounded in both thighs. Undaunted he raised himself upon his bleeding arm, waved his hat, and cried, "Forward!" Another shot . . . in the chest . . . Armant lay dead. Mansfield was a bloody battle, a victory for the Confederates, and the last important battle in Louisiana.

Few people today remember the brave exploits of Colonel Leopold Armant. His picture and his sword are in the Cabildo in New Orleans . . . A poem written about him gathers dust in the files of a New Orleans newspaper . . . silent reminders of one who gave his all for his home, his parish, and his southland.

"How proud he looked that glorious day
When Mansfield dawned; how grandly led
The charge; how with uncovered head
From his brave horse that fallen lay.

*Residence of Valcour Aime. His niece is standing at the far right. (From a photograph in possession of James J. A. Fortier)*

*Bridge on the grounds of the Valcour Aime residence with house in the background. (Photograph belonging to James J. A. Fortier)*

*Upper left — Valcour Aime (From miniature in possession of James J. A. Fortier)*

*Upper right — Wife of Valcour Aime (from miniature in possession of James J. A. Fortier)*

*At left — The "fort" in Valcour Aime's garden. (Courtesy of Mrs. R. H. Potts)*

*Lower left — Site of Valcour Aime's garden as it looks today. (Courtesy Mrs. R. H. Potts)*

*Below — Valcour Aime's Tomb*

He rose and waved his hat, then sank
With one last "Forward!"...
Louisiana, never son
On any field, lost or won,
A nobler death hath died for you."

(From poem written by Col. Joseph Collins about Col. Armant).

#### FOOTNOTES

1. Cachez les apparences — hide the appearances ... meaning ... do not tell the family troubles.
2. Well, Italy is certainly in France.
3. C'est pas grand chose, mais c'est mon nic — It is not much, but it is my nest (home). The word nic is Canadian-French. It is used here for nid (nest).
4. Les Americains — The Americans ... This expression is still used here to denote English-speaking people.
5. La tite partie — a card game. Un bal — a ball or dance. A pass-the-day — to spend the day. Une causette — A chat. Tit-cou — a dram ... an intoxicating drink.
6. Mary died in 1947.
7. The French name, Bienvenu, is a word which means welcome.
8. Fortier, Alcée — Louisiana II, p. 393.
9. Report of Dr. Watkins to Gov. Claiborne taken from: Fortier, Alcée. History of Louisiana. Vol. 2, p. 312.
10. The Eighteenth.

## XIII

## ICI — ON PARLE LE FRANCAIS

Our early settlers were French and the French language has survived in St. James. No doubt the proud aloofness of the Creoles and the Acadian dislike for change contributed much to its survival. Added to that, were the educational opportunities provided by the Sacred Heart Convent and Jefferson College, both of which were administered by French societies. So it is not surprising that French is still spoken — some of the cultured French of the Creole and much of the more picturesque French of the Acadians.

Many of the descendents of John Law's early German settlers eventually moved from St. Charles and St. John into St. James. Indeed Vacherie, almost exclusively French in culture, is preponderantly German in name. Often when an Acadian-German is questioned as to his ancestry, he will reply proudly: "Me, I am a blue-bellied Cajun!" And it would be a death-blow to his pride to reveal his German lineage. These people were completely absorbed by the French, proving, even at that early date, that there is no such thing as the German conception of a master race. Their mannerisms, speech, customs, etc. have become French by Acadian, or Creole, absorption, and the only Germanic traces which remain are their blue eyes, blonde hair, and their French-spelled German names.

Certainly the greater number of St. James natives speak French and many who do not, usually understand it. There are still quite a few who speak no English and it is only within the last decade, or so, that French is not used for prayers, sermons, and announcements in most of the Catholic churches.

The French spoken in various sections of the parish differs. For instance, the French spoken at Union — Central is different to that spoken at Vacherie, which in turn, is still more unlike that spoken at Convent. Yet the French spoken in one section may be spoken by many persons in another section, because modern transportation has moved people from one place to another much faster than language changes take place. Then, too, few sections of the parish were settled entirely by German, or French, or Acadian, with the possible exception of Grande Pointe, Bellemont, and Vacherie. Rather the three root stocks settled along the river, the one adjacent to the other — an Acadian here, a Creole there, and a German on the other side. These people lived in complete harmony in religious, agricultural, commercial, and even political relations, but with a flat dead line dividing them in educational and social associations.

Unfortunately the French language is slowly dying in St. James and it is still more regrettable that so little is being done to preserve it. The younger children speak little French. Often the parent speaks French and the child answers in English. It is interesting to note how people change from French to English, and vice versa, with facility, naturalness and ease. They do not realize at all that a bi-lingual conversation is more of an oddity than a general occurrence. But more amusing is the employment of both languages in one sentence. One frequently hears: "J'va aller back",[1] or "Il est no-count, lui",[2] or "Mind-out tu v'attraper ain black eye",[3] all of which is neither French, nor English, nor Acadian, but rather a semblance of all three.

And too, there are many words of Spanish origin which we use in speaking French here. Some follow: *jambalaya*,[4] *savanne, tomate, grégue, ouragon, piroque, patate* and *chocolat*. *Piastre* is still used instead of dollar but piastre is Italian in origin, not Spanish. Among the perplexing words of St. James are *toise* and *arpent*. A toise is an old French measure approximately 6 2/5 feet. An arpent, too, is an old French measure, but here it is used as lineal or square. As a square measure an arpent is a little less than an acre. As a lineal measure an arpent is 192 feet.

The people of St. James are great talkers — not only with their tongues, but with their eyes, their hands, their arms, their whole bodies. In relating an incident the reconteur dramatizes his story and there is much mimicry and badinage. Some people are so anxious to talk that they sit on the edge of their chairs anxiously awaiting a break for breath. Often everybody talks at once and frequently one hears, "Clara, tais-toi, c'est mon tour."[5] They especially enjoy political gossip and an election year is most favorable for talk with loud bantering and hot argument. When the peak of the discussion is reached, everybody breaks into explosive laughter, and the principal participant, if he has won his point, will slap his knee, jump up, throw his arms up into the air, and turn completely around. These gregarious people love life. They like talk. They enjoy company and the oldsters find their animated conversations much superior to radio and television entertainment. And when some one begins: "Est-ce que tu te rapelle ———?"[6] Then they are in for a really big session.

An amusing incident is that of two elderly sisters, who visited each other every afternoon. Both were in their eighties, but none-the-less spry and talkative. One late afternoon Celeste came to see Delphine, who was just getting into her old-fashioned corset. She heard Celeste at her door and went to meet her tugging at the corset strings. At once they both began to talk as though they had not seen each other in years, Delphine backing and Celeste going forward — both very close, eye-to-eye, and quite oblivious to everything else. They traveled thus all the way to the back of the house and automatically retraced their steps to Delphine's room, so that she could get into her jupon[7] and her dress.

Yes, they love talk, these St. Jamesians, where they be eight, eighteen, or eighty . . . Creole or Acadian . . . and those Creole-Acadian-Germans, too. And though French has ceded its place to English in many homes, the French roots are still here. A native St. Jamesian says "Chat",[8] to his cat, and, "Passez",[9] to his dog. To illustrate:

A teen-age girl of Acadian descent was brought up in a town where she cultivated a disdain for French and always denied her Acadian extraction. One day while making a house-to-house canvas for votes in a Carnival-queen-contest she came to the farmhouse of an old French-speaking Acadian woman. In her best airy manner the girl began to solicit the old woman's support. With many signs and much laughter the genial old lady explained that she did not understand one word of English. At this the haughty young girl with a cynic disdain and a borrowed Texas twang began to tell that she could not speak *one* word of French. Just then a big shaggy dog came around the house with a menacing growl. With one loud yell "Passez", the girl jumped into her car and drove off. Her fright had brought out her French!

The cows, too, seem to be bi-lingual here. And in the evening dusk one can hear the farm boy clear over the country side: "Cha, cha, cha,[10] Mignon, cha Mignon!" And Mignon raises her head from her levee-grazing and slowly wends her way homeward, swatting the flies with her tail, while softly answering, "Moo!" Yes, the French roots are still here!

## As We Say It

Like all rural areas in French Louisiana, St. James has many peculiar and amusing expressions. Some are Acadian and others Creole in their origin, but many are common to both have been the spontaneous outbursts of a moment which required an unusual description. Many of the expressions used here are not local, but are in general use in Creole or Acadian families of French Louisiana. In listing a few examples, I shall give the expression, if possible its origin, and the locality where it is used.

*Du jololo* . . . weak coffee. The natives of a small Pacific island, Jolo, drank very weak coffee. The expression is a corruption of eau de Jolo (water of Jolo). Used at Convent.

*Les gros yeux à Dédé* . . . Dédé's big eyes. This expression here denotes clear vision. Dédé Jacob was a river pilot, who had such extraordinary sight, that he missed seeing nothing up and down the river in daylight and in darkness. Used at Convent.

*Il a toujours la fale vide* . . . He always has an empty craw . . . meaning that he is always hungry. Used at Romeville.

*J'vais coté Tantôt* . . . I am going toward the hereafter. It means getting old or contemplating death. Used at College Point.

*Il a une grande babinette* . . . He has a long face. Babinette is a corruption of a babine-lip . . . Used generally.

*Un tit cou* (un petit coup) . . . a draught of wine or other intoxicating beverage. Used generally.

*La bricaillerie* . . . Scraps. Used in describing teen-age boys. Used at Central — Union.

*Des maquillon d'cordelle* . . . clothspins. Usually termed *des épingles à linge*. Used at Vacherie.

*Tu as un tit morceau d'Bertaut*. You have a little piece of Bertaut. Auguste Bertaut had a plantation almost directly across the river from his sister on Rapidan Plantation. But Auguste had a very loud voice also. Whenever he and his wife decided to cross the river to spend the day with his sister, he would go to the river's edge and yell: "O, Dada, on vient diner, tue des poules."[11] To this day anyone who speaks in too loud a voice is said to have "un tit morceau d'Bertaut!" Used at Convent, Romeville, and St. James.

*J'vais poudré mon estomac* . . . I shall powder my stomach, meaning I shall eat a little snack. This is derived from the habit of a spinster, who arose and ate at all hours of the night. She gave as an excuse that she had a gnawing feeling in her stomach and that food quieted this. The expression now denotes the act of eating a little snack when one shouldn't. Used at Convent and Romeville.

*Granman Alexandre* — A very miserly old woman had many children, grandchildren, and great grand children to whom she was known as Granman Alexandre. No doubt she possessed some good qualities, but her many descendants remembered nothing of her except her extreme stinginess. That trait was handed down to one or another in each successive generation. To this day the parsimonious person is always called: Granman Alexandre. Today the name is applied to any stingy woman. Used at Convent, Central and Romeville.

And here is an English expression to complete the story: "This ain't from the kitchen, but straight from the parlor." This expression is used among Negroes here to emphasize that the information given is authentic. It originated among the slaves who used it to show the difference between slave kitchen gossip and overheard parlor conversations of the masters. It is probably in use in other sections of America. Used at Convent.

FOOTNOTES

1. J'va aller back . . . I am going back.
2. Il est no-count, lui . . . He is no good.
3 Mind out, tu v'attraper ain black-eye . . . Mind. you will get a black eye.
4. Jambalaya . . . A creole dish whose main ingredient is rice. Savanne . . . pasture. Tomate . . . tomato. Grégue . . . coffee biggin. Ouragnon . . . hurricane. Pirogue . . . dug-out, skiff, or other small row-boat. Patate . . . sweet potato, but generally used here for any potato.
5. Clara, hush, it is my turn.
6. Est-ce-que tu te rapelles? . . . Do you remember?
7. *Jupon* . . . petticoat.
8. *Chat* . . . Scat.
9. *Passez* . . . go away.
10. *Cha, cha, cha,* . . . used to call cattle.
11. *On vient diner, tue des poules* . . . We are coming to dinner . . . kill some chickens. The Creoles uses *volaille* for chicken and the Acadian uses *poule*.

## XIV

## LA VACHERIE

Vacherie is a French word meaning cow house or ranch. It is a word which is frequently used in old records here, so it is not surprising that a village bears this name. The surprising part is that this little community is almost exclusively French in language and culture, yet almost entirely German in name and appearance. Here one finds stocky, blue-eyed, blond boys playing football in French: "Quand tu attrapes la plotte,[1] galope!" and "Si tu peux, coionne le!"[2]

Shortly after the founding of New Orleans, John Law's German colonists settled on the lands above the city in St. Charles and St. John Parishes. From these German settlements there came to St. James three families — the Steins, the Zellers, and the Ockmanns. They rowed across Lake des Allemands to fish. Here they found a ridge, and as higher land was always desirable because of the Mississippi River floods, the fisher folk stayed to farm. The first house was a cabin built by Stein just across the street from the present school house. Stein was soon followed by others and thus Vacherie was settled by Germans. Then the Acadians arrived, many of whom settled on the ridge among the Germans, and proceeded to absorb them. Acadians raised cattle. Such a ranch or stock farm was a "vacherie" so the settlement became La Vacherie.[3]

The story is told that one day a Chickasaw Indian came to trade with the frugal and hard working Germans. He became critically ill and a German settler, Joseph Weber, nursed him back to health. A few weeks later a woman in the Weber household went out into her garden to cut a cabbage for dinner. Instead she was bitten by a rattlesanke. The Chickasaw ran to his pirogue and returned with a small, flat, blackish-brown stone which he applied to the wound and the woman recovered. This was the mad stone of Vacherie described in the chapter on Indians.[4] The Chickasaw stayed a year. When he left he gave the stone to Weber who had befriended him. And so it is that the Vacherie stone has belonged to the Weber family for about one hundred and fifty years.

More than any other place in St. James, Vacherie has preserved its old French culture while it has acquired the modern conveniences of the American way of life. Today it is a sprawling village of German-Acadian Americans who have the laughter, the friendliness, and the love of life and color of their Acadian forbears, mixed with the industry and the thrift of their German ancestors. Soft musical French is spoken. Families are large — there are three sets of twins in the Anthony Gravois family. And like most French-Louisiana towns the coffee pot is never empty and the women make the best chicken gumbo this side of Heaven.

### FOOTNOTES

1. Quand tu attrapes la plotte, galope — When you get the ball, run. The word plotte is used here for ball . . . The French word for ball is "balle."

2. Si tu peux, coionne le — If you can, get him. The word coionner is used here meaning to box . . . or to knock out.

3. It is quite probable that Vacherie was the first settlement in the parish, but no proof is available. The older people in Vacherie claim that the Indians who built Shell Hill came here after the white people. Since some of these Indians came here in 1764 and the Vacherie settlers preceded them, the Vacherie settlement would ante-date that of the Cantrelles.

4. She was bitten on the finger. The stone has been applied to various parts of the anatomy and some claim that it was once used on the human tongue.

## XV

## NAMES: PEOPLE AND PLACES

Although the greater number of St. James families have French names, there are a trace of Spanish, many German, a few Swiss, and some others. Under French rule there were Swiss troops in Louisiana. When their period of service was completed many of them settled among the Germans of the German Coast. In time they, as well as the Germans, came to St. James in fairly large number.

Many of the names of the first settlers such as Cantrelle, Judice, LeBlanc, Poirier, still survive, but in some cases changes have taken place in the original names. The Chauvin-Delery family has branched into Chauvins and Delerys. Of the German names most were spelled phonetically by French priests and in this process, Wagensbach became Waguespack, Foltz became Folse, etc.

In reading early French records one is surprised to note how many persons had aliases. For instance one of the first wardens of the St. James Church was Joseph Hubert, *dit*[1] Laparde. One wonders if there is any connection there with the present profusion of nick-names among the French-speaking people of St. James. Nearly every one has a nick-name, whether he be Creole or Acadian. Some have several and in many cases the given name is seldom heard. A boy is Christened Joseph, is called Jo-jo, grows up to *M'sieu* Joe[2] and his wife becomes *M'am* Joe.[3] Surely the peak of nick-names was reached when Benjamin was called Bében, his father became Gros-Bében,[4] and his son Tit-Béhen.[5] Then when Theodule married, his wife became Tante Theodule.[7] This last custom is slowly disappearing. Today we have a decided trend of coupling English names with French surnames. One hears Eldred Laplanche and Wilton LeBlanc. But the favorite is still Joseph and Mary and every large family has a Joseph and/or a Marie.

Below are a few St. James surnames which have survived through many generations:

*French*
Roman
Trudeau        Cantrelle

*Canadian*
Scionneau
Chauvin        Verret

*Acadian*
Landry
LeBlanc        Martin

*Spanish*
Vegas — formerly — Viga
Rodrigue — formerly — Rodriguez
Sanchez

*German*
Haydel — formerly — Heidel
Vicknair — formerly — Wichner
Weber — formerly — Vebre

*Swiss*
Toups — formerly — Dubs
Kinler — formerly — Kindeler

The following St. James names appeared in the New Orleans census of 1726: Lambert, Simon, Bourgeois, Poirier, Bergeron, Saunier, Martin, Bernard, Vincent and Dupuy. These names are usually classified as Acadian and there were, in fact, many Acadians of the same name, but since these people lived in New Orleans as early as 1726 and as the Acadians did not arrive until many years later, the people bearing these names are as likely to be French or of Canadian, as of Acadian stock.

There are many in St. James today who are the direct descendants of the survivors of the Natchez massacre. While only twenty men escaped, most of the woman and children were made prisoners and were later rescued. Of their descendants who later settled in St. James were the Judice, Cantrelle, Rousseau and Lambremont families.

Other names not given elsewhere which appeared in Louisiana between 1720-1730 and which are still found in St. James today are: Alexandre, Gaudin, Mericq, Huguet, Robert, Plaisance, Millet, Jacob, Goudeau, LaPlace, Sarazin, St. Martin, Petit and others.

Among the early and influential settlers of the Acadian Coast who came here in the late 1700's and the early 1800's and whose names are scarcely mentioned elsewhere in the story are the following: Patrice Uriell, François Croizet, Hubert Rémy, François Meffre Rouzan, Jean Baptiste Boucry, Joseph Constant, James Mather, Justin Terrell, J. B. Tete, Jean Baptiste Poeyfarré, Richard Fowler, Joseph Laurent Fabre and Jean Gourdain. With few exceptions, most of these names have entirely disappeared from the parish.

One of the oldest Louisiana names which has survived in St. James is Trudeau. François Trudeau, his wife, and child were listed in the Louisiana census of 1706. At that time there were but eighty-five white persons living in Louisiana. The later census of 1721 finds Trudeau well established. There he is listed with his wife, seven children, two French servants, thirty-two slaves, nine head of cattle, and four horses. To own a horse in New Orleans in 1721 was something of a marvel. In fact there were only nine horses in New Orleans and Trudeau owned four of them. Trudeau's holdings were surpassed by few persons of that time. Among these few were the three Chauvin brothers, whose descendants still live in St. James. In very recent years some of the Trudeaux moved from St. James into Orleans and St. John Parishes. The old Trudeau home at Convent is still standing and it is presently occupied by the Poché family. Poché, too, is quite an old name — Jacques Poché was living near the river above New Orleans as early as 1724.

It was one of François Trudeau's daughters, Marie Thérese, who provided Louisiana with a stirring and adventurous romance in the early 1730's.

She fell in love with an army officer, Alphonse La Buissonnière. At that time regardless of rank, French officers in the Louisiana service had to obtain official government permission to marry. This the governor refused. Undaunted Marie Thérese and La Buissonnière eloped to Spanish-governed Pensacola where a Franciscan priest married them. The Louisiana clergy and government officials were furious and La Buissonnière was recalled and ordered to report for duty to isolated Fort Chartres in the Illinois Country. Marie Thérese was forbidden to accompany him.

At that time traveling from New Orleans to the Illinois Country was by boat in convoy twice a year. Usually three or four months were required for the up-river trip. La Buissonnière left in the convoy of 1733 with Marie Thérese secretly embarked in another boat. When out of sight of the city she joined her husband on his boat. But misfortune tagged on and at Natchez she was striken with small-pox. Discovered she was compelled to return to her father's house while a sad La Buissonnière continued to Fort Chartres and military duty. Two years elapsed before the marriage was finally confirmed by the court and Marie Thérese was allowed to rejoin her husband proving that love laughs at locksmiths . . . small-pox nothwithstanding.

And for those who would like to know the end of the story: For once good fortune smiled upon them and La Buissonnière became commandante of the Illinois Country in 1737. Life in Louisiana was hard and short in those adventurous days and La Buissonnière died on December 11, 1740. But time mends even broken hearts . . . and Marie Thérese Trudeau La Buissonnière married again . . . and to another officer . . . Louis Robineau de Portneuf.

But the oldest name in St. James by far is Hébert. In fact some of the Héberts of the parish date their ancestry to the first white French child born in America, one hundred years before the founding of New Orleans. The story: In the spring of 1605 Louis Hébert, Parisian chemist, whose father had the distinction of being in the service of the queen of France, Catherine de Medici, came to Quebec with his family. They and a couple named Vienne were the only permanent French colonists and Mrs. Vienne died shortly after her arrival. Although glowing promises had been made to the Héberts by a French trading company in order to induce them to come to America, these promises were not kept. In fact the company treated the Hébert family more like slaves and it was only because of their untiring work that they managed to raise enough food to keep themselves alive. But they survived and in 1629 it was the produce from Hébert's farm which helped to save the garrison of Quebec from starvation. Over three hundred years later Louis Hébert's direct descendents, the Camille Héberts, were native-residents of St. James. There are other Hébert families in the parish today, some of whom, no doubt, trace their ancestry to that first French family in America: the Louis Héberts. In the census of 1766 we find the name of Francois Hébert. In 1779 Joseph Hébert,

Acadian, followed Galvez in the fight to capture Baton Rouge during the Revolutionary War Hébert is indeed an old name... and a good one!

But the name of names in St. James Parish is neither French nor Spanish, but German. Many stories of its origin have been written but no one has yet solved the problem of its spelling. In the church and court records here one finds many variants of the name of one of John Law's early immigrants. He settled somewhere along the German Coast, but many of his prolific descendants moved into St. James bringing with them this orthographic puzzle:

| | |
|---|---|
| Sechnedre | Seixnaydre |
| Seckjedre | Seckgeneidre |
| Sechenedre | Sexchnaildre |
| Secknejedre | Scheckschneide |
| Chesnaeldre | Sickneyeder |
| Chisnaildre | Sexchjeneider |
| Checnaitre | Sexneyder |
| Chetaildre | Schexnayder |
| Chitaildre | Schexnardre |
| Chisnailder | Schexnailder |
| Chexnaitre | Schexnaildre |
| Sixchnaidre | |

And to further complicate the matter one of the clan who wrote in a clear bold hand signed thus: Jean Seckjehneidre. And *that* looks a little like it sounds.

The place names of St. James are curious too, and there is much variety and legend. Since many of the place names have appeared elsewhere in this story, I shall add only a few more.

*La Longue Vue* is today known as Paulina. There is a long stretch of the Mississippi where it is very straight affording a long view of the river. The French called it *La Longue Vue*. Incidentally this is one of the oldest names of the parish. It appeared in the records of 1785. The transition to Paulina is not clear. Legend says that a nun named Pauline lost her prayerbook with her name inscribed therein. The place where it was found became Paulina.

Many of the place names of St. James were changed when the railroads and postoffices were established. For instance the plantation was *Welham,* the railway station became *Oneida,* and the post office *Hester.* This is rather confusing.

*Belmont* is the location of a large Indian mound. The French said, "Qu'elle belle moule!" In time belle moule became Belmont.

*Burton* and *Lutcher* were named after the owners of saw mills established in those places.

*Gramercy* was named after the Gramercy Park in New York by Mr. Spellman, who was connected with the Colonial Sugars.

*College Point* is deduced from the college built on the point — a big bend in the river.

*Welham* was a poor-working man who longed for a plantation. By hard work he acquired three adjoining tracts of land and named them all Welham after himself. Evidently he became quite prosperous as when his daughter entered the convent to become a nun, she was said to have brought a dower of fifty thousand dollars with her. A subsequent owner, Mr. Leon Keller had long desired this plantation. When he finally realized his wish and acquired it, a son was born. He was christened: Leon *Desiré Welham* Keller.

*Convent* for a long time was simply St. Michel, but later became Convent because of the Sacred Heart Convent built there.

*Timberton* was a saw mill and village built away from the river near the swamp — a town in the timber: Timberton.

*St. James* was first called Cabahannocer — later Cantrelle — but it finally held on to the name of the St. James Church.

*White Hall* was first the domain of the Bringier family and was named after their big white house, or White Hall.

*Romeville* was once the site of the Webre plantation. The Webres intermarried with the Romes and because of the many Rome families, the village became Romeville. The Romes, by the way, are the descendants of one of John Law's early colonists, Johann Rommel, and they still retain the family characteristic of beautiful reddish-blonde hair and large blue eyes. The name was changed from Rommel to Rome. Johann Rommel, his wife, and two children were among the forty Germans who arrived in Louisiana on the ship, *Deux Frères,* on March 1, 1721. Of the 213 persons who sailed for Louisiana on this ship only forty survived the voyage.

*Union* was first called Pointeville. This was because the land there spreads fan-like from centric point sixty-six far back in the woods to the river. Later because of the famous gambling place, Pape Vert, Pointeville became known as Pape Vert. Then it took the name of the church, Sté. Marie du Fleuve ... from vice to virtue so to speak. The first postoffice in that section was on Union Plantation. Later the postoffice was moved nearer the church and the village became known officially as Union. But Union is still frequently referred to as *La Pointe* and the people as *Les Pointus*[8] ... a name which many resent for some unknown reason.

The Mississippi River, too, which bisects the parish has its history of names. To various Indian tribes it was the *Méchesebe*. Even before its discovery by DeSoto in 1541 Cortez referred to the great river of which the Indians spoke as the *River of the Holy Ghost*. DeSoto named it the *Rio Grande*, but to Joilet it was the *Buade*. As LaSalle floated down its circuitous route to the sea, he named it the *Colbert*. Iberville referred to it as the *St. Louis* and to some it was the *River of the Immaculate Conception*. But finally with many spelling variants, it has remained the *Mississippi*. The word Mississippi is Algonquin — Misi (great) sipi (water). To the world, the father of waters is the Mississippi, but to us it is "le fleuve"[9] or the river — as though there is no other. And for that matter there is none like it!

## Plantation Names

The names of the plantations, too, were interesting and as they changed owners, they often changed names. First there were the saints: *ST. JOSEPH, ST. JAMES, STE. EMMA, STE. CECILE, STE. AMELIA, STE. ROSE, ST. LOUIS, ST. MICHAEL, STE. ELMO, STE. CLAIRE, STE. ALICE, STE. VICTOIRE*, and *STE. MARY*. Then came the ladies: *LILY, LAURA, ADELE, STELLA, MINNIE, CONSTANCIA, CELESTINE, FELICITY, BESSIE K., NITA, FAUSTINIA, ELINA, ANITA, HESTER*, and *ELMA*. The trees were not forgotten: *OAK ALLEY, BAY TREE*, and *GOLDEN GROVE*. Popular, too, were the good old French names: *BELLEMONT, BAGATELLE, BOURBON, COTEAU, BEAU SÉJOUR, LONGUEVUE, BOISJOLIES, BELLEVUE, BON SECOUR,* and *BONNE ESPÉRENCE*. Some of the owners perpetuated their names through the names of their lands: *ARMANT, WELHAM, FOR-*

*STALL, VALCOUR AIME, DE LOBEL, AYMAR, CABIRO,* and *DELOGNY*. And Michel Bernard Cantrelle, looking forward to present day alphabet trends, gave his initials to his vast domain: *B. B. C.* Some names were rather incongruous: *PIKE'S PEAK, LAUREL RIDGE, MT. AIRY, GOLDEN RIDGE,* and *SHELL HILL* in a land that is as level as a floor. *RICHBEND* wound with the torturous Mississippi. There were two called *HOME PLACE* — one on each side of the river. Many French Creoles, not to be outdone by their American neighbors, gave English names to their plantations and seemingly sorry for such rash acts, forever after pronounced them with a French twang: *WHITE HALL, UNION, STAR, GREEN, COLUMBIA, CRESCENT, WILTON, UNCLE SAM, RAPIDAN, BURTON, MAGNOLIA,* and *SPORT*. Three names were Indian: *BILOXI, TIPPECANOE,* and *KABAHANNOSSE* (Cabanocey). Although *ALTA VILLA* was owned by Spaniards, its origin is Italian: alta: meaning high or deep, and villa: country house or garden. *HELVETIA* was the Latin word for Switzerland. *GOLDEN STAR*, the sugar planter's set goal, spread its sugared self into neighboring St. John Parish. *ACADIA PLANTATION* was right in the middle of the old Acadian Coast. Mere man had his inning with *SIDNEY* and *DAVID*. *LAUDERDALE* was Scottish and *SALSBURG* was German. The bagasse-mortar constructed gate at its entrance made *COLOMB PARK* look like one. Perhaps the only trace of long Spanish occupation remained with *BUENA VISTA*. Since nothing succeeds like success, one planter called his plantation: *SUCCEED*. And there was a *TEXAS* in St. James, too. Long preceding the eighteenth amendment there was *MOONSHINE* in the parish, but not to be outdone by predecessors, or contemporaries, one plantation was simply: *RED HOT*.

From saints to moonshine the plantations of St. James have had varied names. The owners, too, have ranged from cosmopolitan to ultra ultra: French, Acadian, Spanish, German, Creole, carpet bagger, freedman — even *JOHN McDONOGH*, the well known New Orleans philanthropist. But the strangest owner of them all is the American Red Cross to whom was bequeathed the *BUENA VISTA* plantation in 1943.

What's in a name is an ageless adage, but how a person signs it is something else again. Some interesting signatures of old and new St. Jamesians are shown in another place.

At left—Colomb Park. (Courtesy Mrs. R. H. Potts)

At right — Armant Plantation House (Courtesy Mrs. Potts)

Below — Home of Francois Trepagnier — late 18th Century (Courtesy Mrs. Potts)

Above — St. Joseph — built for Valcour Aime's daughter (Courtesy Mrs. Potts)

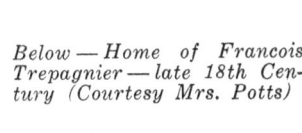

*Pape Vert*

*Charles Chauvin, present owner of Pape Vert, built 125 years ago by his ancestors. Picture made on Tezcuco Plantation in front of old slave cabin.*

*Welham Plantation house as it is today. (Courtesy of Mrs. R. H. Potts)*

*Rapidan Plantation at Central, La. Old house later used as a private school.*

## FOOTNOTES

1. *Dit* — said or called.
2. *M'sieu* — Monsieur — Mr.
3. *M'am* — Madame — Madam.
4. *Gros* — big.
5. *Tit* — Little.
6. *Nonc* — oncle — uncle.
7. *Tante* — aunt.
8. *Les Pointus* — the pointers — people of the point.
9. *Le fleuve* — the river.

## XVI

## EDUCATION

The history of early education in St. James is almost synonymous with the history of the Sacred Heart Convent and that of Jefferson College. Indeed, these two institutions were among the pioneers in the educational field in Louisiana and St. James was fortunate in having two such schools within its borders.

Before their founding, and to some extent after, education in St. James was in the hands of private tutors on the plantations. In this regard it is interesting to note that the first tutor listed in the parish was one Joseph Bouchard, age forty-three, tutor at the home of Louis Judice and Jeanne Cantrelle in September 1769. Since the Judices had only one child of school age, Michel, eleven, it is quite probable that Bouchard taught other boys of the Cabahannocer settlement. At any rate it is safe to assume that he was St. James' first teacher. Sometimes the tutor taught only the children of the big manor, but in other cases, he taught all the white children of the plantation, or even the combined groups of children of several plantations. The tutors were well-educated persons, many of whom were political exiles of France, or in some cases, French exiles of the West Indies. The smaller children usually had a tutrix — A Creole gentlewoman, who had seen better days and who was glad enough to teach in exchange for a good home and her bread and butter. The store of knowledge which she imparted was not confined to the three R's, but rather it included the broader lessons of Christianity, culture, and polite behavior with "Les Lettres de Madame de Sévigné" as final authority on P's and Q's.

Then, too, there were private schools which flourished here and there at various periods. One such school was that taught by Mr. Henri Ménuest prior to 1815. Tuition was $12.00 per quarter and no English was taught. The books used:

        Un trésor des enfants
        Un trésor de la jeunesse
        Un abrégé de la grammaire
        Un alphabet syllabique
        Un catéchisme du Père Antoine

However, in 1848 Mr. J. B. Menny conducted an all-English school known as the *Louisiana Model School*. This was probably the first English school in the parish. Mr. Menny, not satisfied with the progress that his French-speaking pupils were making, decided to do something about it. He wrote a textbook: *First Book in English of the American School Method* which he sold here and in New Orleans at #24 Canal Street. It was advertised in *Le Messager* as . . . ."framing a system rapidly teaching children to read." The price: ten cents per copy. Mr. Menny also taught night classes for adults. French St. James had become interested in English!

Educational opportunities were not equally distributed and the Acadian children shared little with the wealthier Creoles. The latter, not only had better schooling at home, but when grown were sent abroad, or to colleges on the Atlantic sea-board. However, the early 1800's saw the establishment of a convent and a college, and St. James was for sometime the leader in education in Louisiana.

When Father de la Croix came as pastor to St. Michel, he remembered the excellent work of the Sacred Heart nuns, whom he had met at Florissant, Missouri, where they had established their first American convent in 1819. Father de la Croix asked the Religious of the Sacred Heart to found a house at St. Michel, but they had just recently opened a convent at Grand Coteau and had neither money, nor religious, to spare. But Father de la Croix was undaunted and he decided to raise the money and build a convent. He soon collected $7,000. Added to this was his persuasive zeal and the nuns finally obtained permission from the mother house in France to accept his offer.

Reverend Mother Eugenie Audé was sent to found the convent and with her came Mother Hamilton, Sister Mullanphy, Sister Labruyère, and three novices, one of whom was young Mary Hardy of St. Louis. They arrived by boat on Hallowe'en in 1825 and *La Toussaint*, always a big day in St. James, was long remembered because on that day the Sacred Heart nuns filed into the little frame church of St. Michel. Their building was not quite complete, so the nuns did not take possession until November twentieth and the school did not open until the following April.

The convent, to which the nuns had no title, was a two-story colonial building and, strange to say, without a stick of furniture. From this small beginning sprouted the beautiful convent, known for over a hundred years as St. Michael's, and the noble work of Les Dames du Sacré Coeur began in St. James.

In 1838 there were two hundred girls at the convent and under the leadership of Mother Aloysius Hardy, it was decided to build a new and larger convent. A plantation, about a half mile above the church, was bought from the Joseph Landry heirs, but before the building began, some of the heirs challenged the validity of the sale and it was then proved that Joseph Landry had never held clear title to the land. In time this legal tangle was straightened and the erection of the new convent began. The nuns moved into this new building on January 28, 1848. For years it was the outstanding example for the Christian education of gentlewomen in south Louisiana and the convent was so beautiful, so clean, and so restful that to this day the people of St. James, use this expression: "C'est beau comme le convent du Sacré Coeur."[1]

But the growth of free schools, the successive failures of the sugar crop, and the rural location brought slow decadence to St. Michael's. In 1926, when a disastrous hurricane wrought great damage to the convent, it was closed — only one year after it had celebrated, with pomp and ceremony, the centennial of its founding. Later it was re-opened as a school for Mexican refugees and after that it served to house a girls' N.Y.A. unit.

A word or two about this fine old building: It was of French-Gothic architecture, three stories high and three hundred feet wide. On each side were battlemented wings and the central building had upper and lower galleries supported by unusually beautiful columns. It stood in a lovely garden surrounded by flowers, shrubs, and trees — peaceful, grandiose, and proud.

Again the convent became vacant. It was offered for sale and as there were no satisfactory buyers, it was decided to demolish it. It is certainly not a credit to the people of St. James that nothing was done to preserve it. We sat idly by and watched its dissolution brick by brick. First, we lost Uncle Sam, then the convent, and next — so it is rumored — will be the Trudeau house. Shall we lose all that our fathers built at such a sacrifice? Where is the courage of old Jacques Cantrelle, the determination of the Houma Indians, the patience of the Acadian exiles, and the pride of our staunch Creoles?

There are so many stories about the Sacred Heart Convent, that it is difficult to select one or two for the telling. First: Here is the unique story of Madame Gallitzin.

She was a Russian princess and a non-Catholic, who became a convert. She left the gay life of the court of the czars to become a nun. In time she was sent to America to visit the convents of the Sacred Heart order, and in this capacity, she came to St. Michael's. Although she was reared in the cold climate of Russia, she seemed to suffer strangely here from the cold and she wrote to a friend that she could never get comfortably warm in Louisiana. During one of her visits, the terrible pall of yellow fever settled over the convent. Mother Gallitzin contracted the fever and died. She lies buried in the little convent cemetery where a small iron cross marks her final resting place — a long way, indeed, from the glittering halls of the czars to the silent sod of St. James.[2]

Another story, more humorous, but none-the-less true: When the centennial was observed at the convent, old alumnae came from many parts of America and from all over Louisiana. There were some, who had attained their old age without ever having set foot in the convent since their graduation. Among these was Marie S. She and Clara B. had been classmates, had parted at seventeen, and were now in their seventies. They searched for each other in all the old familiar places, each knowing that the other was there, and neither knowing the other's married name. Finally Clara asked a very old nun to locate Marie. Within a few minutes the reunion was staged. They embraced each other with a smacking kiss on each cheek — and then holding each other at arms' length, they looked longingly and lovingly into each other's eyes and then Marie cried: "Mon Dieu! Clara, que tu as changé!"[3] What did she expect after fifty years?

## JEFFERSON COLLEGE

The story of Jefferson College is the story of a school that started without a struggle. Indeed, Jefferson was born with a gold spoon in its mouth, although through the near-century of its life, it often ate from one of tin. There were hard times and lush times, but it always came through. Floods, storms, fire, plague, poverty, and war could never conquer the courage and inspiration of its various leaders. St. James had seen the light of education in the founding of the Sacred Heart Convent and now its dreamers began to dream of a university for its young men. The story:

In 1831 Jefferson College was founded by Etienne Mazureau, Dr. F. Burthe, J. H. Sheppard, and a few others. Like a temple, its Greek architecture arose on the land of the Vavaseurs near the banks of the Mississippi. It cost $124,000 and it was named after Thomas Jefferson. Nothing was lacking: it had the finest library, an excellent museum of natural history, complete laboratories, and beautiful paintings. The state legislature appropriated an annual grant of $15,000 and professors came from West Point and Paris. But its glory was short-lived: On March 6, 1842, of a bright Sunday morning, Jefferson College burned completely and entirely, except the one building now occupied by the Godfrey Champagnes.

But Jefferson arose anew — more slowly and with more difficulty the second time. The college struggled, the legislature ceased its appropriation, and hard times closed the college in 1855. Valcour Aime, Governor A. B. Roman, and other prominent St. Jamesians re-opened the school under the name of the Louisiana College, but in 1859, it was closed, seized, and sold at auction. From $124,000 Jefferson had fallen to a paltry value. But another corporation was formed and in 1861 the school was reopened under its old name: Jefferson College.

Then war came — the terrible Civil War. The little boys went home to safety and the big ones went off to fight. The following letter[4] written one week before Farragut landed at New Orleans and about two weeks before the Federal gunboats tied up in St. James shows something of the spirit of the time.

       . . . . . . . Plantation
       21st April 1862

Pres. Jefferson College
Dear Sir,

My children return to Jefferson College today. Henry is over eighteen years and consequently hath to be called any day to serve his country in the field. He is anxious to start for the seat of war and I will go to New Orleans this week to see what arrangements I can make for his departure. In the meanwhile as I would not want him to be idle, I send him to the college with the request that should he be called away before the expiration of the session you will allow him . . . . ."

The Federal troops arrived and beautiful Jefferson College became a military post occupied by Union soldiers, who wrecked everything but the buildings. In 1864, the stock-holders sold the property to a group of priests, the Society of Mary, and Valcour Aime donated his share of $20,000. The war was nearing its end and the college reopened on July 12, 1864. In spite of Reconstruction, financial difficulties, yellow fever and depressions, the college prospered and from its halls came many men who became leaders in Louisiana's cultural and civil life.

But like the convent, with the coming of free high schools, other difficulties set in and in 1928 old Jefferson College permanently closed its doors as an educational center. It was bought by the Society of Jesus, who now operate Jefferson as a retreat for laymen under the name of Manresa House.[5]

But the old school has never ceased to play a useful part in the lives of men. Today retreatants — some of whom are not Catholic — gather each week in meditation and in prayer to renew their faith in God. Jefferson has simply changed from Christian education to Christian rehabilitation.

Of the amusing incidents of college life, here is the tale of Madame Quarante-Poules.[6]

Madame Quarante-Poules was a frugal Acadian housewife, who lived very near the college. At that time the grounds were enclosed within a high brick wall, which irked the students. Whenever an opportunity presented itself, some of the boys would sneak out, make a foray on the neighboring chicken yard, slip out to the batture, and cook the chickens. This went on for a long time, but in one week, several parties of boys, all unknown to each other, made way with forty of the Acadian woman's chickens. She could stand it no longer. She snatched her garde-soleil from the hook back of the door, stalked straight to the president's office, and walked in, unannounced. Beginning in plaintive tones and rising to the crescendo of a woman's fury, in Acadian French she blurted the story of her forty chickens — mes quarante poules — The president offered to pay for the chickens, but she indignantly refused. She wanted the boys punished! The story soon spread — each group of boys believing itself to be the only guilty crowd. For days each delinquent student awaited the dreaded summons to the padre's office, but the wise old man understood boys better than women or chickens. He said nothing, knowing that he held a trump card. For a long time after that, the mere mention of a chicken was enough to temporarily straighten a wayward scholar. And as for the good Acadian woman, to this day, she is remembered only by the name of Madame Quarante-Poules.

Then there is the story of the happy-go-lucky boy from New Orleans, who always poked fun at the students because of their strict religious rules and exercises. There is a very dangerous eddy in the river just across from the college and many persons have drowned there. One day this boy and several companions secretly rowed across the river. Engulfed by the eddy, they lost control of the boat and seemed doomed. His companions were panic stricken and began to scream. "Shut up," yelled the boy. "Pray, you so-and-so, pray." And the boat righted itself and all were saved.

Education is surely reflected in the writings of a people and many St. Jamesians, native and transient, have left on the parish the stamp of their successful literary activities. In addition to the files of its many newspapers are other works of literary, historical, or entertainment value. A list of the better known writers follows:

| | |
|---|---|
| Jules Choppin | — Poems |
| Alcée Fortier | — History, biography, folklore |
| Jean Gentil | — Poems, essays, serials |
| Desirée Martin | — Autobiography |
| René de Senéguy de la Peichardière | — Local history |
| John L. Peytavin | — Articles, essays, stories |
| Henri Rémy | — History |
| Alfred Roman | — Military writings |

### The Public Schools

During a January night in 1904 the courthouse at Convent burned and with it practically all the records of the various St. James Parish School Boards. Because of this, little authentic information on the early public schools of the parish is now available.

*St. Michael's Church today.* "*Consecrated in the past, blessed by the present and hopeful of the future.*" *Rectory at left of Norman architecture. Built in 1875.*

St. Michel de Cantrelle, 1831, Convent, La. This picture was taken the year it snowed. It shows the first Sacred Heart Convent (right) and the old presbytere (left). At lower left hand corner Chouquette is seen selling her "ba-bas."

St. Michael's Church — interior today. (Photo by Joe Lucia)

Prior to 1850 state laws pertaining to public education were passed, but little was accomplished here as in other parishes. It is to the credit of St. James that its native son, Governor Alfred Roman, was greatly interested in education and worked untiringly to that end when serving his two terms as governor of Louisiana.

Probably the first free education offered in St. James was at Jefferson College. The state appropriated $15,000, annually for Jefferson, but in return the college had to educate seventeen students gratis. The Sacred Heart Convent maintained an orphanage whose enrollment rose and fell with yellow fever years, but these two institutions were private schools and the free schooling which they offered reached but few.

There is no record of the first free public school in St. James Parish except an article which appeared in the parish paper, *Le Messager,* on September 10, 1849. Translated from the French it follows: "The inhabitants of the fifth scholastic district learn with pleasure that Mr. J. B. Menny, the excellent English professor, has been duly commissioned by the superintendent of this parish and authoribed by the directors of this district to open a free school near the old St. Michael Church. There are already fifteen pupils enrolled. Mr. Menny teaches English only, but his colleague of the superior district teaches French only." The name of the colleague is not given but in another issue of *Le Messager* (May 6, 1848), there is a card inviting the public to attend the trimester examinations of the Primary School of the Second District conducted by Messrs. Brulatour and Como. Although there is no proof that these two schools were the first public schools of the parish, they were undoubtedly among the first.

In 1854-60 there were ten public schools with an enrollment of 370. French was taught in the morning, English in the afternoon, except at Vacherie, where no English was taught. The school day lasted six hours and the teachers' pay ranged from $14.00 to $50.00 per month. But the public schools of the Reconstruction Era fared worse. Very few white children attended as the whites and Negroes were not segregated. It is said that Miss Desiré Martin's salary at Grande Pointe was discontinued because she refused admittance to Negroes. When the carpet bag rule came to an end in 1877, separate schools for the two races were established.

In the 1880's interesting data are noted. The more advanced pupils taught the younger children. Christmas holidays were instituted. Although the unbelievably low salaries were cut to $30.00 per month, there were more applicants than jobs available. A big leather strap was part of the standard equipment in all schools. At one time meteorology was taught. The superintendents salary was $125.00 per year. It was common practice to build and equip a school for $350. And one school erected near St. James station in 1874 cost only $130. In 1885 the enrollment was 339 and the average attendance was 68%. Almost always there were fewer children in school than out of school. The teachers for the session of 1880 were:

  Ward 1. Ben P. Bourgeois
  Ward 2. Mrs. Rosa Guadin
  Ward 3. Mrs. Louisa Dornier
  Ward 4. W. Bauvais
  Ward 5. Mrs. Labertaut
  Ward 6. D. J. Richard
  Ward 7. E. Beauvais
  Ward 8. F. Brignac, Sr.

The text books of 1877 were:
  Swinton's Elementary Geography
  Swinton's Reader
  Robinson's Progressive Arithmetic
  Wilson' Dictionary
  Swinton's Analysis of English Grammar
  Dimitry's History and Geography of Louisiana
  Holmes' United States History
  Poitieut's French Grammar
  - - - - - Speller

But great oaks from little acorns grow! Today St. James has six public schools for whites and eleven for Negroes. One hundred thirty-eight teachers are employed and the school session is 180 days with an average attendance of 96%. There is a supervisor, as well as a superintendent, and the well equipped school plants are valued at more than half a million dollars.

Private schools other than parochial schools no longer exist. There are no tutors on the big plantations and Jefferson College and the Sacred Heart Convent have closed their doors. Private schooling for the chosen few have been replaced by public education open to all!

N.B. The information for the above articles on public schools is taken from the thesis: A History of the Public Schools of St. James Parish by Richard P. Lowry.

Incomplete List of Superintendents of Education in St. James Parish:

| | |
|---|---|
| J. J. Roman | 1848 |
| E. S. Stoddard | 1872 |
| James C. Wingard | 1873 |
| John R. Gallup | 1875 |
| Dr. George W. Johnson | 1878 |
| Alfred Plaisance | 1882 |
| F. B. Dicharry | 1888 |
| P. M. Lambremont | 1889 |
| J. N. Gourdain | 1897-1921 |
| R. P. Lowry | 1921-1937 |
| E. L. Roussel | 1937- |

### FOOTNOTES

1. C'est beau comme le couvent du Sacré Coeur — It is as beautiful as the Sacred Heart Convent.
2. The convent property was recently sold and the remains of the nuns were moved to the St. Mary Cemetery at Union.
3. My, God, Clara, how you have changed!
4. This letter was found in the attic of one of the buildings after the closing of the college.
5. The old college buildings were recently repaired, redecorated, and refurnished at a cost of about a quarter million dollars.
6. Madame Quarante-Poules — Mrs. Forty Chickens.

## XVII

## GOVERNMENT

During World War II people complained of bureaucratic government and its attendant restrictions. The meat shortage had everybody on edge, yet few people know that meat was rationed in Louisiana's earliest history by this simple expedient: It was illegal for anyone to kill a cow. Then we have the story of two New Orleans women, Madame Flamade and Madame La Chevalier, who were charged with the extortionate sale of eggs. For punishment they were fined one hundred francs, given fifteen days in prison, and threatened with expulsion from the city. It is a long way from then to now, but government is still vital, although many changes have taken place in its administration.

When the parish was settled, government was to a great extent a law of self-preservation. It was dangerous to wander far afield and almost suicidal to cross the river. But as has been mentioned before, the parish expanded within a very short time and organized government became a necessity.

Under French rule Jacques Cantrelle was appointed commander of the post at Cabahannocer about 1765. Perhaps his most urgent duty was that of establishing the swarming Acadian settlers on new land. He was, in addition, a preserver of the peace and a judge of very limited authority.

When the parish passed under Spanish rule in 1769, new laws were promulgated. Each district became a commandantcie and the superior officer of the post was a commandante,[1] with various military, judicial, and civil powers. A commandante, Nicholas Verret, was reappointed by O'Reilly in 1769. His duties were of wider scope than that of the commander under French rule. Assisted by syndics, who were stationed every three leagues, the commandante preserved the peace, examined traveler's passports, helped settlers obtain land grants, prevented smuggling, registered the sale of lands and slaves, acted as judge in minor cases, and performed the office of notary public.

Perhaps of greater interest were some of the peculiar laws of that early day. To illustrate: Real estate sales were made in front of the church after high Mass on a Sunday morning. If a man owed the government, one of his slaves could be imprisoned until his debt was paid. Debt for food was a privileged one. Dogs were not allowed in church. People of bad morals were expelled from the settlements. Indians could not be enslaved, but Negroes could. Articles necessary to soldiers had to be sold at a cheaper price. A settler had to give legal proof that the wife he took with him was his lawful wife. All new-born babies had to be Christened Catholic. And in order to encourage people to settle in Louisiana the Spanish government gave each new settler the following:

1. A land grant of five arpents front.
2. Enough maize to tide over the settler until his crop could be harvested (one barrel for each adult and one-half barrel for each child in the family).
3. A hoe, a scythe, an ax, and a spade.
4. Two hens, a cock, and a young pig.

Nicholas Verret died in office and was succeeded by Michel Cantrelle, who served as commandante under Spanish authority until St. James, as part of the Louisiana territory, was sold to the United States. When Dr. Watkins, representing Governor Claiborne, visited St. James in 1804, he reappointed Michel Cantrelle. Under the new territorial government, the Acadian Coast (St. James and Ascension) became one of the first twelve counties and it was named Acadia.

A new government had to be provided and according to instructions sent by W. C. C. Claiborne, governor of the territory of Orleans, the parish government was reorganized in 1805. At a meeting held at his residence at Cabahannocer on May 27, 1805, Michel Cantrelle presided. He was still acting as commandante of St. Jacques de Cabahannocer, but actually he was commissioned as judge of the new parish of Acadia. Acadia was divided into twelve districts and the commissions, which had been sent by Claiborne, were issued as follows:

| | |
|---|---|
| Parish Judge | — Michel Cantrelle |
| Sheriff | — Robert Wederstrand[2] |
| Clerk of Court | — L. Rémy |
| Treasurer | — A. D. Tureaud |
| Coroner | — Gaspard Debuys[3] |

Justices of the Peace — Louis Mollere, William Conway, W. C. Scott, Christophe Colomb, Daniel Blouin, Étienne Reynes, and Joseph Landry.

After that meetings were held regularly, usually at the Cantrelle home, but occasionally at some other residence in the parish. It was decided to raise money but the assembly voted against a tax on real estate. Instead it was decided to tax slaves, dogs, and carriages as follows:

1. Any one having the use of a carriage of two or four wheels had to pay $5.00 per year.

2. Each inhabitant was allowed five slaves without payment of impost. Any person owning more than that number had to pay a tax of two escalins per slave.[4]

3. Each inhabitant was allowed to own three dogs. Any over that number were known as "luxury dogs" and were taxed two escalins each.

4. Each inhabitant was compelled to report annually on his number of carriages, dogs, and slaves and was taxed an additional $5.00 if his report were not forthcoming.

The following article describes the beginning of the police jury system in St. James: An act of the Territorial Legislature, dated April *, 1807, provided that the parish judge, the justices of the peace, and a jury of twelve persons appointed by the parish judge meet on the first Monday of July, or oftener at the call of the judge, to make regulations in regard to parish roads, levees, fences, cattle, improvements, police, etc. At first this body had no special appellation, but in time it became known as the police assembly. By 1811 this jury became elective and was constituted solely of twelve jurymen elected at large by the voters of the parish for a term of two years. The parish judge presided over this body and nine members constituted a quorum. In 1813 the parish was divided into wards and the police assembly became officially known as the police jury with one member from each ward. All the acts of the police jury had to be posted in front of the church and had to be enforced by the parish judge.

As there was no courthouse at first, court sessions were held in the St. James Church presbytery and in private homes. Michel Cantrelle's sugar house was used as a prison. At a meeting in

July 1806, William Donaldson offered to furnish a courthouse and prison at his expense providing that the sessions of the court were held at the head of Bayou Lafourche where Donaldsonville now stands. The court accepted and "la maison de ville pour les séances de la cour"[5] were erected. Later, when St. James and Ascension became separate political units, the court was moved back into St. James near the St. James Church.

In 1835 the parish contracted to pay Hudson E. Burr $6,300 to erect a forty-foot courthouse and jail just below the St. James Church. This was probably the building which served until the Reconstruction era when Convent became the county seat.[6] The building then erected at Convent burned in 1904. The present courthouse was erected in 1904.

The first election held in the new parish of Acadia was on September 16 and 17, 1805, for the purpose of electing the representative of the parish to the territorial legislature. Two days were required for the balloting because of the poor transportation then available. In the afternoon of the seventeenth the judge, the sheriff, and the clerk of court met at the St. James presbytery to count the ballots. Two hundred twenty-six votes were cast and since Joseph Landry[7] and William Conway received more ballots than the others, they were duly certified as the representatives of Acadia and instructed to report to New Orleans for the meeting.

In 1807 the Orleans Territory was redivided into nineteen parishes and Acadia became separately St. James and Ascension. Michel Cantrelle continued to serve St. James as the parish judge until 1812. The office of sheriff had been abolished in 1807 but was recreated by an act of March 16, 1810 and made appointive. The broad Constitution of 1812, which by the way, covered only fourteen printed pages, was never amended, and served until 1845, provided for an appointive sheriff for a term of three years. The first recorded sheriff of the reorganized parish was Antoine Maurin and the first judge was none other than Augustin Dominique Tureaud of White Hall renown.

The present system of electing a sheriff was inaugurated by a proviso of the Constitution of 1845. In earlier years the office of sheriff changed hands often and during the period of Reconstruction, it was held successively by three Negroes. Since that time only four men have held the office. Mr. Livain Bourgeois and Mr. Louis LeBourgeois, each served sixteen years and Mr.

— 91 —

Joseph B. Dornier[8] completed thirty-six years in office. This is the longest tenure in any office in St. James with the exception of Michel Cantrelle. Cantrelle not only served as commandante and judge, but also a member of the Louisiana legislative council of the first territorial government.

The carpet-bag government of the Reconstruction period presents unbelievable details. Parish expenditures rose with the years as did the parish indebtedness, while the cash in the treasury dropped to $16.35 in June 1875. Where the money went nobody knew as the roads, bridges, levees, and public buildings were in a deplorable condition. The jail was such that the prisoners had to be kept in irons to prevent their escape. At a Republican Convention held at the courthouse in July 1873, the walls were "defaced by obscene, vulgar, and revolting inscriptions and like caricatures of the officers of the court and prominent citizens of the parish."[9] Benches, chairs, and banisters were reduced to shambles.

Lands were expropriated, illegal taxes were collected, and justice was mis-carried. Eleven out of fifteen members of a grand jury impanelled in 1875 were illiterate. The president of the police jury without legal authorization sold the old Vacherie road at a private sale to an ex-judge for $500 — and this payable in scrip which was almost worthless. In 1873, although all the public schools had been closed for some time, the school board spent some $9,000 in two months. A few of the officials of the parish could not sign their names. Some official names appear in the court records in various handwritings — sometimes in big bold characters and at other times in fine slant. Apparently whoever was conveniently near at hand signed for them. But the height of indignity was reached in 1874 when the old courthouse was seized and sold for $541.

Since Louisiana has had nine different constitutions, the parish, too, has had many changes in its form of government. St. James has been a part of the following judicial districts: second, fourth, twenty-second, twentieth, twenty-seventh, and twenty-third.

Of course, people always think of a court in terms of stiff decorum, but the parish has had at least one judge who was a most colorful, though perhaps not so dignified, a personality. To begin: He served some where along in an unstable period

Old St. James Church

Sanctuary of St. Michael's Church, showing hand-carved communion railing. (Photo by Joe Lucia)

*Grotto of Our Lady of Lourdes at St. Michael's Church. Built in 1876 of bagasse clinkers, according to Roger Baudier, N. O. Diocesan historian, this grotto is the first in the United States.*

*St. Mary's Chapel at Union—served by St. Michael's priests. (Photo by Joe Lucia)*

and, as was often the case, two judges claimed the office. Whether he was actually elected we do not know — but sit he did. He was a beady-eyed old man who had a coughing habit which only an alcoholic sip could assuage. It is said that he sat "en banc" with a large newspaper spread wide upon his desk. When the yen for a *ti-cou* struck him, he raised the paper, leaned over, and took a swig from a bottle of Vermouth which he kept under his desk for just such a purpose. At any rate one day when he had had more "sips" than usual an attorney questioned one of his decisions. He quickly took his dram, calmly ordered the sheriff to adjourn the court, and boldly called the attorney out in the public road to settle the argument man-fashion.

In passing we should stop to pay tribute to three prominent St. Jamesians, who have held high office in Louisiana. Elsewhere in this story we have mentioned André B. Roman, who was twice governor of Louisiana and, incidentally, one of the best in the history of the state. In 1880 Felix Pierre Poché, direct descendent of Pierre Chenet of Périque tobacco fame, was appointed associate justice of the Louisiana Supreme Court and served with distinction. In more recent time, 1908-1912, P. M. Lambremont, direct descendent of the first Pierre Lambremont who perished in the Natchez massacre, served as lieutenant governor of Louisiana. Many other St. Jamesians have served their state and county in lesser capacity, but these are too numerous to mention.

La politique[10] is still a pertinent topic in St. James and yet provides a conversation piece, but through the years the parish has been primarily a peaceful place in which to live. And to date we have not had to resort to the treatment accorded one butcher of New Orleans who, because he sold dog meat, was compelled to parade around the city for several hours with this inscription placarded upon his back: "Master eater of dogs and cats;"

### Footnotes

1. Under Spanish rule the commandante received a salary of $300 per year, the surgeon $360, and the pastor $240.
2. Wederstrand served only one month. He was replaced by Gasper Debuys.
3. Most of the above named officers served only a short time as the Territorial Legislature abolished the offices of parish judge, sheriff, clerk, coroner, and treasurer on March 31, 1807. In their stead a parish judge, who was invested with their combined duties, was appointed by the governor

for a term of four years. Michel Cantrelle was appointed for St. James.

4. Escalin — money worth 12½ cents.

5. La maison de ville pour les séances de la cour — courthouse.

6. On May 4, 1869 a tract of land was sold by Anastasie Poché, widow of Joseph Landry, to the Police Jury of St. James Parish for the express purpose of erecting a courthouse and a jail.

7. Joseph Landry resigned and in July 1806 an election was held to replace him. The election lasted three days, 141 votes were cast, and William Donaldson was elected.

8. Mr. Dornier did not run for office in 1948 and Mr. Gaston Brignac was elected. Mr. Brignac was not a candidate in 1956 and Mr. Gordon Martin was elected.

9. Taken from the official reports of the grand jury.

10. La politique — politics.

## XVIII

## THE RIVER

Surely there is no more beautiful scene anywhere than the sun-set beyond the Cabahannocer Church across the Mississippi River from Convent. There the soft pinks and icy blues cast their reflection in the mirror-like Mississippi with only the dark outline of the levee separating sky and water. It is a peaceful scene — its calm serenity belying the disastrous tricks which the great river has some times played on St. James.

When Iberville came up the Mississippi in 1699 it was at flood stage. It presented a picture so different to that which he expected, that he doubted for a while that this was the great river for which he was searching. And the Mississippi has been thus always: peaceful, beautiful, helpful at times, but deep, sinister, and treacherous at flood time.

When the early settlers were issued grants of land along the river, one of the conditions stipulated was that the settler had to build and maintain a levee fronting his land. Thus the first levees, which were only a few feet high, were built.[1] As the settlements spread, the levees were extended until each side of the river was lined with a continuous levee. There were many floods as the years went by, but la crevasse Nita[2] is still a big topic of conversation among the older St. Jamesians.

Nita was a plantation just below Romeville. Legend tells us that it was named after the song, "Juanita." No doubt it was a prosperous plantation because, so the story goes, $80,000 in cash was found in a little walnut armoire[3] and desk when the owner died. The little armoire is still in use in a Convent home— minus the $80,000, of course. After the owner's death the plantation passed into the hands of one of the sons, where he and his family continued to live.

In 1890 there was a severe cold wave in March, which is unusually late for a south Louisiana freeze. All up and down the river the planters were up at the crack of dawn to estimate the damage. One planter, who had just recently sold his share of Nita, arose at three o'clock in the morning. Coffee was served and the whole house was astir. He consulted the thermometer then he said, "Go back to bed, the cane will grow again, but I know not what's coming with the flood above."

In those days the rice crop was irrigated through a wooden trough across the levee and road. This was a rice flume, but French St. Jamesians called it "la dal de riz." At Nita there was such a flume and the river being very high, water flowed through it over the levee and into the rice canal on the plantation.

On March 12, 1890 an old Negro, known as Neega, attended a wake on the Bonne Ésperance Plantation of the Boucrys. On his way home at midnight, there was so much water across the Nita road that the old man had to walk back to the railroad track, which was slightly elevated, in order to get across to his home at Rapidan. At a nearby store several men were having a *tite partie*[4] and some one went to tell them that the flume at Nita was leaking badly. Such things were not uncommon in those days and the card game continued. But at two o'clock the levee blew out and the torrent came rushing in. Piercing screams were heard from one house to another arousing the occupants for miles. At the wake pandemonium broke loose . . . each one rushing to rescue his family and possessions . . . and leaving the sorrowing mother alone in vigil over her dead daughter.

For days every effort was made to plug the gap, but Nita was a sandy place and nothing could stop the flood. The plantation home was just below the break and the water came rushing in so fast that some of the members of the family had to be evacuated in a cart and others in a skiff. All that the owners saved was a silver pitcher and a painting of three grandchildren.[5] Weeks later the family layette[6] was found in an old-fashioned chest safely anchored in a tree-top in the swamp.

And one can not but wonder what poor Madame Flagil thought when she saw the swirling waters of the angry Mississippi carrying mud into her spotless Nita home. It is said that she was, by far, the most meticulous person in the parish and that her pet hate was dust. Whenever she left her home for a few days her first inspection upon her return was the floor of the Nita house and woe to them who had let dust accumulate. She went from room to room and rubbed her finger on the floor to check. Once when she was visiting in New Orleans some one accidentally dropped boiling hot lard upon the kitchen floor and there was consternation in the house. Every means was employed to remove the spot to no avail and in final desperation the plantation carpenter was summoned to plane the floor to remove the stain.

But Madame Flagil could not cope with the mighty Mississippi! When the levee broke she was carried off in a three-mule cart much against her will. As they slowly slushed their way down the watery road, she looked back at her deserted house . . . an island in a rushing sea. Just then a curtain from an open window blew perilously near a lighted lamp. Gasping, she covered her eyes with her hand and begged that a servant be sent back to extinguish the forgotten lamp. She feared fire more than flood. But the water had already reached the axle of the cart wheel and the mules were barely able to feel their way out of the deluge. Soon the murky water rushed in and smeared its mud on floors and walls and ceiling and then collapsed the house like a flimsy deck of cards.

The back waters flooded the east bank from St. Gabriel to New Sarpy. As the land here slopes away from the river, the homes and crops nearer the levee were saved by building small embankments all around the fields. Many such little protection levees are still seen in the plantation fields today. Months later the breach was closed, but the planters had lost a fortune and Nita was completely ruined — as can be seen to this day.

The river has been the friend of St. James as well as its foe. Before the coming of the railroads, it was the only means of transportation, other than horse-drawn vehicles over muddy, or dusty, local roads. The 1800's saw the hey-day of deluxe packet travel. It seemed as though the river boats were trying to out-do the luxurious plantation life, and one still hears that on the packet *la Belle Creole*,[7] dishes were never washed. It was easier to throw them overboard.

In addition to carrying our water-borne commerce, the river furnished many of our people with most of their wood for fuel. This drift wood comes racing down the river at "high water." Indeed, catching drift wood, towing it to shore, cutting and cording it was a picturesque operation carried on up and down the levee at flood time. Mr. Valcour Aime tells us in his plantation diary that his slaves salvaged 95 cords of drift wood during the January-February rise of 1840.[8]

And since the days of the Indians the river has provided the people who have inhabited its banks with fish and shrimp. The river shrimp is unlike salt water shrimp in that it is smaller and has a finer flavor. People here eat shrimp in every fashion — boiled, fricassée, gumbo, cocktail, salad, in stuffed tomatoes, etc. In season, May through July, nearly everybody eats shrimp nearly every day. And in the early morning, one hears the cry of the shrimp peddler, "Swimp! Swimp!"

But to return to floods! There have been many floods through the years. In 1892 there were thirty-seven crevasses in Louisiana and the one at Bellemont flooded considerable property, although it was not nearly as disastrous as that at Nita. The highest stage ever recorded on the Mississippi here at the College Point gauge was in 1927, when the river rose to thirty-two feet. As a general rule people here love, rather than fear the river, but there were many that year who slept with both ears off their pillows and with their clothes on a chair near-by.

Since the building of the Bonnet Carré spillway all danger of flood has vanished. The muddy Mississippi peacefully courses down its winding bed to mingle with the clear, blue waters of the Gulf. This is just as it did four hundred years ago when De Soto's tattered band of explorers hopefully paddled through St. James in search of liberation from the forested lands of the valley. Only now, the river is always a friend, no longer a foe!

### FOOTNOTES

1. In the early 1800's, the levees were but twenty feet wide at the base and only five feet high.
2. Crevasse — break in the levee causing a flood.
3. Armoire — clothes press.
4. Tite partie — card game for stakes.
5. These articles are now in the possession of Mrs. Oscar Daspit of Houma, La. and Mrs. Atole Sarrodet of New Orleans.
6. This layette had been hand made in Paris, France, for the advent of a recent superintendent of New Orleans schools, Mr. Lionel Bourgeois.
7. La Belle Creole — packet plying the river in the early 1800's.
8. Sugar houses then used wood for fuel.

## XIX

## CURIOUS CUSTOMS

The customs of St. James are as varied as were its early settlers. As the many groups or families settled here, their culture spread and their customs were handed down through the years. Some of the better-known practices, such as *La Toussaint*[1] and *le charivari*,[2] are the same as those generally observed through French Louisiana. Others, such as the duel and *lagniappe*, have become obsolete because their usage has been legally forbidden. But the French St. Jamesians who dislike frequent changes, have, for the most part, clung tenaciously to their old customs, be they of Acadian, Missouri-French, Creole, Spanish, French, or West Indian origin. Some are quite humorous and others sacred. To illustrate:

### LA PRIERE EN COMMUN[3]

Mémère was a proud matriarch of the old school — a mixture of Louisiana Creole and Virginia ultras — and to boot, she married a prominent St. Jamesian. It was not necessary to arise early in her household, because there were servants to perform all the necessary tasks of a well-ordered home, so Mémère arose and dressed at leisure. When she was ready she knelt at the foot of the stairs, clapped her hands, and cried in a loud voice, so as to be heard upstairs as well as down: "La prière du matin!"

Perhaps you had a hang-over from the night before; maybe you were just sleepy; or too, you may have been in the middle of your morning ablutions, but you rolled out of bed, or you dropped everything, and down on your knees. There was no waiting — no absentees — not with Mémère.

To an outsider the morning prayer at Mémère's presented a never-to-be-forgotten spectacle. At the first clap of her hands, there was a shuffling of feet and general clattering all over the house. Some appeared in their *jupons*,[4] the little ones in *camisoles de molleton*,[5] but usually almost every one was dressed for the day.

The prayers were said in French with piety and devotion. Mémère was a firm believer in the efficacy of prayer and she did not stop with spiritual offering. Often she ended with special supplication for temporal favors. Imagine the surprise of a house guest one morning when Mémère, after pious and humble exhortation, ended with "Et faîtes que je puisse acheter la vache de Monsieur Tel-et-tel aujourd'hui!"[6]

In poorer families, the morning prayer by group was often omitted, because, by dawn, each had gone to his task, but the evening prayer was a ritual. Everyone was present. In summer it was said on the *gallerie*[7] with the children sleepily leaning on the *garde-fou*.[8] In winter all gathered around the open fire of the mother's bedroom. The mother usually said the prayer, and when death removed her from the scene, perhaps the most disconsolate session was that first family prayer without her. Each tried hard to answer the rosary with the futile bravery of pent-up emotion. Each remembered the little things she had done and said. Her very presence hovered over them all.

The beautiful custom of family prayer was still observed by many families in St. James, but what with the youth scattered to the far corners of the world and many of the oldsters tuned in to radio and television this edifying custom was gradually passing away. However, the recent *Crusade for Family Prayer* has brought back this custom to the fore and the St. James families are again united in "la priére en commun."

## LAGNIAPPE

*Lagniappe*, which indirectly means a little gift, is a custom which we have inherited from the Spanish. Up to a very recent day, when a purchase was made, a trifling gift was added. It was not always, as if often believed, a bit of something sweet. An additional pepper, a sprig of parsley, or even an extra crab, is a lagniappe when added gratis to a purchase.

Little children, some of whom were totally ignorant of mathematics, devised an ingenious way of getting lagniappe. If a child were sent to the store to buy three articles, two of his pals would join him. Each would buy one article so that each one would get lagniappe.

The legislature finally put a stop to lagniappe, but in many rural areas its practice was continued. However, the war rationing of sugar and the subsequent scarcity of cheap candy, gave this custom a death blow. And I am sure that the mothers of the parish, both white and colored, have more trouble in inducing their offspring to run errands to the country store now that the prospect of lagniappe is almost nil.

## DUELS

Winston's Simplified Dictionary defines a duel thus: "A duel is a fight between two persons, usually planned before-hand, and fought with deadly weapons before witnesses." It is just that! The people of St. James, being of Latin extraction and consequently hot-tempered, engaged in duels, as did men in other parts of French Louisiana.

A man resenting an affront, or provocation, would challenge the aggressor to a duel. A challenge, called a cartel, was written in red ink and delivered by special messenger. A letter written in red ink is a deep insult in St. James to this day. The aggressor, whether he believed in dueling or not, was bound to accept the challenge or be forever dishonored. Seconds were chosen by each party. The seconds met and arranged the details of the duel such as time, place, weapons, distance, etc.

One of the noted duels of St. James was that fought by Doctor Charles Gray and Mr. Denis Richard. Dr. Gray and Mr. Richard were neighbors and quarreled over a newspaper publication. Dr. Gray did not believe in dueling but was honorbound to accept Mr. Richard's challenge. The following article taken from the Donaldsonville Chief dated August 22, 1874 describes this duel.

A fatal duel occurred in the parish of St. James, last Sunday morning, in which Dr. Charles Gray and Mr. Denis J. Richard appeared as principals, Messrs. J. R. Gallup and E. N. Bean acting as seconds for the former, and Messrs. F. P. Poche and Camille Mire for the latter. The weapons used were Smith & Wesson revolvers, distance fifteen paces. Two shots were fired without effect, and it was supposed that the affair would be amicably settled at this juncture, but Mr. Gallup insisted upon another fire, contrary to evident wishes of both principals and the other seconds. At the third fire, Dr. Gray fell dead, shot through the heart, and Mr. Richard received a very serious wound in the stomach which may yet result in his death, although he was alive at last accounts and the physicians expressed hope of his recovery. Dr. Gray was a popular and experienced physician, having served with credit in the British and Union armies, and his death is universally deplored in St. James. He was charitable and kindhearted, and his loss will be severely felt among the poor and needy. The difficulty grew out of the recent misunderstanding between Messrs. Richard and Jackson of the *Sentinel*, and was not of such a nature as to demand the blood of either party.

In case the reader is interested, Mr. Richard recovered and continued to live near the Grays, but his health was very poor. Dueling was practiced in St. James even after it was prohibited by law, but gradually the hot-bloods of the parish came to the conclusion that death in a duel didn't settle an argument. It only prevented further parley. And did it really matter that much what one thought of trivialities before, if after, one could never think again?

## LE CHARIVARI

*Le Charivari* shows best the spontaneous gaiety and love of mimicry of the Acadians. Whether this custom was brought to Louisiana by the French or the Acadians, I do not know, but it is one of the long established customs of St. James, and it is one in which Creoles and Acadians participate.

When a widow, or widower, re-marries, a crowd, usually composed of the friends of the couple, serenades the newly-weds with a noisy demonstration of music, yells, ringing of bells, clattering of tin pans, etc. In fact, anything which will make a noise is employed, and the *charivari* is a custom in which the children particularly delight. After the noisy outbursts subside, the bridal couple invites the crowd in and treats everyone to a drink — more often hard than soft. After much toasting, many pleasantries, and often some buffoonery, the crowd retires.

Often as people sit on their galleries on a warm summer night, they hear the sudden outbursts of a *charivari*, sometimes coming from across the river, and they know that a widow or widower has re-married. No doubt the largest *charivari* staged in St. James in the last fifty years was that led by Mr. George Huguet of Convent for Mr. and Mrs. Alexandre Brignac in 1928. Word leaked out that Mr. Brignac, a widower, and Miss Lucie Schexnaydre were to be married at St. Michel's Church in the evening of March nineteenth. Mr. Huguet with a few men, women, and children, about thirty in number, walked to the church, which was just a short distance, and planned to stage a *charivari* that night. The couple got wind of the story and sped away in automobile and since a *charivari* does not begin after nine o'clock, the disappointed serenaders went home.

The second night they went to the couple's home in greater number, but they were not received. The third night about seventy-five persons went by automobile. Still no invitation! It was then learned that Mr. and Mrs. Brignac refused to receive the serenaders, because in calling the *charivari*, their nick-names had been used instead of their given names.

Then the *charivari* began in earnest. Mr. George (Huguet) was determined and the crowd, which returned every night, increased by leaps and bounds. On the seventh day, Mr. George got out an old plantation bell, mounted it on his truck and paraded from Union to Gramercy, ringing the bell, and proclaiming the *charivari* all along the way. The effect was magical. From all sections people came that night to see as well as to join in the fun.

The parade, which was over a mile long, formed at Mr. Huguet's. First was the plantation bell with Mr. George himself. Then came a truck bearing a coffin surrounded by lighted candles, a most weird sight in the dim moonlight. Mr. George explained that this was to signify the death of the friendship of the Brignacs for their friends, whom they would not receive. Upon reaching the house a young man impersonating a preacher, preached the funeral of the friendship in comical mimicry, once falling over the coffin, in pretense that he had had too much tafia.

Word of this comédie-non-pareil spread far and wide and on the eighth night over three hundred cars and trucks and one thousand persons made up the *charivari*. What with the tooting of the horns, the clamor of the bell, the incessant clatter of tin pans, music on combs, and what not, the sleepy little village of Convent was wide awake indeed. Court was in session and Mr. George gave orders to cease all noise in passing the court-house.

When the serenaders arrived at the darkened little Brignac house, the huge throng, blocking the road and extending all over the levee let loose —

"Charivari![9]
Pour qui?
Monsieur Alexandre Brignac!
Avec qui?
Mademoiselle Lucie Schexnaydre!
Sonnez[10] les bourgots!"

And then the din - - - - - - - -

After a few minutes, a faint light crept through the half-opened door of the cottage. Mr. Brignac came out and invited the serenaders in. Of course, the little home could never contain but a small number of that immense crowd and Mr. George and about fifty other persons entered the house. Root beer, which had been made in a large tub, was served, and after a few gay sallies and much merriment, the crowd slowly dispersed.

All *charivaris* are not nearly so spectacular and neither do they conform to the same pattern. Since that day most marriages of widows, or widowers, are kept secret and a small group of intimatese gives a *charivari* preceding the wedding. Since two *charivaris* cannot be given to a couple, this precludes the possibility of another such tumult.

## LA TOUSSAINT — LE JOUR DES MORTS

La Toussaint is All Saints' day and comes on November 1st. It is St. James' most beautiful custom. It is as its name implies — the day of the dead — a memorial day.

For weeks before La Toussaint there is much activity in the cemeteries — white-washing the tombs, cutting the grass, and cleaning the graves. On the appointed day crowds of people, from all walks of life, visit the cemeteries to bring beautiful bouquets of fine chrysanthemums or, as circumstances permit, pathetic little handfuls of half-faded flowers — all to be placed before the graves and tombs. There are services in all the Catholic Churches, which are followed by orderly processions to the cemeteries where "Le Libera" is chanted.

But once the service and procession are over, the crowd begins to disperse. And one meets old friends and the many *tantes*,[11] and *cousines*,[12] and *parains*.[13] Between the tombs and in the *grande allée*,[14] there are reunions of old friends and distant relatives with much kissing and many introductions. Here one sees for the first time "le petit bébé du grand garçon de Tante Titine"[15] and there is much animated conversation with enough "do-you-remembers" to wake up the dead.

In years gone by *La Toussaint* was the big day of the year at St. Michel. The Jefferson College band, the faculty, and the students, the clergy and acolytes, and followed by the laity, formed a long procession which filed slowly and mournfully to the *cime-*

*tiere*. All Saints' was a day of mourning and stiff decorum. Even Hallowe'en parties were never given then, because it was considered poor taste to attend a party on the eve of the day dedicated to the dead of one's family.

It is not strange that the chrysanthemum has become the symbolic flower of the dead. It is one of the few flowers which blooms profusely at that time and so closely has it become associated with the dead that I know some persons now residing in St. James who would not, under any circumstances, decorate their homes with large chrysanthemums.

The first cemeteries although taken up by the river, were between Mye Braud's house and the church. In the present burial ground there are several tombs which are over a hundred years old.

When a needed levee swallowed the old *cimitieres*,[16] the new one was already in existence, but little was done to transfer the dead to the new plot. It was better, perhaps, to be finally consigned to the great Father-of-Waters, which long before had mercifully embraced the tired, fevered body of that intrepid Spanish explorer — Hernando de Soto.

## LA TITE CAUSETTE

*La tite causette*[17] is a conversation, but as often as not, it is the relation of a choice bit of hot gossip. It is still a favorite St. James pastime, whether it be on *la gallerie* at eventide, or across the back fence in the hot noonday sun. No sooner is a piece of news apprehended than one calls Pélagie next door, and over the fence the news travels from this one to that. *La tite causette* often lasts an hour or more with much added or subtracted, depending on which side of the fence — literally and figuratively — the narrator happens to be.

## STRANGE FLAGS

There is a curious custom here of putting out a white flag on the front gate post if it is necessary for the doctor to call. I do not know why a white flag is used, unless it be that the patient has surrendered to the attacking germs. At any rate, the country doctors rarely miss seeing the white flag and as each one knows the locality of his patients there is seldom the embarrassment of the wrong doctor stopping in.

Here we have the story of a nimble old lady whose eighty-four years and high blood pressure did not prevent her from climbing over high fences and giving cows a quick chase when needs arose.

One day she felt very badly so she put up her white flag. The doctor called and ordered her to bed. In fact he said: "Remain in bed until I call again." Two weeks elapsed and no doctor. The old lady was better, but bored. Again she hoisted her white flag.

She was having a barn built and curiosity got the best of her. She slipped into her dressing gown and went out to the barn. In the middle of an animated conversation with the carpenter, she heard the doctor's car come to a stop. Panic-strciken, she ran from the barn to the house, jumped into bed, and covered herself up just as the doctor entered the room.

Finding her blood pressure higher than ever, he ordered her to remain in bed. This she did until his car was out of sight beyond the bend in the old river road. Then she went back to her carpenter while the doctor continued his stops where waved the little white flags.

The red flag is another matter. It, too, is posted on the front gate post, but it is used to halt the "coal-oil man."[18] The red flag means the kerosene tank needs re-filling. In this case the red flag seems symbolic enough, since the kerosene eventually does get red-hot.

## LA TITE PARTIE

*La tite partie*[19] is a card game — always for stakes — sometimes very big, but usually very small. Men assembled, and still do, on a Saturday night for a gumbo, or a shrimp boil, or a court-bouillion[20] and *la tite partie*. In days gone by, they played ramps, euchre, and poker. The last two are still favorites. I don't know why it should be called *la tite partie*, because it often begins in the late afternoon and continues through most of the night. In some homes it has been the subject of violent quarrels, because friend-husband occasionally came home with a *tignon*[21] because he had had *trop des tit-cou*[22] and *la tite partie* had cost a whole lot more than its name implied.

At any rate we have the story of a gay young Creole, whose father gave him $10,000 for a trip to Paris. After much preparation and many farewells, the young blade started out. He went to New Orleans, via river packet, to board a steamer. But when he reached New Orleans, he had to borrow money to come back to Bellemont. *La tite partie* on the river boat had cost him his trip to Paris.

## LES BILLETS D'ENTERREMENT[23]

Another old custom, still generally observed in St. James, is that of the black-bordered poster announcing a person's death and inviting the acquaintances, relatives, and friends to attend the funeral. These little papers are about five by seven inches and are issued as soon after a person's demise as can be conveniently arranged. They are tacked up in general stores, in the church portico, on telephone poles, post offices, but a notice is also delivered by special messenger to every house where there are relatives or friends of the deceased. And the Creole, who is a naturally sensitive individual, usually will not attend a funeral if a notice has not been delivered into his home. If inquiry is made as to his absence, he will draw himself up proudly and say: "Ils nous ont pas fait part!"[24]

## THE WAKE

A wake means to keep vigil through the night over the dead. Years ago a wake was the assembly of all relatives and friends of the bereaved family. There was silence and mourning and sorrow. In more recent years the wake offers a gathering place for the curious, as well as the sympathetic. One sees little groups huddled in corners — the women always in the house, and the men always on the porch and on the lawn — giving each other the news and bringing each other up to date on the doings of their friends. And one hears such as: "Just think, Telesphore died only six months ago and *Marie fait déja la veuve.*"[25] Coffee is served at all hours of the night and one swaps news, gossip, and political information over those demi-tasses.[26] But be that as it may, *une grande enterrement*[27] is still something to be proud of in St. James Parish.

## A TIRE LARIGOT

Another odd custom is that of rocking oneself in a comfortable old-fashioned rocking chair. The favorite place for this simple diversion is the porch in summer and the fireside in winter. In fact one straight-laced old spinster is so fond of rocking herself that she gives up this pastime as a Lenten penance of self-denial. And a common expression heard here is "Je me berce à tire-larigot." This means to rock until one is dizzy.

## The French Calendar

Through the years there is nothing which has remained so unchanged and so typically St. Jamesian as the French calendar. It is distributed here by the local merchnats about Christmas. It is printed in French on both sides of a stiff white cardboard 10½ x 13½ inches. In addition to the regular tabular arrangement of the days, weeks, and months of the year, it supplies other useful information. It gives the latitude and longitude[28] of New Orleans in relation to that of Paris and the difference in Paris and New Orleans time. It furnishes the exact time of the sunrise and sunset for the year, as well as all information on the waxing and the waning of the moon. It chronicles the beginning of the seasons to the very minute. It includes the movable feasts of the Catholic Church, the ember days, and a saint's feast for each day. It lists the daily weather forecast and, surprisingly, contains practically no advertising — only the name of the merchant who distributes it.

These calendars are still a part of St. James life and there are many homes where the calendar hangs in a conspicuous place on the wall or graces the mantel. In homes where there are several adults, each one has his own calendar and woe to the merchant who forgets to give Nonc Eusebe, Tante Jojo, and Malou their calendars. When a child is born, the calendar is immediately consulted for his saint's name (usually his middle name) and this accounts for some of the strange appellations in the parish: Apolinaire, Monique, Euphrasie, Eusebe. . . . .

But the oddest use of the calendar is that to which it is put by the good housewife. Here it becomes a sort of family diary. A ring is drawn around March 12th with the notation: *poule à couver.*[29] January 16th: *Mignone a eu son veau.*[30] June 15: *marriage de Marie.*[31] August 24: *planter des pommes de terre.*[32] Sept. 25: *ouragon.*[33] March 28: *fait nos Pâques.*[34]

Sometimes a family keeps its calendars. Yellowed with age and disfigured by marks, they chronicle affairs, both public and private, right spang on the wall. And the little child who innocently destroys or mars a calendar is really in for it. *C'est mon calendrier!*[35]

## La Gallerie

One of the pleasantest customs in St. James Parish, and in other Acadian communities too for that matter, is life on "la

Blessed Duchene's well dug for the Ladies of the Sacred Heart upon their arrival in St. James at St. Michael's. (Courtesy of Rev. Robert Morin, S.M., Pastor of St. Michael's Church at Convent. Father Morin is seen drawing a pitcher of water from the well. Photo by Joe Lucia)

St. Joseph's School for colored people. Established by the Ladies of the Sacred Heart in 1866 it is the oldest Catholic school for colored children in the State. Moved to St. Michael's in 1932 Rev. Francis Georzelin, S.M., is the pastor. (Photo by Joe Lucia)

## OUR FLAGS

St. James, with its complex history, has had correspondingly numerous flags. Since the history has already been given, the flags are here reproduced with explanatory notes.

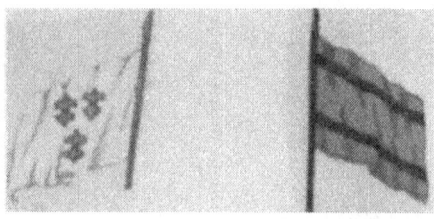

*1*     *2*     *3*     *4*

**1.**
The flag of the French kings appeared in St. James as LaSalle sailed down the Mississippi River in 1682 and claimed Louisiana for France.

**2.**
Although St. James, as part of Louisiana, had been ceded to Spain in 1762, the Spanish flag was not raised until 1769 when Spain took formal possession of Louisiana.

**3.**
The tri-color of the French Republic became the flag of St. James on November 30, 1803 when we again passed into French hands. This flag was probably never flown in St. James proper.

**4.**
Twenty days later St. James, as part of Louisiana was sold to the United States. We then unfurled the fifteen-star flag of the United States.

**5.**
Louisiana seceded from the United States on January 26, 1861 and became an independent state. The above flag was adopted on February 11, 1861. This flag, too, probably new flew over St. James as we soon joined the Confederacy.

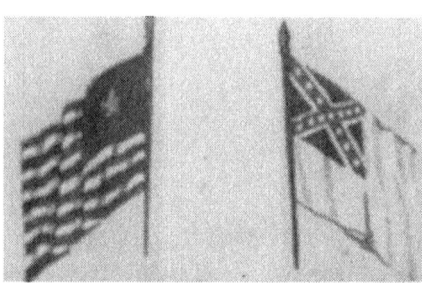

*5*     *6*

**6.**
A few weeks later Louisiana became a part of the Confederate States of America and the flag of the Confederacy flew over St. James until it was taken over by Union troops in 1862.

Today St. James is no longer French or Spanish, Acadian or Creole, Yankee or Confederate. It is American. And Old Glory proudly waves its protective folds over St. Jacques de Cabahannocer!

Gallerie." *La gallerie* is the front porch and no home is so poor as to be without one, though porches here range from the large encircling galleries of Oak Alley to the creaky, rough boards of a dilapidated old cabin. Here the baby is rocked to sleep, the housewife shells her butter beans, Mémère simultaneously makes her *tite causette* and her tatting, and several ladies join in the co-operative effort of a quilt. Occasionally a man is seen cutting his neighbor's hair and giggly little girls sit and shell pecans to make *des bonnes pralines*.[36] An old Negro slowly sharpens his hoe while his wife, with her pipe in her mouth, patches a shirt and the ever-present dogs lazily sleep in the sun.

In more recent times, screens have enclosed many porches and most of them have electric lights, but life there is still vital though sometimes a little uninhibited. The porch is frequently picturesque, too. Red peppers hang on the wall, pecans and seeds are spread on the floor to dry; pot plants, toys, and fishing nets are about — and in some cases even wash tubs. But almost always clothes are strung on the *garde-fou* to sun. In fact this custom of sunning clothes on the porch railing has had some rather complex results.

Recently crisp fall weather put in a sudden appearance. This was the signal for the housewives to sun those camphor-smelling winter woolens. One St. James lady quickly unpacked her winter clothing and hung it out on the front porch. Immediately after dinner, she retired for her usual siesta. While she was sleeping, the laundryman from a neighboring parish made his regular Thursday call, but she did not hear him. There is no railing on this porch so the clothes were swinging about on coat hangers with a blanket draped across the swing. The laundryman cried his usual stock-in-trade, but as there was no answer he surmised that the housewife was out and that she had placed the clothes there for him to collect. He piled suits, coats, dresses, skirts, sweaters, and what-not into the blanket and left, bending under the weight of the huge bundle.

In due time the lady woke up, leisurely dressed, and went out on her porch to gather her clothes. She was dumbfounded, aghast, frantic . . . . her whole stock of winter clothing had simply vanished. Then it slowly dawned upon her that this was the laundryman's day to call. The telephone solved the riddle, but not without a little hard feeling . . . the laundryman, not a native St. Jamesian, taking the stand that he was correct in his surmise and the housewife insisting that it was *her* prerogative to sun *her* clothes on*her* porch without his packing them off.

A few days later the clothes were returned "as was" ... all tied up in the blanket ... and the housewife sunned them all the more because of the trip they had taken. And life goes merrily on on *la gallerie*.

### MARIE LAGRAINE

And who is Marie Lagraine? Well, Marie Lagraine is an Acadian puppet ... only she is not a real puppet, but a real human being ... part of one, anyway. Before Christmas Marie Lagraine comes to visit some of the St. James homes in order to check up on the children's behavior and to ascertain their Christmas wishes.

Marie Lagraine is in reality the forearm of an Acadian mother, whose doubled fist is a painted face with a little white cap perched on its head, while a flowing *gabrielle*[37] hides the woman's arm which forms the body of the puppet.

Marie Lagraine comes out from behind a thick suspended quilt dancing to the children's singing. Then they ask her direct questions, which Marie Lagraine answers by shaking her head up and down for yes, and horizontally for non, with a special heave-to for *I don't know*. She gets very angry by stomping at the bad children and dances for the good ones to their great glee.

Recently all the grandchildren of a large St. James family were assembled in the plantation home for a séance with Marie Lagraine. One three-year-old youngster was so fascinated that he was spellbound and could ask no questions. Egged on by some adults to ask what he wanted for Christmas, he finally opened his mouth to match the width of his eyes and blurted: "I want one like that." At this naive suggestion Marie Lagraine shook her head but danced with joy.

To the children Marie Lagraine is Santa Claus's mother. Years ago an ex-St. Jamesian, a naval officer long stationed in the North, visited the parish with his family. It was arranged to have his *Yankee* children see Marie Lagraine and they were delighted with the performance. A few days later they returned to their northern home, and soon it was Christmas time again. The children were taken to a large department store to see Santa where the little St. James visitor stumped Santa with: "Oh, Santa Claus, I saw your Mama in Louisiana." And since Santa

Claus is supposed to be a native of the North Pole, he was quite puzzled as to the origin of his Louisiana mother. His ruddy face reddened all the more, because, for once, he could not make the proper comeback. And after all what could a Yankee Santa Claus know of an Acadian Marie Lagraine? That is a secret joy known only to the little children of the Acadian communities of south Louisiana.

FOOTNOTES

1. La. Toussaint — All Saint's Day — November First.
2. Le Charivari — a confused noise — a serenade.
3. La prière en commun — group prayer.
4. Jupons — Petticoats.
5. Camisoles de molleton — This is a Creole, or Acadian, expression meaning flannelette night-gown. The word blouse (a loose frock) is also used here for night gown.
6. Et Fâites que je puisse acheter la vache de Monsieur Tel-et-tel aujourdi'hui. And make it (possible) that I buy Mr. So-and-so's cow today.
7. Gallerie — gallery — here used for porch.
8. Garde-fou — railing or bannister.
9. Charivari!
Pour qui?
Monsieur Alexandre Brignac.
Avec qui?
Mademoiselle Lucie Schexnaydre.
Sonnez les bourgots![10]
Charivari!
For whom?
Mr. Alexandre Brignac
With whom?
Miss Lucie Schexnaydre.
Blow the horns!
10. Sonnez means to ring or blow and bourgot is some sort of a horn once used to announce the arrival of the butcher. Sonnez les bourgots is used here to start off the noise in a charivari. Before the advent of a truck delivery in St. James, the butcher used a horn, the baker a bell, and the ice man a whistle, in order to announce their approach or arrival.
11. Tantes — Aunts.
12. Cousines — Cousins.
13. Parains — Godfathers.
14. Grande-Allée — main aisle — often called the big alley.
15. Le petit bébé du grand garçon de Tante Titine — The little baby of the big boy of Aunt Titine.
16. Cimitiere — Here used for cimetiere — a cemetery.
17. La tite causette (petite) — a little conversation, a chat.

18. Coal-oil-man — person who delivers kerosene.
19. La tite partie (petite) — a little game.
20. Court-bouillon — fish cooked in special Creole style.
21. Tignon — a little drunk.
22. Trop des tit-cou (petit coup) — too many drinks.
23. Les billets de'enterrement — funeral posters.
24. Ils nous ont pas fait part — They did not invite us.
25. Marie fait déja le veuve — Marie makes the widow. That is, Marie is looking for another husband.
26. Demi-tasse — small after-dinner coffee cup.
27. Une grande enterrement — A big funeral.
28. St. James has practically the same latitude and longitude as New Orleans.
29. Poule à couver — Set a hen.
30. Mignone a eu son veau — Mignon had her calf.
31. Marriage de Marie — Marie's marriage.
32. Planter des pommes de terre — planted Irish potatoes.
33. Ouragon — Hurricane.
34. Fait nos Pâques — Made our Easter duties.
35. C'est mon calendrier — That's my calendar.
36. Pralines — pecan candy.
37. Gabrielle — full flowing wrapper — or house coat.

## XX

### STRANGE PLANTS

St. James is part of Louisiana's famous sugar bowl and, certainly, the sugar industry has played an important role in the history of the parish. But there are smaller and more colorful industries and less-known and stranger plants: Périque, moss, filé, and vetiver. And since Périque tobacco is grown here exclusively, I shall begin with its story.

#### PÉRIQUE TOBACCO

Probably there is no plant of such minute acreage and such vast renown as Périque tobacco. Wrapped in romance, mystery, and hard work, it has brought St. James into world repute.

The story begins way back with the Indians. Some say there were Choctaw, others Chickasaw, or even Acolapissa, or Houma. Nobody really knows, but everyone seems to be agreed on two things: They were Indians and they lived near Gramercy. The first settlers found these Indians smoking a tobacco that was different. They taught the white man the method of cultivating and the odd process of curing this distinctive tobacco. This, we might say, was the gift of the St. James Indian to the world.

There are many amusing legends and startling true stories concerning Périque tobacco and Pierre Chenet, the man who introduced it commercially. Pierre Chenet, a wandering little Acadian exile, was adopted by a Spanish family, who nicknamed him Périque.[1] Thus the tobacco which he introduced to the outside world after settling in St. James became Périque tobacco.[2] Périque had four daughters who married four Poché brothers. Many of the descendants of the Chenet and Poché families still reside in St. James.

In 1803 Pierre Chenet lived on a tract of land which is now part of the town of Lutcher as shown by authentic parish and state records. It is certain that he owned and cultivated this land and it is probable that this is where he first produced the tobacco which made St. James famous. But Périque was not only a farmer and a business man but he played some part in the community. When the first church was built at St. Michel, he became one of the wardens. His wife was sponsor at the christening of the first bell, which was named la Pierre-Suzanne. The other sponsor was an eighty-year-old Acadian, Pierre Michel. Périque, himself, lived to be eighty six.

But stranger still is the story of Périque tobacco. It grows in an area in St. James which extends about fourteen miles on the left bank of the Mississippi River, in soil that, apparently, is not different from the soil around it. Yet this plant grows nowhere else in the world. The seed is so small that it is mixed with fine ashes to be sown in well-prepared beds at about Christmas. In approximately three months, it is transplanted into the open field in wide rows. After some growth it is topped, and later, the new buds, called suckers, are nipped off by hand. Only a few large leaves are left to develop and mature. About June-July, the tobacco is cut and gathered. It is then hung in sheds to dry for some three weeks. Then the stalks and stems are stripped off, the tobacco is slightly moistened, and packed by layers into heavy oak barrels.

Here begins the strange method of curing, which entails time, patience and hard work. Pressure is applied by the use of heavy jack-screws, which are tightened daily. Every few weeks the pressure is removed, the tobacco is taken out, aired, replaced in the container, and repressured. This is done three or four times before winter sets in and again in March. During this process, the tobacco gets very dark, unbelievably strong, and delightfully fragrant. It is then packed in carrottes,[3] in tins, and in barrels to be shipped.

Périque is no crop for laggards and lazy folk. In fact such intensive cultivation is required that a farmer plants but a few acres, yet much of the work is done by the children of the prolific Acadian families. But Périque is a money crop and it keeps indefinitely — two good reasons for its culture. Its price has fluctuated from ten cents to two dollars per pound, but the average price is more nearly thirty cents.[4] And if there is no sale, why the farmer keeps it — Périque only improves with age. For a long time practically the whole crop was shipped abroad — especially to Britain and to Sweden. In more recent years domestic tobacco companies purchase much of the crop, which they use as a blend in high-grade pipe tobacco.

Although some natives smoke or chew pure Périque, it is much too strong for the average smoker. Indeed the fun-loving Acadian long ago learned the loaded cigar trick — only this cigar was not explosive. It was unadulterated Périque, but a knockout, just the same. In riding in from New Orleans one day, a jolly young Acadian boy from Belmont gave a fine cigar to a man on the train. The man was delighted, but long before he reached Baton Rouge, he was stretched out on the platform — genuinely tobacco sick. Yes, sir, pure Périque knocks the new smoker cold, yet it has no more nicotine than other tobaccos. Many connoisseurs of distinctive smoking demand a Périque blend — and how and why it's different, nobody knows. Perhaps Pierre Chenet did, but even at that distant day, he was too good a business man to tell. And now, like la Pierre-Suzanne, it can never more be told (tolled).

### Spanish Moss

Long ago the French and Spanish explorers marveled at the long, graceful garlands of Spanish moss festooned about the trees. The French derisively called it Spanish beard, and the Spanish, not to be outdone, called it Frenchman's wig. Today it is known as Spanish moss, but its real name is *tillandsia usneoides*.

There is a well known legend in Louisiana that the moss is the hair of an Indian princess, who was killed by enemy Indians during her marriage ceremony. As was the custom among the people of her tribe, before her burial her hair was cut off and spread on the limbs of a huge oak tree, under whose gnarled old branches she was buried. In time the wind blew the hair from tree to tree, where it grayed into Spanish moss.

Moss is attached to the trees, but feeds on air, so it is not a true parasite. It is long, stringy, and greenish-gray and as it sways in the trees, it resembles a deep fringe. Some Indians used it for scant clothing in summer. The early settlers daubed it with clay, or mud, to form old-fashioned walls and chimneys for their pioneer homes. It was much used, and still is, for mattresses, but today most of the moss sold is used in overstuffed furniture. An unusual use of Spanish moss was its employment by the Indians in giving sweat baths. The patient, completely enveloped in several layers of moss, was placed on a slightly elevated cane bed. A low charcoal fire, over which boiled herbs smouldered, was then set under the bed. The heat and steam seeped between the canes and through the moss, producing a profuse sweat.

About six pounds of green moss are required to make one pound of cured moss. It is gathered from the trees in the woods and swamps where it grows wild. When cured, moss is no longer gray, but black. It grows on cypress, pecan, oak, persimmon, ash, gum and other trees and its average price is six cents per pound. Moss is best gathered in the early daylight hours of the fall and winter months.

The moss industry, though very picturesque, is not very important in St. James. There is a moss gin at Lutcher, but the owner, Mr. Alvyn Woods, says that ninety-five percent of the moss ginned there comes from other sections than St. James, yet almost all within a radius of seventy-five miles.

Moss contributes much to the beauty of the trees in St. James. The moss covered trees at College Point, Jefferson College, Helvetia, and Bellemont are particularly beautiful. But moss is at its best in the old crape-myrtle trees of the parish. Nothing can outdo the pleasing combination of pink blossom, green leaf, and gray moss.

## Gombo Filé[5]

*Filer* is a French word which means "to run thick and ropy." Too much *filé* added to gumbo makes it thick and ropy, so evidently *gumbo filé*, derived from the word *filer* is well named.

The sassafras tree, from which filé is made, grows wild in south Louisiana. In examining early colonial records, one finds that sassafras was an important item of trade in those pioneer days. The sassafras tree, which belongs to the laurel family, grows quite large in good soil. The birds eat the blue berries in mid summer and the root is used for flavoring extract. However, filé is made from the sassafras leaf and it is with filé with which we are now concerned.

After August fifteenth, the leaves are gathered in clusters, or twigs, and hung in a shed to dry. A few weeks later, they are pounded very fine in a pilon made of a hollowed log and pestle. The product which ensues is a dull green powder. This is sifted through an ordinary flour sifter and packed into glass containers. Since filé making is not a commercialized industry here, discarded beer bottles, jelly glasses, and mustard jars are used. One might say that the making of filé is a little *métier*,[6] which brings in a few extra dollars a year to the frugal Acadian house wife. There are people at College Point and Romeville, who make

*First Page of Marriage records, St. Michael's Church, 1809.*

*Third page of Marriage records, St. Michael's Church, 1810.*

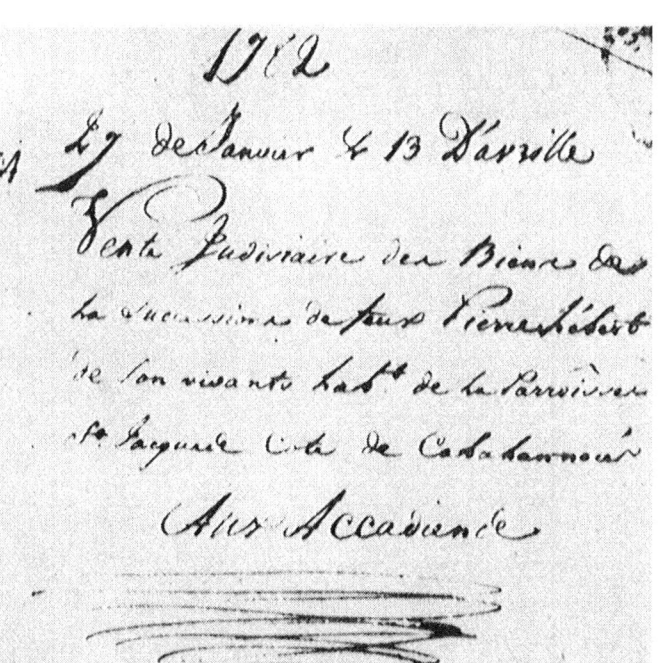

*First page of Court Record of Succession of Pierre Hebert, 1782.*

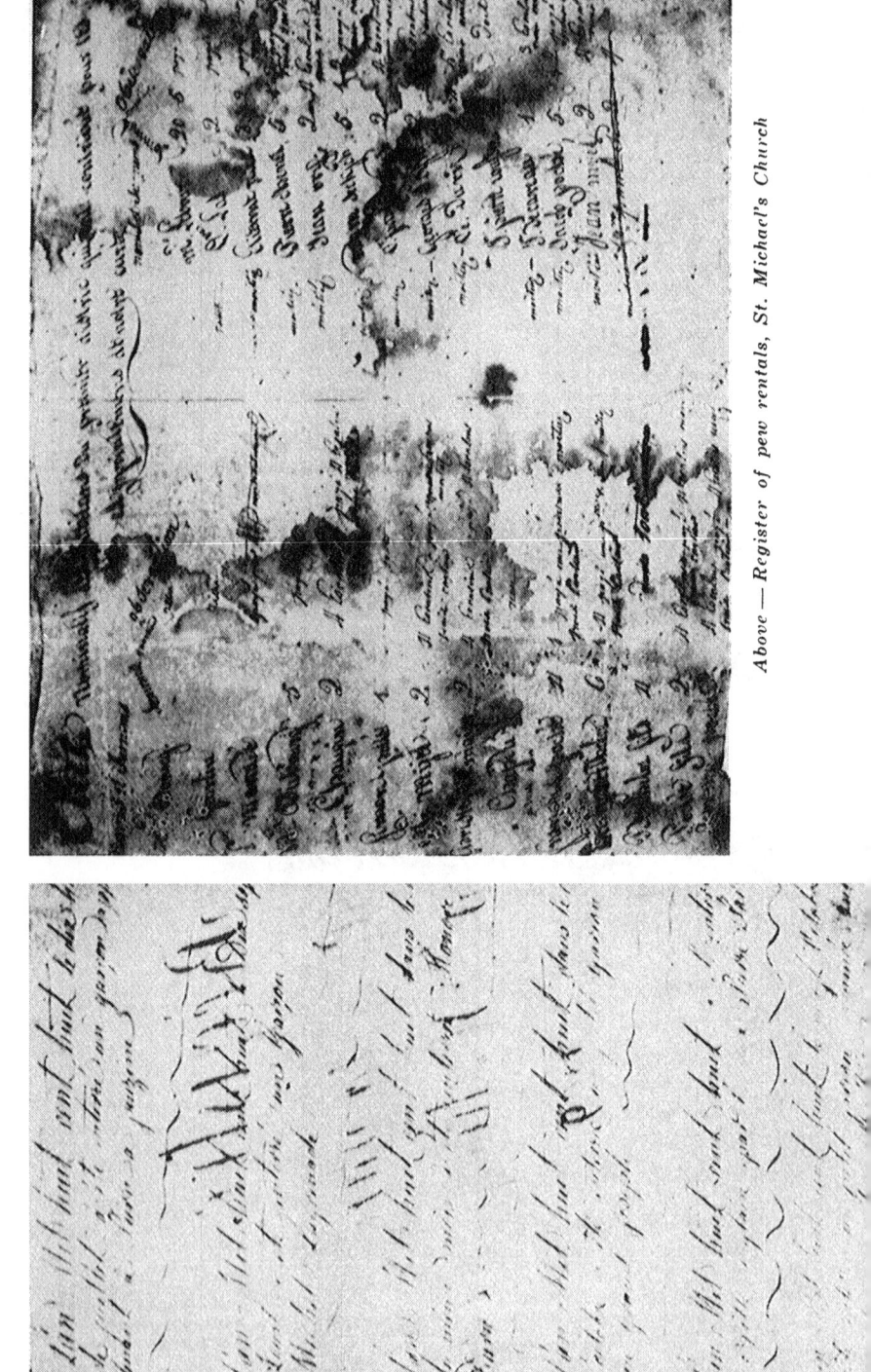

Above — Register of pew rentals, St. Michael's Church

excellent filé and during the fall many New Orleanians drive here on Sunday afternoons to get their year's supply of pecans, red pepper, and filé. Each local vendor has her regular customers.

A few months ago an old lady from Convent visited in New Orleans. Upon leaving, her hostess gave her a dollar and said: "Give this to Emma, she will know what it is for." Now, it happened to be near la Toussaint and the dollar had been sent to be expended in white-washing a tomb, but Emma was so accustomed to buying Adele's filé, that she took it for granted that the dollar was for that purpose. This little tangle was happily straightened out before the filé was sent to Adele. And fortunately, too, one could make an enormous amount of gumbo with a dollar's worth of filé — usually a pinch — whatever that is — suffices.

## VETIVER

If Périque tobacco is St. James' romantic plant, surely *vetivert*[7] is its aromatic plant. This native of the East Indies has been grown in St. James since the early history of the parish. It is quite possible that it was introduced here by Valcour Aime, who brought to St. James plants from all over the world. It has become one of the most popular garden plants in the parish, but not grown commercially. It is deciduous but during our long, warm summer, it reaches a height of eight feet or more. Vetivert has long slender, sharp-edged, green leaves and the whole bush looks very much like a gigantic clump of overgrown grass. Sometimes it is used as a screen, but more often in clumps to decorate the lawn or to fill odd corners. But vetivert's popularity lies underground. Its small snake-like, raffia-colored roots have the mildest, sweetest fragrance, and have long been used in madame's mahogany armoires, especially among the bed and table linens.

The roots, which are very hard to dig out, are thoroughly washed and sundried. Then they are cut and tied into little bundles, which weigh next to nothing. When the fragrance wanes, the little bundles are lightly sprinkled with water and placed in the sun for a while. This gives them new life, or at least, a new fragrance. Some people weave them into mats, and others fashion them into palmetto-like fans, but their greatest use is that of a sachet.

Growing vetivert is not an industry of St. James. Here and there people have what we might call their free customers — that is, persons from the city, who annually get their vetivert supply from their St. James friends. And since the root retains its fragrance for three years or so, vetivert is a sort of lovely, lingering lagniappe.

### Footnotes

1. Périque — This name has many spelling variants. It is even spelled Perrick in some of the court records, but since Périque was illiterate and signed his name with a cross, no one will ever know who was right.

2. In more recent years Christophe Roussel, whose direct ancestor, Christofle Roussel, was a prominent citizen of the parish as early as 1807, became known as King Périque. King Périque is not to be confused with the original Périque . . . Pierre Chenet.

3. Carotte — a method of packing this tobacco into a twist called a carotte.

4. Price in 1954 was about 60c a pound.

5. *Gombo* — gumbo.

6. *Métier* — trade.

7. *Vetivert* — The correct spelling is vetiver but many people here add the final "to" to the word.

## XXI

## THE FOURTH ESTATE

More than eighty years had passed since the founding of the parish and yet no local newspaper had been established. This seems strange in a community whose people had built the finest schools in the state. This was due in part to the poor means of communication and transportation then available. And, too, the parish was served by the New Orleans papers delivered by boat several days old.

The first parish paper, *Le Messager*, was established by Charles Moroy and A. Lagardère on July 24, 1846. It was printed entirely in French and covered only four pages. The subscription price was $5.00 per year, but the subscribers had the privilege of advertising gratis for their runaway slaves. *Le Messager* was the first official journal of the parish. Prior to that time official notices were printed on large sheets divided in two. On the left side of the sheet notices were in French but on the other half was the English translation. These notices were posted throughout the parish. *Le Messager* at first was published at Bringier, but in 1851 *L'Imprimerie du Messager* was moved to an old building known as the St. James Exchange just above the college. Let us look at some of the early editions of St. James' first newspapers.

A serial covered one-fourth of the paper, the ads and official notices, one-half. This left but one page for news and, strangely, *Le Messager* contained little local news. Even so copies of a century ago give us an interesting picture of that day. The ads listed articles which have disappeared from present day stores: blanc de baleine,[1] orgeat,[2] la prise,[3] eau de vie,[4] mantillas, wigs, walking canes, cotton and wool cards, mourning dresses, and cholera medicine. One store whose name was *Hard Times* advertised champagne. But more surprising to modern readers, butter was quoted at twenty-two cents a pound and molasses at fifteen cents a gallon.

Although Mr. Godchaux had moved his store from Convent to New Orleans a few years before, he advertised in *Le Messager*. At 107-108 Rue de la Vieille-Levée he offered fine coats at six dollars and the best trousers at eleven. A good linen shirt could be had for a dollar, but the best cost four.

The Postmaster at Convent, Mr. Leon Blouin, published a card giving the day of the departure and the arrival of the mail thrice weekly. Rewards were offered for run-away slaves, and an auction, in March 1850 listed 257 slaves for sale. The president of the college, Mr. Louis Dufau, invited the public to attend the weekly examinations given to the boys "in their studies made at this institution." And places were reserved for the ladies. Some occupations seem strange to us today: Dealers in carts and carriages, harness makers, and stiffeners of cloth. The packet boats operating between New Orleans, St. James, and Bayou Lafourche covered one column. And the names of the boats sounded more like a list of the passengers: The Fanny Sparhawk, the Mary Foley, the Dr. Batey, the C. D., Jr., the Eliska, and the F. M. Streck.

But in spite of the fact that the old copies of *Le Messager* are at least one hundred years old, they are remarkably well preserved and some are not even yellowed with age. The paper is fine and light and the print is clear.

The establishment of others newspapers followed *Le Messager*. These early papers were not confined to news. They included serials, poems, essays, discussions, and a variety of articles. California news was found in almost every issue because of the recent discovery of gold there. Politics, then as now, was a favorite topic and duels were often the result of political writings. The newspapers of a century ago were more literary and cultural. They were usually published by French political exiles who found refuge here and who were among the well educated men of that period.

At first all the newspapers were in French but as time rolled on, they became bi-lingual. The present local papers are in English. The last French-English newspaper in St. James was *L'Interim* suspended in 1942 — a casualty of World War II. At the time of its demise it was published in English only. None of the earlier St. James newspapers has survived.

The predecessor of *L'Interim* was *Le Foyer Creole*. Mr. Florian B. Dicharry, one of its publishers, was involved in a law suit, so he changed the name to *L'Interim*. The suit dragged on for a long time and although Mr. Dicharry finally won, his paper did not resume its former name. In examining the issue of

*Le Foyer Creole* of May 18, 1881, one can but note the number of articles and the variety of topics included. That copy contained write-ups on diamonds, religion, the French language, Russia, cotton, Tunisia, electricity, money, and misbehavior in church. In addition were New Orleans gossip, local news, cards, ads, a serial, and what not. Perhaps the most interesting ad was that of a syrup which claimed to cure ten unrelated diseases. This paper also carried the official directory of the state and parish officials and a panel of 110 jurors, giving us an interesting register of the men who lived here seventy-five years ago.

Probably the best paper ever edited in St. James was *Le Louisianais*, published and written by Mr. J. J. Gentil, 1865-1891. In fact, this paper ranked as one of the best newspapers published in Louisiana. Mr. Gentil was a political exile of France. He was highly educated and had graduated from the College of Blois, France, his native home. He taught at Jefferson College but when the Civil War closed this school, Mr. Gentil began the publication of *Le Louisianais* at his home in Convent. He is said to have been a fearless critic and a prolific writer and he wrote countless poems, essays, and serials. An interesting true story concerning Mr. Gentil follows:

When World War I began, Mr. Marcel Part, native and resident of Convent, was engaged to marry Miss Luce Olivier, granddaughter of Mr. Gentil. In time Mr. Part arrived in France. The St. James boys had the advantage of speaking French. One day Mr. Part's commanding officer was in search of a billet and as he could speak no French, he called on Mr. Part to accompany him and to act as his interpreter.

They knocked at a sturdy French home and the door was opened by an old, old lady. Mr. Part conveyed the message and they were let into an adjoining bed-room. Imagine Mr. Part's surprise when he saw Mr. Gentil's picture — the very replica of the one he had seen so often in Miss Olivier's home in Convent. After the matter at hand was disposed of, Mr. Part said, "Monsieur J. J. Gentil, is it not?"

"Yes, my brother," answered the woman incredulously. And from then on Mr. Part was a frequent visitor in that quaint French home, where the little old lady in wooden shoes always opened the door.

The first all-English newspaper published in St. James was the Reconstruction weekly, *The Republican*, established at Convent in 1870 with George E. Bovee and L.E. Bently as editors. After printing a few issues the name of *The Republican* was changed to *The St. James Sentinel*. It was the misunderstanding over *The Sentinel* which caused the tragic duel at Welham in which Dr. Gray was killed by Denis Richard. The publication of *The Sentinel* continued from 1870 to 1877. At one time it was edited by M. T. Jackson and at another by A. F. Hunsaker, but George Bovee continued as owner. *The Sentinel* was published at Convent and as it was the official parish journal of the Reconstruction era, frequent references are made to it in the various local court records.

The following is a list of newspapers published in St. James Parish at one time or another:

| PAPER | DATE ESTABLISHED | PUBLISHERS |
|---|---|---|
| Le Messager | 1846 | Moroy and Lagardère |
| St. Michel | 1854 | Henri Rémy |
| L'Autochtone | 1855 | Moroy and Lagardère |
| Le Rappel Louisianais | 1865 | A. L. Roman |
| Le Louisianais | 1865 | J. Gentil |
| The Republican | 1870 | G. E. Bovee and L. E. Bentley |
| The St. James Sentinel | 1870 | G. E. Bovee and M. T. Jackson |
| Le Foyer Creole | 1880 | Renaudier, de la Peichardière, and Dicharry |
| L'Interim | 1888 | F. B. Dicharry |
| Le Courier de St. Jacques | 1888 | Joseph N. Gourdain |
| La Gazette | 1895 | Joseph N. Gourdain |
| St. James Voice | 1914 | A. Miles Coe |
| The News-Examiner | 1938 | David Reynaud |
| River Parishes Journal | 1930 | Sigur Martin |
| The St. Jamesian | 1944 | Joseph Lucia |

FOOTNOTES

1. *Blanc de baleine* — spermaceti — used in making candles.
2. *Orgeat* — a popular drink made with sugar, almonds, etc.
3. *La prise* — snuff.
4. *Eau-de-vie* — brandy.

## XXII

## FOLKLORE

There are legends, stories, superstitions, and myths that have been handed down from generation to generation in St. James. Much of the folklore of the parish is similar to that of other sections of south Louisiana because the origin is the same: the Negro slave.

Mr. Alcée Fortier, native St. Jamesian and grandson of Valcour Aime, compiled the "Folk Tales of Louisiana" and told them in the patois of the French-speaking slave just as he had heard them as a little boy in his antebellum home. Several of the stories in Mr. Fortier's book came from an old negress who lived near Vacherie. Probably the most widely known folk tale in St. James is the story of Jean Sot.[1]

Jean Sot was so stupid that he wore his overcoat in summer and fanned himself in winter. One day he heard that the King would give his daughter in marriage to anyone capable of answering the King's riddle. However, the condition attached was that he, who tried and could not answer in three guesses, would have his head chopped off. Jean Sot determined to try in spite of the supplications of his mother, who realized how simpleminded he was. He set out and with the help of Compère-Lapin,[2] he not only managed to answer the King's riddle, but to ask a riddle of the King, who could not answer it. Thus Jean Sot won the King's daughter and the kingdom. And because he had been so clever, his name was changed from Jean Sot to Jean L'Esprit.[3]

Even more colourful, and certainly endless in number, are the superstitions about *gris-gris*. A *gris-gris* is a charm which works evil as well as good. It is usually made by a practioner of voodooism to suit the occasion or as needs arise. It takes any shape or form and is composed of a variety of articles, but nearly always it contains a little salt or pepper. Sometimes just the word *gris-gris* is used with proper timing. This is generally done by the smaller fry — especially in a marble game. When the opponent takes his shot, a little fellow will yell "gris-gris" and quickly make a little cross in the marble ring. And if the marble is missed, there is eminent satisfaction that the gris-gris didn't fail.

Another true story of the gris-gris concerns Jenny. She was an excellent cook in the employ of a prominent St. James family. She liked her work and she loved her "white folks," but she simply could not get along with their old yardman. She was convinced that he was trying to *hoodoo*[4] her. One morning she arrived for work, as usual, but when she lifted the stove lid, she found a gris-gris — a little white feather tied in a scrap of red cloth and carefully sprinkled with blackpepper. She never went back to work and a few weeks later she moved to New Orleans.

Many years later her old employer died and he was laid out in deathly grandeur in a fashionable funeral parlor in New Orleans. At nine that evening an old white-haired negress in immaculate white dress slowly entered and walked noiselessly to the bier. Tears coursed down her cheeks and her lips moved in fervent prayer. Her heart was broken. As she turned to go a mature woman tapped her lightly on the shoulder. Through her tears Jenny saw the little girl who she had so long ago loved and nursed — the little girl whose mud cakes she had baked — the little girl grown up — her old employer's daughter. Instinctively Jenny folded her into her arms, as she had done so many years before, entirely oblivious as to time, place, and people — their sorrow a common bond. Few of the prominent Louisianians gathered there could keep away their tears, yet none knew how Jenny had missed her white folks — all on account of a gris-gris.

And speaking of gris-gris, here is a voodoo rhyme good enough to scare anybody:

"L'appé vini, li grand zombie,
L'appé vini, pou to gris-gris."

Translation:

He is coming, the big zombie (devil),
He is coming, to gris-gris you.

The superstitions are too numerous to list, but here are a few common ones:

Drop a dish towel and company will come.

A screech owl in the yard means impending death in the house.

A crowing rooster on the door-step indicates company.

If you desire to be rid of boring company, stand a broom, straw up, in a corner and the company will leave at

*Lieut.-Gov. Lambremont and his family. Direct descendants of Pierre Lambremont who perished in the Natchez massacre.*

*Above — Swamp scene. From design for a tile created by the author.*

*Middle left — Tante Tinia, famous originator of mouth-watering confections. (See chapter on Cusine for Connoisseurs)*

*Lower left — Old Slave Cabin (Courtesy of Mrs. R. H. Potts)*

*Nita Crevasse — March 13, 1890 — still a vital topic of conversation in St. James Parish.*

*The Court House of St. James Parish today. This is the fourth court house of the Parish. (Photograph by Charles O. Subra)*

once. And then if you sweep after them, they will never come back.

Cat tails brought into a house bring death with them.

Two table knives at one cover denote an early wedding.

Never mend a sheet as the person sleeping on it will never wake up.

Never cut out a dress on a Friday. You won't live to wear it.

A family portrait falling from a wall is a bad omen.

"If red garters you do wear
You will be a millionaire.
If your garters are all yellow,
You will never want for fellow!"

This jingle has been the occasion of much speculation and one young lady, who could not make up her mind whether she preferred man or money, decided to wear a garter of each color with the secret hope that the result would be a rich husband. But there was a slip — perhaps of the garter — and now she is happily married — but not to a rich man.

A wealthy old lady, who was a stickler for detail and who was noted for her stiff decorum, had a plantation which she could not sell, although she was very anxious to be rid of it. After many years she heard the red garter ditty and instead of being duly horrified, as everyone expected, she surprised her intimates by wearing a pair of bright red garters. This was indeed a shocking thing for *cette grande dame*,[5] who had always been so properly precise that she was delighted when three-cent stamps were issued. They were purple and since she was in mourning, her black-bordered letters could then be posted *en demi-deuil*.[6] But back to the magic of her red garters: she soon sold her plantation and that was that!

And then there is a person whose marked success in nearly every poker game she attributes to her red garters. Often in the course of an evening's game, some poor unlucky player will beg and beg to borrow just one red garter, until in final desperation she will slip it off and fling it across the table, her very knees shaking in mortal dread that her own stack of chips will soon diminish.

Superstitions, too, are often used to frighten little children into good behavior and *le gros loup-loup*[7] is frequently called upon to castigate in dire fashion the little miscreants. *Le gros loup-loup* varies in form and potential evil from place to place, but a modern touch, indeed, was added when *le gros loup-loup* was none other than the noisy road machine. And always when a certain little girl heard it coming down the road, she would run into her home and burst into violent weeping, her panic lasting until the road machine was once more out of sight and sound.

The moon also plays its part in other than its romantic and luminary role. When a new moon appears with the crescent pointing up it is the opportune time to make a wish for money as follows: A silver dime is placed in the palm of the right hand and held down by the thumb. Touching the forehead and then extending the arm out, palm up, one bows low three times and says: *Salut belle lune, je vour demande la charité.*[8] And so the story goes before very long money will be received or found.

The St. Jamesians have always been very fond of music and in the old days every Creole family had its musicians. The daughters played the piano and the sons played the flute, the cornet, or some stringed instrument. The Acadians, too, loved music, but since few were fortunate enough to possess a piano, they substituted with song and many an Acadian girl whiled away a dull evening singing her favorites, as she rocked to and fro on *la gallerie*. Some of the old songs still heard in the parish are: "Malbrough s'en va t'en guerre," "Cadet Roussel," and "Fais Dodo." The words vary a little in different places, but a common version follows:

> *Fair dodo, Colas, mon p'tit frère,*
> *Faïs dodo, t'auras du lolo.*
> *Papa est en haut*
> *Qui fait des sabots.*
> *Maman est en bas*
> *Qui fait des bas."*

It means: —
> Go to sleep, Colas, my little brother.
> Go to sleep, you'll have some candy.
> Papa is upstairs making wooden shoes.
> Mama is downstairs making stockings.

This was the song sung to the little Acadian and Creole babies as they were rocked in their little *berceaux*. A berceaux is a little wooden crib on rockers. Mrs. Leo P. Hymel of Convent has one, which was hand made by one of Mr. Hymel's ancestors. It is said to be over one hundred years old.

Then I must add a word about *la vieille traiteuse*.[9] In those by-gone days doctors were scarce and medical supplies were few so *la vieille traiteuse* made tisanes, cataplasms, and compresses for fevers, aches, and pains. She used herbs, bark, roots, orange rind, brandy — not entirely without success. She treated sprains with mumbled words, little signs, and much massage. In fact, St. James still has some *traiteuses*, who have quite a few patients. But, as often as not, the treatment given has no medicinal value whatever, but is instead as superstitious and as preposterous as the practices of the earlier Indian medicine man. And long ago, I heard of a *traiteuse* who advised a patient with toothache to put a raisin in the cavity, and *"Bois clous rouilles."*[10]

And perhaps an equally grotesque idea was advanced when a person suffering from herpes (shingles) was advised by several old persons to kill a black chicken and let its warm blood drip on the herpes blisters. But a man in a neighboring parish who received the same advice solved the problem in a more practical way: "Bring me the chicken and be sure its a fine one," he told the well-wisher. And in an aside to his wife he added: "I have an idea that chicken will do me more good inside than out." And a delicious dinner was enjoyed by all.

And, too, we have at least one St. Jamesian, who quite a few years ago, hired a voodoo doctor to come all the way from New Orleans to free her tormented soul from an evil spell — and incidentally, she was freed also of a twenty dollar bill. The voodoo practitioner, by the way, came in a luxurious car adding a touch of modern ease to the age-old cult, better known as fleecing.

I have but touched on the fascinating folklore of the parish. It is amusing and fantastic. And I often wonder what would happen if Jean Sot, lustily singing "Fais-Dodo" down the river road at midnight, would meet a gros loup-loup with a bunch of cat-tails in his hand! OOOOOOOOOO!!

FOOTNOTES

1. Jean Sot — John Foolish.
2. Compère Lapin — Brother Rabbit.

3. *Jean L'Esprit* — John Sense.
4. *Hoodoo* — The word should be voodoo — but people here say hoodoo.
5. *Cette grande dame* — That grand lady.
6. *En demi-deuil* — in half mourning.
7. *Le gros loup-loup* — This expression is used here to denote anything which will frighten a child — a monster of some kind.
8. *Salut belle lune, je vous demande la charité.* — I salute you, beautiful moon, I ask of you, charity.
9. *La vieille traiteuse* — an old woman who administered simple remedies.
10. *Bois clous rouillés* — drink water in which rusty nails have been steeped.

The following ad is taken from the files of *Le Moniteur de la Louisiane* dated April 22, 1809:
(Translated from the French)
RUNAWAY SLAVE: Left from the plantation of the undersigned, on March 29, County of Acadia . . . young negro, named Apollon, of Congo nation, five feet, three inches, twenty-two years, good figure, name of owner tattooed on chest, speaks French and English, attired in blanket coat and black Kerseymere trousers. It is assumed that he went to New Orleans. Honest reward to finder who will return him to M. Claude Treme, New Orleans or to the undersigned on his plantation:

             Chevalier Marlarcher
             Comte d'Acadie, April 2, 1809

## XXIII

## CUISINE FOR CONNOISSEURS

In the 1850's just prior to the Civil War, life in St. James reached its peak of lavishness. On the big plantations with their many slaves, the kitchen was usually in a building detached from the house. The kitchen was large and there was much to be done as the cook never knew just how many would be present for any meal. All travelers were lodged and fed gratis and then, too, Tante Doudouçe might unexpectedly arrive with her brood of ten "to pass the day."[1] The family gathering at meal time was the occasion of much animated conversation and to this day St. Jamesians like to sit around the table after dinner — just to talk and drink coffee.[2]

And while a stranger traveling through was given food and shelter in almost any house where he happened to stop, a Creole family never sat down to a meal with an acquaintance, whose social status was below its own. Only friends, relatives, and social equals were invited to join the Creole family at meal time. A meal was not a modern "gulp and go," but rather a very pleasant part of the daily life with curtains drawn to shut the scene off from curious passersby.

There was once a prominent St. James family whose fortune had been lost in the Civil War. They managed to hang on to their beautiful old home and some of their land, but they owed money to almost everybody including a patient Acadian butcher, who had long supplied them with meat. One day the butcher and a Creole gentleman happened to call at the same time. The butcher was trying to collect the meat bill and the Creole a loan. Both arrived as the family was about to dine. The Creole was invited to dinner, but not the butcher. He waited outside and cooled his heels, while they ate the meat which he had supplied for the meal. The family was too proud to eat with the butcher, but not too proud to eat his meat.

It may be of interest to know something of the favorite foods of the people of St. James from long ago to now. To begin I shall tell what was eaten at a feast of the Houma Indians and St. James' first settlers.

    *La creme de noix* — almond flavored syrup
    *Le jambon d'ours* — bear meat
    *La sagamité* — a coarse hominy

Some of the foods of particular local renown are: *les babas de Chouquette*,[3] *les brioches de Tante Tinia*,[4] *les pralines de Mimi*,[5] *le café*,[6] *le gombo*,[7] and *la boucherie*.[8]

## LES BABAS DE CHOUQUETTE

When the name Chouquette is heard here, the old-timers unintentionally smack their lips. Chouquette and good things to eat are synonymous. She was a small, thin woman of quick step and agile movement. She was part Indian, Negro, and white. She and her mother had been the slaves of the de la Chapelle family and lived on their farm just below St. Michel's Church at Convent.

Now a *baba* is a coconut-cream cake. According to Felisca Braud, who lived near by, Chouquette made a soft sweet dough which she covered with a thick, rich custard. Over this she placed a layer of finely grated coconut. This she cut into oblong pieces the size of a hand and baked. When done, she topped each part with a fluffy meringue. But best of all a baba was sold at the unbelievably low price of five cents.

Babas were not Chouquette's only confection. She made delectable cream-puffs — large round ones for a nickel, too. And there were cup cakes, all kinds of pies, and, of course, pralines — deep pink coconut pralines and those of brown-sugared pecans.

At that time the Jefferson College boys used to walk from the college to the church on Sunday and Thursday afternoons and the spacious church grounds became a meeting place for beaux and belles of that day. All week Chouquette was busy grating coconut, shelling pecans, buying, baking, and cooking. But on Thursdays and Sundays she appeared with a big, flat laundry basket covered with a clean white cloth. She always wore a bright-colored tignon and a deeply-flounced, stiff, white apron. She spread her goodies on a table on one side of the church grounds, and while she waited for her customers to arrive she slowly waved her huge *latanier*[9] back and forth to shoo the flies away.

After many years Chouquette's mother died and she went to live with her sister at White Hall about six miles above St.

Michel. She continued to ply her trade and often walked from White Hall to Convent, her big flat basket on her head and her arms swinging leisurely at her sides.

Chouquette died about thirty years ago. She was then in her eighties, but the memory of her babas lingers still. And when one describes something good to eat here, one says: "C'est bon comme les babas de Chouquette."[10]

### LES BRIOCHES DE TANTE TINIA

Tante Tinia was a widow and person of much refinement. She always wore a stiff, black silk dress with bit of white lace around its high neck. Her widow's cap was tied with long black streamers beneath her firm chin. She was a pretty, old lady — tall, straight, proud, white-haired and rosy cheeked. After her husband's death, she visited this relative or that for long periods — a custom much employed at that time by widows and spinsters. Tante Tinia sewed beautifully and as she visited the many relatives, she sewed for them. To the children, though, her coming was a source of elation — not because of a new *peignoir*[11] or a fine *pantalon*,[12] but because she made the most delicious *brioches*.

Nearly two days were required to make the brioches, but on the second morning, you woke up with a pungent fragrance of anise in the air, and no alarm was needed to get you out of bed that day. With innumerable "ohs" and "ahs" the *déjeuner*[13] was enjoyed by everybody. Some of the hot brioches were sent by special delivery (Negro boy) to a neighbor or two, because one of the most gracious Creole and Acadian customs is to share the good things of life with others.

### LES PRALINES DE MIMI

Dr. W. A. Reed tells us in his fine book, "Louisiana-French," that pralines were first made by the chef of the Maréchal du Plessis-Praslin in the early 17th century, and that this confection bears his name. Often English-speaking people and Acadians erroneously say *plarine* for *praline*. The first St. Jamesians found wild pecans here and later sugar became the main crop, so it is not surprising that pralines have long been a favorite.

Various recipes are used, and the commercial praline sold in New Orleans is usually made of brown sugar, but a local favorite is the praline known as *les pralines de Mimi*. They are a creamy white and have a different flavor. And here we have the story of a young school teacher, whose beau requested a batch of those good pralines. She went to work to deliver the goods, but as she bent over the pot to stir it, a hairpin fell in. She had no more pecans and very little time, so she fished out the pin and sent the candy off. He proposed soon after that and today the story is beginning to spread in St. James, that if you want your beau to pop the question, you must send him a box of *"pralines-de-Mimi"* in which a hair pin has been dipped. As for the school teacher in question, she married her beau and her own candy-haired little girl is called Mimi — not after the pralines, but after her own grandmother — the entire matter being quite co-incidental.

## Le Café

Since long ago when slaves awakened the members of the household with cups of steaming black coffee, this delightful custom has prevailed in St. James. With the passing of slavery and the present scarcity of servants the coffee is now made by some member of the household. In some homes, there is a family bargain: The father makes the coffee in winter and the mother makes it in summer.

What a pleasant way to be awakened — with a cup of hot, black coffee! Even the smallest children open a hopeful eye at the first stir in the house. They get theirs in bed, too, only the children drink *jololo* — weak coffee which is well diluted with water.

The people of St. James are coffee drinkers and, no doubt, the exigencies of war rationing proved to be quite a hardship. There are many families where the coffee pot stays on the stove from which coffee is drunk at any time of the day. In other homes, coffee is served in bed, at breakfast — here it becomes *café-au-lait* — at ten o'clock, after dinner, and in the early afternoon. A social gathering known as a "morning coffee" is a pleasing way of introducing a house guest. In fact people of St. James can always devise a way to call for the serving of a cup of coffee.

While much of the coffee here is drunk black and strong, some people use cream. But the Louisiana custom of café-au-lait is inherited from the French. This is hot, boiled milk, colored with strong black coffee. Served with biscuits, corn-bread, or *pain-perdu*,[14] it is the mainstay of the parish breakfast.

Black coffee is usualy served in small cups, but café-au-lait is served in a large cup. In days gone by, each older person had his own individual cup, which nobody else ever dared use. And when Nénaine Louisa's personal cup was accidentally broken it required a diplomat to tell her the bad news. And for days after, Nénaine Louisa talked o fnothing else but *ma petite tasse*[15] and why she called it *petite* nobody ever knew, because surely it contained nearly a pint. There are still many oldsters who insist on a large personal cup, and when Christmas brings a gift of a big cup and saucer of fine china,[16] it's a big day, indeed, for *Mémère*.

But to return to coffee, almost every family has its own blend — a pound of this and a pound of that — and they never deviate from that adopted mix. Often there are violent discussions as to whose coffee is best, and Tante Mérante will bring a drip of her blend to Nonc Mathurin to prove her point. But the argument is never convincing enough to change one of those inveterate coffee drinkers.

## La Boucherie

Now that *is* something — *la boucherie*! For weeks the hog is fattened in a special pen, so constructed that he exercises very little while he eats very much. The necessary cold weather is anxiously awaited and when the weather turns,[17] the hog's squeals can be heard. Everyone in the neighborhood smacks his lips and claps his hands. He knows that tomorrow he will have some bit of good boucherie to eat. Since a boucherie is quite an undertaking, several persons, in addition to the family and servants, are required. Everybody helps — even the children — and usually, friends and relatives will come to give a *coup-d'main*.[18]

One group will make *la gelée*,[19] another will devote its energies to the *boudins*. *Le boudin rouge* is blood pudding and *le boudin blanc* is a sort of liver sausage. Both are eaten with hot grits for breakfast or supper. Still others make *les saucisses*[20] and *les grillades-fumées*. Since no English word could adequately describe *les grillades*, I shall tell how they are prepared.

The grillades are thick slices cut from the choice pieces of pork. They are, more or less, three inches thick and five inches long. They are highly seasoned and then smoked as follows: A fire is made of corncobs over which is sprinkled sugar or molasses. A barrel, open at both ends, is placed over this smoldering fire and across the barrel-top are rows of thin laths. The grillades are laid across these laths and smoked. Then they are cooked in deep fat in enormous open kettles over a fire in the yard. When well-done, they are poured into big crocks and entirely covered with hot lard. They will keep indefinitely — if there are not too many gourmands in the house.

Other products of a boucherie are *gratons* (cracklings), which are eaten as is, or baked with corn bread. Then there is that mysterious *andouille* made of tripe, ground meat, fat, garlic, etc. This is smoked and then boiled. It is especially good in making gumbo, but it is also sliced very thin and eaten cold.

After the boucherie is finished the partition begins: *une gelée pour le déjeuner de Nonc Sosthene*,[21] *a boudin rouge pour Tante Sésé*[22] — and on and on until there is little left of the boucherie.[23] But the boucherie one sends out is really an investment. The next cold wave somebody else will make a boucherie and send a share all around. And so it goes through the winter — each getting a treat from the other until it's your turn to treat again. Pig squeals and curling smoke in anybody's back yard are a good omen in St. James — but not for the pig!

## SAGAMITÉ

*Sagamité* is sort of gruel made of cracked corn. The Indians taught the first settlers how to make it and it was an article of food much used in the parish for many generations. In some sections it is still eaten. In early times the corn was cracked in a *pilon*. The fine meal was used in making bread, but the large cracked kernels became the sagamité. In many parts of the parish corn and rice are still pounded in home-made pilons.[24]

## LE GOMBO

*Gombo* is a word of Congo origin which means okra, so it is possible that the slaves gave us *le gombo*. But filé was first sold by the Indians in the New Orleans markets. In St. James gumbo is made with, or without, okra or with whatever else one has on hand and filé.[25] It is the favorite dish of the parish. It is the pièce-de-resistance at all fairs, the mainstay of our meatless Fridays, and the central object of many an evenings' frolic. In fact a gumbo supper is one of the enjoyable customs carried down from long ago to now.

A gumbo supper usually consists of *un bon gombo*,[26] *une bonne salade, du bon vin,* and *des bonnes pralines*. That word *bon!* It is a good word and how our French-speaking people use it! Only here one says, "bon-bon-bon." Our people always repeat a word at least three times for emphasis and one speaks of a gumbo with a vivacity, which requires oft-repeated adjectives and much gesticulation.

Gumbo's main ingredient can be turkey, chicken, or ham — crab, oyster, or shrimp — sausage, grillade, or andouille — and in a pinch, yesterday's left-overs. Almost always it is a combination. Chicken and oyster is a favorite as well as shrimp and okra gumbo. To an outsider gumbo is a thick soup served with rice. To a native it is *un bon gumbo*.

Even the sassafras tree, from which we get filé and which, incidentally, grows wild in this parish, is a symbol of the mélange which makes up a gumbo. Three distinct forms of the leaf often grows on one branch signifying that, at least, three good ingredients are needed to make a real gumbo. Filé is a grayish-green powder made from the dried leaves of the sassafras tree, as described elsewhere in this story.

Mr. John Peytavin in his unpublished memoirs tells an interesting story of *le Pape Vert*. Every Saturday night there was a Fais-dodo at le Pape Vert where Capt. Jacque Chauvin's boat always stopped to let his passengers enjoy the evening. Promptly at eleven o'clock, gumbo was served and it was announced — not by servant, not by bell — but by playing Bellem's Grand March. At the first notes the dancing stopped and the couples marched to the supper room — so called because supper was the only meal that was ever served there. Few people ever knew the name of the march. Locally it was known as *la marche du gumbo*.[27]

### FAVORITE ST. JAMES RECIPES
#### LES PRALINES DE MIMI

Ingredients:
- 2 cups pecans
- 2 cups white granulated sugar
- 2 tablespons white Karo corn syrup
- 1 cup pet cream or rich milk
- 1 teaspoon vanilla

Procedure:
Place all ingredients except vanilla in saucepan and cook until syrup makes a very soft ball when tested in cold water.

Remove from fire, add vanilla, and beat until thick and creamy. Drop by spoonful on moist board. Let cool.

### CREOLE PLANTATION CHERRY BOUNCE

Ingredients:
- Louisiana wild cherries
- Pure grain alcohol
- 3 lbs. sugar

Procedure:
- 2 qts. water

Fill 4 to 6 quart bottles with Louisiana wild cherries which have been stemmed, washed, and drained. Pour enough pure, best grade grain alcohol to fill each bottle and completely cover the cherries. Cork and let stand for 3 months. Then drain (do not mash cherry pits) and strain.

Syrup:

Place 3 lbs. sugar and 2 qts. of cold water in saucepan and boil for 2 minutes. Let cool and strain through fine cloth mesh. Add syrup to cherry juice as per taste for sweetness and alcoholic content. Bottle and let set. Serve chilled in cordial glasses.

### GOMBO de ST. JACQUES

Ingredients:
- 2 heaping tablespoons lard
- 1 heaping tablespoon flour
- 3/4 cup chopped onion
- 5 stalks chopped celery (with leaves)
- 1 large chopped green pepper
- 1 diced fresh tomato
- 1 teaspoon salt
- 1 1/2 qt. hot water
- 2 cans shrimp or like amount of fresh shrimp
- 2 doz. oysters
- pinch red pepper to taste
- 1/2 teaspoon gumbo filé

Procedure:

Heat lard and add flour, stirring constantly, to make a brown roux. Add onion, celery, and green pepper. Brown. Add boiling hot water, salt, red pepper and tomato. Boil 1/2 hour. Add shrimp and cook 15 minutes. Add oysters 10 minutes before serving. Remove from fire and add filé. Stir well. Serve hot with rice.

## LES BRIOCHES DE TANTE TINIA

Ingredients:
- 1 yeast cake
- ½ cup tepid water
- 5 eggs
- 1½ cups sugar
- butter
- ½ cup milk
- ½ teaspoon salt
- flour
- anise seeds

Procedure:

Levain: To make levain, dissolve yeast cake in ½ cup tepid water and add enough flor to make soft batter. Set aside and let rise for 2 hours.

Dough: Beat well 5 eggs and add sugar. When thoroughly creamed add one tablespoon butter, then milk. Pour in levain and mix well. Sift flour twice with salt and fol din enough to make a soft dough. Set aside in warm place to rise for about 4 hours. When well risen, roll dough very thin on slightly floured board. Spread butter generously over ½ of rolled dough and fold in two. Roll again, butter as before, and fold over. Roll very thin again, butter, and cut into strips 1½ inch wide. Roll as for jelly roll and place on greased or buttered tins. Set aside in warm place to rise about four hours. Sprinkle sparingly with anise seeds. Bake in moderately hot oven. Serve hot with café-au-lait.

And speaking of foods, the parish has had its gourmands as well as its gourmets. One day a tramp, or a traveler — perhaps he was a little of both — stopped at a plantation for refreshment and rest. He liked the cooking so well that his stay lengthened into days and then into months and years. He told no one from whence he came or who he was, except that his name was Monsieur Brochet. Two other facts became apparent: he was absolutely trustworthy and he had an enormous appetite that could never be satiated. In time he became the yard man, doing odd chores, watching over the children, acquiring little responsibilities, and always, always eating. He stayed twenty years. But one day the wander-lust seized him again and he simply vanished, unannounced and unnoticed, just as he had come. The children missed him — but not the cook. How she had hated that master gourmand! And today when one eats too much, somebody is sure to say "Il mange comme le vieux Brochet!"[28]

FOOTNOTES

1. To pass the day. This is a local expression taken from the French "passer la journée." It means to spend the day.
2. An old colored man still living in the environs of the Uncle Sam Plantation was in childhood the punkah boy of the Jacobs (descendants of the Fagots). He relates: "Dem white folks never knewed when to git up fum dat table. Mah arms used to hurt fum pulling dat rope. De coffee used to git em hot and mah fan used to cool em off."
3. *Les babas de Chouquette* — a cream and coconut delicacy.
4. *Le brioches de Tante Tinia* — sweet rolls.
5. *Les pralines de Mimi* — candy confections.
6. *Le Café* — the coffee.
7. *Gombo* — gumbo.
8. *La boucherie* — various dishes made by the Creoles when a hog is slaughtered.
9. *Latanier* — Palmetto fan.
10. *C'est bon comme les babas de Chouquette.* — It is as good as Chouquette's babas.
11. *Peignoir* — tight fitting underwaist.
12. *Pantalon* — trousers.
13. *Déjeuner* — breakfast.
14. *Pain-perdu* — Lost bread — French toast.
15. *Ma petite tasse* — My little cup.
16. These big cups are still sold in the New Orleans department stores. Some at $10.00 each.
17. The weather turns. Expression used here to indicate a sudden change in the weather, usually from warm to cold.
18. *Coup d'main* — a helping hand.
19. *La gelée* — Hog's head cheese. Delicious hog's head cheese is now made commercially by Veron's at Lutcher.
20. *Les saucisses* — the sausages.
21. *Une gelée pour le déjeuner de Nonc Sosthene* — A cheese for Uncle Sosthene's breakfast.
22. *Un boudin rouge pour Tante Sésé* — a blood pudding for Aunt Sésé.
23. The scarcity of servants and the high price of feed are reducing this parish-wide custom to a minimum.
24. *Pilon* — pestle and mortar for pounding rice, corn, and filé.
25. Filé is not used with okra. Either filé or okra is used to make gumbo.
26. *Bon* or *bonne* — good.
27. *La marche du gombo* — the gumbo march.
28. *Il mange comme le vieux Brochet* — he eats like old Brochet.

## XXIV
### SOCIAL LIFE IN ST. JAMES

*C'est une bonne vie!* Yes, it was just that: a good life .... that is, the social side of it, anyway. The people of this parish have been, and are to this day, gregarious, hospitable, and sociable. No wonder that one still hears of the brilliance and the éclat of their entertainments with a wishful thought of those pleasant-used-to-be's.

Perhaps the first notable social event of St. James was the visit of the three French princes, one of whom, the Duke of Orleans, became Louis Philippe, King of France. René de Sennegy in *Une Paroisse Louisianaise* relates that the princes, accompanied by Monsieur de Marigny, arrived unannounced at Cabahannocer in 1798. The commandante, Monsieur Michel Cantrelle, received them most graciously and a grande fête was arranged. Among these present were the Cantrelles, the Verrets, and the Bringiers, but no doubt the most interesting guest who arrived to greet the princes was none other than the chief of the Houma, attired in beaver moccasins, a bark coat, and a headdress of hawk's feathers. And at his invitation the princes and their entourage returned the courtesy by calling on the chief at his humble home at the Houma. It was on this trip that the princes were lavishly entertained by Marius Bringier at le White Hall.

Emanuel Marius Pons Bringier was certainly one of the most colorful St. James personalities of any era. One of twenty sons he left France carrying his possessions in his own ship and settled in the West Indies. Dissatisfied with this locale he reloaded his ship and came to New Orleans. In the newly expanding St. James he purchased first one, then several plantations. Here he established his home and lived on a prodigal scale, entertaining some of the important persons of that day, including Andrew Jackson and John James Audubon. And to make life more exciting, perhaps, he married two of his daughters to persons equally as fabulous as he. His daughter, Françoise (Fanny), married the French exile, Christophe Colomb, who was more interested in the arts than in the business affairs of their plantation, a gift of Marius to his daughter. Colomb, completely detached from boring business, went up and down the river in a boat rowed by slaves .... the boat, by the way, had velvet armchairs and a red-fringed canopy which were the talk of the countryside.

Elizabeth Bringier (Betsy), as before recorded, married the adventurous exile, Augustin Dominique Tureaud. Unlike his brother-in-law, Christophe, Augustin took charge of Betsy's plantation, also a gift of Marius. Tureaud operated the Union Plantation like a military unit. At the sound of the plantation bell, the slaves poured out of their cabins, each reporting for an assigned duty. The ploughmen, drivers, hoers, ditch-diggers, even the senile water-boy, with their mules, carts, plows, and other equipment lined up in a straight row down the plantation road. On his prancing horse Tureaud made his inspection and no one dared move until his command to go was given. No wonder the oldsters of that section still refer to him as *Little Napoleon.*

The Bringiers had a town house in New Orleans where they spent the winters to attend the balls and the opera. And even an artist was brought from Europe to paint the family portraits. Not to be outdone by his sisters, Marius' son, Michel Douradou Bringier, married the glamorous fourteen-year-old Louise Elizabeth Aglaé Du Bourg de Ste. Colombe, niece of the famous Archbishop Dubourg of Baltimore. And one more Bringier plantation unit was established, this one inside Ascension Parish at The Hermitage.[1]

Marius Bringier died April 23, 1820. And what happened to le White Hall? Just before the Civil War it was gutted by fire. It was restored only to be damaged by Yankee shells from a Union gunboat and after being stripped by carpetbaggers it was finally demolished.

The second cycle of social life in St. James is best depicted by the events at Valcour Aime's. It was but natural for the almost legendary Monsieur Valcour to inherit the mantle from the equally incredible Monsieur Marius. The story of that era has been covered in the chapter, The Great Plantations. At Valcour Aime's, life was rosy indeed .... literally and figuratively.... Here one was awakened by a slave bearing a cup of steaming black coffee and a lovely red rose.

A later period of social life is described by Adele Le Bourgeois Chapin in her interesting book, *Their Trackless Way.* The Le Bourgeois domain was the Belmont Plantation. After the first plantation home burned, Mrs. Le Bourgeois gave her son

*Old Acadian House. From a Painting made by the Author.*

*Trees with moss. Moss is not a true parasite as it feeds on air. (Photo by Charles O. Subra)*

*Ruins of an old Acadian house showing type of construction of 175 years ago. The walls made of moss and mud still fight the ravages of the damp Louisiana climate. (Photo by Charles O. Subra)*

*Field of Perique Tobacco at Grande Pointe — Acadian settlement where it is extensively cultivated. (Photo by Charles O. Subra)*

one hundred thousand dollars to build a new house. This one was of brick covered with stucco . . . not ordinary stucco . . . but stucco made with milk. Like Valcour Aime, Mrs. Le Bourgeois had had a great and unforgettable sorrow. Her daughter, Louise, died while attending school at the Sacred Heart Convent. From then on, Mrs. Le Bourgeois rarely left her house except to attend church services at St. Michel where she went in her liveried coach lined in white brocade. About her house she was always accompanied by her red-turbanned slave, Lucindy, who opened and closed the doors for Madame and then sat silently on the floor behind her chair.

During the Civil War an arrogant Yankee officer threatened to shell the Belmont house if the whereabouts of the men of the house were not revealed. And then from a chance remark of a slave the officer accidentally discovered that the Le Bourgeois were closely connected with the Charles family of St. Louis who years before had befriended him and paid for his education. Astounded, the officer apologized and sent a guard to protect Belmont and its southern-sympathizing occupants. But though the house was saved, the owners were ruined by the war, and it was only because Mrs. Le Bourgeois inherited a fortune from her northern grandfather that they were able to reestablish the plantation after the slaves were freed. Among the illustrious visitors at Belmont were the Grand Duke Alexis of Russia, Edward Everett Hale, and George Washington Cable.

But life on the great plantations was not always happy. In 1877 yellow fever appeared at Belmont, and four of the Le Bourgeois children contracted the dreaded disease. It is interesting to note that the patients were rubbed with quinine and lard and were given eggwhite in champagne. Mrs. Chapin tells us that once her grandmother Charles became very ill and during this period she was converted to the Catholic faith. At her first outing she attended church services and when the collection was taken she astonished those around her by dropping her diamond earrings in the collection plate.

Belmont was never occupied by other than the Le Bourgeois family. In the late 1800's the levee broke at Belmont. Although the house was flooded and damaged, it withstood the river's rampage, only to be completely burned a short time later. Seemingly revengeful the Mississippi was determined to swallow the Le Bourgeois house. A later levee passed behind the old foundation and the bricks still lie covered with sand in the path of the sometimes turbulent waters. Not even a vestige of its famous columns remain! The columns, incidentally, cost eighteen thousand dollars.

But social life in St. James was not confined to the great plantations and everyone was not "rich like dem Fagots," an expression used to denote comparatively the wealth of the owners of the Uncle Sam Plantation. And so here we come to the tale of Le Pape Vert, the mecca of those in search of amusement. Mr. Charles Chauvin, the present owner and distant relative of the original owner, tells this story.

Jacques Chauvin was a steamboat captain who owned two boats out of New Orleans in the early 1800's. Near the present Church of St. Mary was a steamboat landing where Captain Chauvin's boats made regular overnight stops. Since gambling was the chief form of entertainment on those colorful packet boats, one of the Chauvins conceived the idea of building a gambling house and dance hall where the passengers could land and enjoy themselves. Thus over a hundred years ago Le Pape Vert was built.

Many of the passengers on the boats bought gay little buntings from the local people at the landing. Buntings are delicately tinted little birds which were much in demand as pets at that time. A bunting is known here as a *pape* . . . a green one is a *pape vert* and a yellow one is a *pape dorée*. In time the traffickers in buntings painted a green one on a sign on the batture near the landing. Thus the landing and the place became known as Le Pape Vert and the new dance hall and gambling house assumed the same name.

The original Pape Vert building, which still stands unaltered in appearance and floor plan, had a large dance hall, gallery, bar, and ante-room upstairs. It was in this ante-room[2] that slaves watched over the sleeping children while the pleasure-loving Acadians and the frequently boisterous passengers danced and gambled until the wee hours of morn. Downstairs were gambling rooms, a supper room, and a kitchen. Here fortunes were lost and won . . . even plantations changed hands. Fine liqueurs and champagne were served across that old bar but more often than not it was just a *coup-de-vin*. The music for the dancing was furnished by four musical roustabouts put on the boats for that purpose. Saturday night at Le Pape Vert was gay indeed. What with dancing, gambling, eating, and drinking, the long nights fairly flew. Hot heads even resorted to dueling to settle their arguments and the story is told of one serio-comic duel which provided a conversation piece for many a year.

This duel concerned a trio whom we shall call fictitiously Émérantine, Louis, and François. One Saturday night Émérantine asked Louis to put François out of the Pape Vert dance hall because she objected to his presence. This Louis did, but François called him outside to settle the dispute man-fashion. Louis refused and François, enraged, challenged him to a duel and posted it in front of St. Mary's Church. Seconds were chosen and details were arranged but old human nature was not taken into consideration. The duel was to have taken place after mass. Services over, the congregation nervously filed outside, but Louis, too excited for restraint, fired at François as he walked down the church steps. There was a moment of aimless frantic shooting by both men who emptied their pistols without harming each other. Then tense crowd was panic-stricken. One lady scarcely knowing what she was doing opened her parasol, whether by habit or for protection we shall never know. It was instantly pierced by a flying bullet. Women, without stopping to gather their flowing skirts, ran, dragging their children behind them, while little boys lost their hats and little girls screamed. One grande dame de La Pointe had come to church in her brand-new carriage. It was reduced to shambles by her runaway horse. Terrified, other horses cowered, broke the bonds tethering them, and joined in the mad gallop. What with bullets flying, horses running, women screaming, and people scampering, the ground of Ste. Marie du Fleuve was desecrated indeed on that sunlit Sunday morning. The result: Just a few terrifying minutes of a frenzied melée . . . not one person hurt . . . the quarrel never settled . . . the duel never fought . . . not according to the code duello, that is.

But not all events at Le Pape Vert were as dramatic and as spectacular. Many private balls and wedding receptions were given, some lasting two days and two nights such as the ones for the weddings of Sylvest Reider, Ludjere Dugas, and Florien Lanegrasse. One dance . . . par invitation . . . given for Felicien Ory lasted two nights. Only those with cards were permitted to enter and costume de soirée was a requirement. Pistols and other side arms were checked downstairs along with hats and walking canes. No fooling there!

Le Pape Vert flourished but it changed hands. Mr. Rybiski bought it and operated it for twenty years. But Captain Chauvin's boats were no more and in 1889 Le Pape Vert closed its doors and became a residence. It was purchased by the Joseph Thibodeaux family who ran a store in front of the old building while they used it for their home. Then Charles Chauvin acquired Le Pape Vert and it was restored and re-opened in 1950. Though many repairs were made very few changes were effected. The old kerosene lamps were wired for electricity and the original lamp from Captain Chauvin's boat which once hung over the bar, was placed over the dance floor. The old cypress bar became a bandstand and the original four-place bandstand, a sandwich counter. Pape Vert, 1950, was a variation of a modern night club.[3] But downstairs the gambling rooms were closed. Quaint, petite, and frail, Miss Maria Thibodeaux has the usufruct of the lower floor until her death.

Built in 1849, the property of Eugene Chauvin, Le Pape Vert still lived . . . in 1955, the property of Charles Chauvin. And the Acadians of Pointeville (Union to you) still enjoyed their Saturday night frolic at Le Pape Vert as their Acadian forbears did a hundred years ago. But the *coup-de-vin* had graduated into a highball and the four slave musicians were replaced by a modern juke box. The old name, the old building, and the old Chauvin family still survive and to this day a gay young blade all dressed up for an evening's fun is called: a *Pape Colas*.[4]

FOOTNOTES

1. The Marius Bringier plantation units were at White Hall, Bagatelle, Union, Bocage, and The Hermitage. The last two are in Ascension Parish. Later generations of the Bringiers were at Tezcuco and Ashland. These are also in Ascension. Many of these beautiful homes extending chain-like along the river from Bagatelle in St. James to Ashland in Ascension have been, or are being restored, and are presently occupied. As previously stated White Hall is no more and Union was demolished several years ago because of a new levee. Bagatelle was completely restored by Rev. C. M. Chambon and Bocage by Dr. and Mrs. E. Karlsdorf. Tezcuco is being restored by Dr. and Mrs. R. H. Potts. The Hermitage still in fair state of preservation will be restored by its new owner, Dr. Walter Mattingly, while Ashland is undergoing repairs under the remodeling plan of the Campbell Haywards. The majesty and glamour of these beautiful homes is being preserved by a new generation of appreciative owners.

2. This room was called "parc aux petits" (enclosed space for children).

3. Pape Vert was closed again, June 1951.

4. Pape . . . brightly colored bird — a bunting.
Colas . . . a buffoon, a funster.
A Pape Colas . . . a young man all dressed up for an evening's merriment.

## XXV

## ODD BITS FROM HERE AND THERE

When yellow fever and cholera appeared in New Orleans, these diseases soon spread to the river outposts. St. James Parish had yellow fever as early as 1774 but the years of 1833 and 1853 were the years of the worst epidemics. In fact Mrs. Jean Philippe Boucry, who kept a diary beginning in the early 1800's, marked 1853 with a heavy black cross and called it "L'année de malheur." It was indeed a year of misfortune on the Bonne Ésperance plantation of the Boucry family. Within six weeks Mrs. Boucry recorded five deaths in her family. Maybe the readers would like to know that a thick syrup of watermelon juice was used in the treatment of cholera at that time.

The years of 1853-54-55-56 were surely the most trying in the history of the parish. There were floods, yellow fever, cholera and to add a final blow some St. Jamesians perished in the disastrous hurricane on Last Island. On this page, too, Mrs. Boucry drew a large black cross and wrote "Ile Dernière." Whole families died in the series of misfortunes of this fateful years. Desolation and fear gripped the parish. Several pious inhabitants decided to make a pilgrimage of prayer and expiation to the chapel of the Sacred Heart Convent. This event occurred on October 8, 1854. The original pilgrims were joined by a large concourse of saddened parishoners. The procession filed into the chapel, many clad in the deep mourning of that day. Hymns, special prayers, and a sermon were followed by benediction. In the overflowing throng there were some who had never before set foot in any church . . . all gathered in humility and grief to ask for mercy of the only ONE who could assuage their common sorrow. It is not surprising to note that the dreaded maladies subsided with no new deaths recorded that year.

But Mrs. Boucry's cup of sorrow, already full, surely overflowed the next year when on a bright August morning her little son drowned in the mighty Mississippi right before her very door. And her black-crossed entry ends with "Je l'oublirai jamais." (I shall never forget him). But Madame Boucry has entries in a lighter vein. One tells gaily that her married daughter just moved into her new home . . . a house which is now occupied after one hundred thirteen years by Madame's direct descendant, Miss Lillian Dornier. And adding interest to the old house is the story that its center hallway was used to drill in secrecy by men forming companies to go off to fight in the Civil War.

But many years were to pass before yellow fever was finally conquered. Octave Adam, an old darky now eighty-four, tells this story. When he was a little boy there were so many deaths during a fall epidemic that the church bell rang all day and even into the night for the many funerals. This so depressed the judge who lay ill with the so frequently fatal malady that he ordered the bell ringing stopped. The pastor of the church acquiesced, but not so the fever germ. Octave's own father, who was a servant in the judge's household, contracted the fever the next day. He became ill after breakfast and died before night. The judge recovered.

Over a hundred years ago when St. Michael's Church was being built, a Mr. Thibodeaux was one of the men engaged in its construction. Mr. Thibodeaux always wore a derby. One day when the columns of the church were being put up, he playfully threw his old hat into one of the columns. Unknowingly it was sealed in and to this day there is some guessing as to which column houses the old derby. Perhaps Mr. Thibodeaux knew but he wouldn't tell . . . keeping the whereabouts of his hat under his hat, so to speak.

The first store operated by Leon Godchaux in Louisiana was in a small frame building near the Uncle Sam Plantation.

The Acadians wove a coarse cotton cloth which they dyed blue. This was called cotonnade. Cotton and indigo were important products of the parish. In fact indigo was the main crop to about 1792. Myrtle wax for candles was produced also.

The old well back of St. Michael's Church is the same well which was used by the Sacred Heart nuns over a century ago.

Interesting weather data are noted in the Boucry and the Aime diaries. For instance:
There was very high water in 1844-49-50-51.
It was so cold in 1835 that eggs and vinegar froze.
In 1852 five to twelve inches of snow fell, but the winter of 1826-27 must have broken records in regard to its duration. There was a freeze as early as November 16 with the last frost on May 2 of the following spring. In 1843 sugar cane blossomed but the next year brought sixty-five days of drought . . . men could cross the swamp on horseback. It was so hot on July 6, 1844 that plow horses staggered and died. From unknown causes quantities of dead fish floated down the river in June 1851.

Hot weather was always a part of St. James life, but snow was indeed an uncommon occurrence . . . so much so that Monsieur Gentil, remembering snow in his native France, was moved to writing a poem when a rather heavy snow covered this semi-tropical section.

The poem which appeared in his *Le Louisianais* on January 29, 1891 as follows:

### LA NEIGE

*J'ai vu tomber dimanche*
*D'un ceil gris et couvert,*
*La paquerette blanche*
*Et triste de l'hiver*

*Il a neigé. Les arbres,*
*Surpris et devenus*
*Glacés comme des marbres,*
*Ont blanchi leurs bras nus.*

*Toute chose était blanche*
*Sur terre: le clocher,*
*La maison et la branche*
*Du chene et du pêcher.*

*L'oiseau, l'aile glacée,*
*Ayant faim, ayant froid,*
*Sentait dans sa pensée*
*Monter un vague effroi.*

*Et ma vache Noironne,*
*Voyant le linceuil blanc*
*Qui tombe et l'environne,*
*Bêlait, mais en tremblant.*

*Pour moi, voyant la neige*
*Voler en flocons blancs,*
*Je me disais: Que n'ai-je,*
*Que n'ai-je encor vingt-ans*

*Oui, vingt ans, l'espérance*
*Et le rêve éclatant.*
*O mes neiges de France;*
*O mes neiges d'antan!*
                    J. G.

## TRANSLATION

I saw fall Sunday
From a gray and cloudy sky
The sad white daisies of winter.

It snowed. The trees,
Surprised and frozen like marble,
Blanched their naked arms.

All things were white
On earth: the steeple,
The house and the branch
Of the oak and the peach tree.

The bird with frozen wing,
Hungry and cold,
Felt in his thoughts
A rising wave of dismay.

And my cow, Noironne,
Seeing the white shroud
Which fell and encircled her,
Lowed, while trembling.

Sacred Heart Convent (Le Convent du Sacre Coeur) at Convent, La.

The chapel of the old Sacred Heart Convent.

Old Dòrmitories — Sacred Heart Convent.

Tomb of deceased Religious of the Sacred Heart. Exhumed from St. Michael's Academy Cemetery when the Sisters sold their property, the bodies were placed in this vault at St. Mary's Cemetery.

Study Hall of the old Sacred Heart Convent.

*Jefferson College*

*Family Boarding House at Jefferson College.*

*Chapel at Jefferson College. Gift of Valcour Aime. (Photo by Charles O. Subra)*

*The grounds of Jefferson College — now Manresa Retreat. (Photo by Charles O. Subra)*

> For me, seeing the snow
> Flying in white flakes,
> I bethought me,
> Were I but twenty again.
>
> Yes, twenty, the hope
> And the dazzling dream!
> O My snows of France
> O My snows of yore.

Grande Pointe, center of Périque togacco, has preserved much of its original Acadian culture and charm. Here French is spoken almost exclusively, yet Grande Pointe is not a very old settlement in St. James. On the contrary it was founded rather late—about 1830-50. The tardy arrival of modern ideas there was due to its almost inaccessible location; three miles from railway, highway, and river.

The sugar planters used to go to New Orleans, via boat, to do their shopping. They took slaves with them to care for the children, to carry their parcels, and to serve them. The shopping lists included such items as bolts of pure linen sheeting, because among the fastidious Creoles of St. James there were many who refused to sleep on anything but pure linen sheets.

On the plantations, wine was bought by casks. The cask was placed on little blocks, the bung removed, and the well-beaten whites of six or seven eggs were dropped into the barrel. The bung was replaced and the wine was allowed to set for six weeks before bottling. This process was called "enchanteler le vin." The bottles were then laid on shelves in the wine cellar. This was not a real cellar — St. James is too low for that. Instead it was a large room whose four walls were lined from floor to ceiling with shelves. It contained wine, champagne, Benedictine, curaçoa, anisette, and other intoxicating beverages. The St. James planter never sat down to dinner, company or not, without the proper wine. And, incidentally, little children were served a small glass of wine, too, although they were not allowed stronger drinks as a rule.[1]

And speaking of wine, here is a wine story with flavor: Three sugar planters formed an agreement. Each would take his turn to order from France the yearly stock of wine and liqueurs for the three. The planters would receive the wine, pay for it, and have it bottled, sealed and delivered . . . one-third to each of his partners. In 1890 it was Monsieur Flagil's turn. He had received the wine and had it ready for delivery to his two partners when Nita's Crevasse washed away his home, his wine, his very sod.

Several years later another planter in the course of his plantation routine discovered a quantity of fine wine . . . bottled, and sealed, and buried under a huge deposit of thick sand. Monsieur Flagil knew that it was his wine and he waited in vain for its return. No doubt the finder knew from whence the cache came, but he maintained that he had gotten the wine from an act of God . . . the crevasse . . . and finder's, keepers. And as he drank he said: "À la santé de Monsieur Tel-et-Tel." (To Mr. So-and-So's health) !

The coffee process, too, was interesting. The planter usually bought sacks of his favorite coffee to roast and blend at home. A recent St. Jamesians always used equal parts of Rio and Cordova. Only a few pounds of each — well mixed — were roasted at a time. This insured proper blending and guaranteed freshness.

The span of life was short and widows and widowers remarried. This entailed many family quarrels as to dowries, successions, and inheritances, and it was not unusual for in-laws or blood relatives to carry trifling grievances to their graves. As soon as a person died, his armoires were sealed. As early as possible an inventory was made and every article, no matter how insignificant, was listed to be sold. The old court records here are full of these interesting succession sales with articles listed, the price given, and the purchaser named for every item. With such minute detailing even a small succession covered many pages. The liveliest bidding was not necessarily for lands and slaves, but more often than not, for Mémère's picture, the family's flat-ware, or Grandpère's horse. And when there was dissension in a family, fabulous prices were given for trifles just to keep the other fellow from getting the article which he wanted.

In most families, however, a meeting of all heirs was held and quietly and amicably all possessions were disposed of to the apparent satisfaction of all concerned. An amusing incident in such a settlement: An heir, who was charged with the disposal of all property, was accused of manipulating the division of the estate to such an extent that he received much more than his just share. Three nieces set up such a clamor that he subsequently paid them off to hush them up. They were finally appeased, but to this day, they are referred to as "les trois guêpes de Tante Telle-et-Telle."[2]

In 1860 the postoffice in St. James were as follows: Vacherie Road and Cantrelle on the right bank and Grande Pointe, Convent, and Touro on the left bank.

In 1860 J. W. Dorr, connected with the "New Orleans Crescent", newspaper of that period, made a horse and buggy tour of Louisiana and thus visited St. James. He gives an interesting picture of the parish just before the Civil War. He describes the parish as being very rich with its many sugar plantations, beautiful homes, and fine gardens. He tells us that there were 8,000 slaves with an assessed value of four million dollars. There were two Catholic churches, six sugar refineries, three saw mills, ten public schools, and one newspaper. There were about 250 pupils at the convent and the college had just reopened.

Although St. James lands have been in cultivation for nearly two hundred years they are very fertile. The parish is still divided into little farms and big plantations and remains almost entirely rural and agricultural.

Horse racing was a popular sport in St. James and one of

the tracks was that just below St. Michel's Church. This track was operated by J. O. Millet about sixty years ago. Horses were brought from many St. James plantations, as well as the neighboring parishes. It is said that the two favorite horses were Prince and Scott and that fortunes were lost — and won — on these two horses.

The little children of long ago, too, had to be amused. Among the favorite games which, by the way, required nothing but a good stock of imagination were: "Pigeon volle"[3] and "Pin, pi, po, Laurent." The children's favorite card game was "La pioche", which is still played throughout the parish. But the mysterious "guess what" of an earlier day was a "Si-si à dents dans une bôite sans fond." Literally this means a little nothing inside a box without a bottom, but it was always the source of endless guessing by the children.

But one rhyme which always provoked the smaller fry was when they said "Mam, j'ai faim"[4] and the mother replied: "Manges une main, et gardes l'autre pour demain."[5] This answer often produced wailing and weeping of crocodile tears. Sometimes this childish act had the good result of sending the mother into the kitchen to make some "gran pattes." A gran patte is a soft, greaseless, biscuit dough which is fried in deep fat. While frying, the dough puffs up like little balloons, and the Acadian children always had a lot of fun filling their puffs with café-au-lait before eating them. This played havoc with the red table cloths, which, by the way, are still used in some St. James homes.

Another game which is still being played by the children of St. James comes at Easter. The hard boiled eggs dyed in various colors are hidden about the lawn for an Easter hunt which follows the usual pattern. But when the eggs have been gathered, the children go back to a game played long ago. A child holds an egg firmly in the palm of his hand with his curved fingers hiding all but the tip end of the egg. Along comes a challenger who holds his egg in exactly the same position. Then with one short tap he tries to crack the shell of the first contestant's egg with his own. Whoever holds the cracked egg loses it. Before the game is played the two players decide which end of the egg will be exposed and both players must use like ends as the round-ed end of an egg is more vulnerable than the pointed end. It is then that one hears the children yell: "Points or rounds?" Frequently a child finds but one egg in the hunt, but if it has a tough shell this preliminary misfortune turns to good account. With one egg of hard shell he can win fifteen or twenty. And deep indeed is his chagrin when eventually somebody comes along and "Busts" his champion egg. But stranger still is that though this game has long been played, it has no name.

An interesting little poem which amused the French-speaking children of earlier days and which is still good fun in the parish follows:

*Un petit bon homme pas plus gros qu'un rat*
*A battu sa femme par-dessus ses bras;*
*En disant, Madame, ça vouc montrera*
*A voler mes pommes quand je'en serai pas lá.*

It means: A man no bigger than a rat beat his wife in order to teach her not to steal his apples when he was gone.

The following old riddles, which are a play on words, have been handed down from generation to generation:

Un homme debout, lit.   (A man who is standing, reads.)
Une femme asis, coud.   (A woman who is seated, sews.)
Un enfant assis, joue.  (A child who is seated, play.)

Repeated in fast childish prattle it sounds like: A man boils, a woman has six necks, and a child has six cheeks.


The early Acadians turned to raising cattle here as this had been their main occupation in their old home. Then, and to this day, the younger boys of the family had the chore of driving the cattle home at sunset. Often this became the butt of jokes among the children. When asked if he had seen a certain stray cow, the little Acadian boy replied with:

*Cayette est crevée*
*La bas à Burnside,*
*Les quatre pattes en l'air*
*La tête dans l'fossé.*

This means: Cayette is dead at Burnside (or some place name) with her four hooves in the air and her head in the ditch. In other words: Go look for her, *yourself.*

When the full moon appeared:

*Je voix la lune,
Belle et grande,
St. Laurence qui m'appelle à sa chapelle,
Beauté, charité,
Paradis quand je mourrai.*

This means: I see the big beautiful moon. St. Lawrence is calling me to his chapel (in order to obtain) beauty, charity, and Paradise when I die. It is a wish made on the full moon.

To poke fun at a braggart or a conceited person:

*Henri Quatre, Roi des Macaques,
Suspendu par ses quatre pattes,
Pour avoir volé quatre barils d'patates.*

This means: (You are) Henry the Fourth, king of the monkeys, hanging by his four feet because he stole four barrels of potatoes.

To poke fun at one who complained about minor aches and little hurts and falls:

*Priez enfants, priez enfants,
Pépère appret mourire,
Mémère en bas le lit,
Appret danser en queue d'chemise.*

This means: Pray children, pray, Grandfather is dying but Grandmother is dancing under the bed in her chemise. In other words: You think that you are dying, but we are all laughing at you.

In the old days the biggest celebration in St. James, as elsewhere in south Louisiana, was for New Year. On New Year's eve the clans gathered in the old homestead, had a big gumbo supper, or an eggnog party with plenty to drink. Near midnight huge bonfires were lighted on the batture and there were many fireworks. The bonfire, built of cane reeds, was arranged in cone shape with a heavy pole in the center to hold it up. It burned for several hours and the popping cane reeds added their din to the noisy celebration. On New Year's day there were big turkey dinners and gifts were exchanged.

The children of today have retained the custom of making bonfires, only now they are burned at Christmas before midnight mass. The bonfires are smaller and are built on the levee. Usually a group of neighborhood children will work for several Saturdays building their bonfire. Sometimes a naughty rival group will sneak in and burn somebody else's bonfire a few nights before Christmas — a mean trick which is never forgiven.

The uniforms worn by the girls at the convent in 1838 were made of crimson bombazine (silk and wool twill) and were trimmed in black velvet. Gloves, sashes, and black velvet capes were added as the occasion warranted.

In the early 1800's the school session lasted eleven months with one month's vacation coming in the fall. There was one holiday for Christmas and one for New Year, but the students usually remained at the convent and college.

Twelve students presented themselves for the re-opening of Jefferson College after the Civil War. They were:

| | |
|---|---|
| J. Damaré | A. Robert |
| J. Marlarcher | V. Sere |
| N. Landry | J. Gauthreaux |
| A. Bourgeois | P. Martin |
| A. Jourdan | I. Crane |
| E. Duffel | J. Crane |

A favorite drink of the parish was anisette sometimes made at home by various recipes until it took strange forms from a sort of sweetened water to a high pressure kick. At any rate we have the story of some spinsters who lived next door to their brother who had identical twins. One of the twins inherited his maiden aunt's taste for anisette and early every morning presented himself for his tit-cou. An hour or so later he returned for another drink and the aunt thinking that he was the other twin served him a second glass. This actually went on for months before the aunt discovered the ruse.

In 1871 fortune tellers had to pay a license of $250 to practice in the parish — now the fee is $5.00.

In the old days there were few physicians in the parish. Since distances to be traveled were great and transportation very difficult, doctors were consulted for grave illnesses only. The plantation owners hired physicians by the year to care for their families as well as their slaves and the fee varied with the number of prospective patients on the plantation. At one time Valcour Aime paid his physician, Dr. Mericq, $600.00 per year. Among the earliest doctors in the parish besides the above mentioned were Doctors Philippe Lachausée, Jean Louis Chabert, Jean Marie Mallard, Marie Louis Raoule de Chamanoire, and Pierre Lyon. Dr. Lachausée was the first physician. He was listed in the census of 1769. The licensing of physicians was lax indeed and we have the story of the charlatan who established himself in St. James where he set up his practice at Central with this sign: Docteur Brocard. It was not until several months had elapsed and after he had treated quite a few patients that it was accidentally discovered that he was nothing but an imposter. Of course he left on the next boat, but there are still many people in the parish who refer to a quack as "un Docteur Brocard."

Here is one of the first *Help Wanted* advertisements of St. James Parish. It appeared in a copy of *Le Messager*:

> "Wanted a young man of industrious habits from 15 to 18 years of age as an apprentice to carpenter's business. Apply to R. S. Chadsey, Carpenter.
> N.B. None need apply that is fond of attending at the balls and tables.
> Parish of St. James, December 28, 1848."

## CATHOLIC CHURCHES ERECTED IN ST. JAMES PARISH

| | | |
|---|---|---|
| St. Jacques de Cabahannocer | 1770 | St. James |
| St. Michel de Cantrelle | 1822 | Convent |
| Ste. Marie du Fleuve | 1831 | Union |
| St. Joseph de la Longue-Vue | 1849 | Paulina |
| Notre Dame de la Paix | 1854 | Vacherie (back) |
| St. Philippe | 1873 | Vacherie |
| Ste. Philomena de las Grande Pointe | 1875 | Grande Pointe (Chapel) |

Our Lady of Prompt Succor        1903   Lutcher
Sacred Heart Chapel            1920   Gramercy

The bell of St. Mary's Church was given by Mr. Sylvère Cantrelle, it was christened Marie-Narcisse and the sponsors were Érasmé Landry and Mrs. B. Tureaud.

Certificate of Jacques Cantrelle's second marriage taken from the St. Louis Cathedral Archives, #344:

L'an 1730, le 16 avril. Je soussigné pretre capucin, missionaire apostolique a la Nouvelle Orléans apres avoir publié trois bans de mariage au prone de notre messe paroissiale pendant trois dimanches consécutifs entre Jacques Cantrelle, natif de St. Léger en Picardie diocese d'Amiens, fils de Claude Cantrelle et de Marguerite Eurquin, ses père et mère, veuf de Marie Françoise Minquetze d.cédée aux Natchez d'une part, et Marie Marguerite Larmusiau, Native de Rennes en H.naut, fille de Jean Bte. Larmusiau et de Catherine Hetterniso ses père et mère, veuve de Pierre Houx décédé aux Natchez, d'autre part, et n'ayant pas trouvé d'empechement a l'effet du dit mariage je leur ai donné la bénédiction nuptiale en presence des témoins soussignés, scavoir: Messieurs Rossard, greffier au conseil supérieur: Manadé, chirurgien major: le sieur Michel, employé; Jean Louis, qui ont signé avec moy a la reserve de dite future épouse qui ayant déclaré ne savoir écrire ny signer a fait sa marque ordinaire.

    Cantrelle, Manadé, Rossard, Michel, Jean Louis et
    Fr. Hyacinthe, pretre capucin
    Missionaire apostolique.

Above conforms to the original.

    Gist of above:

Jacques Cantrelle, native of St. Leger in Picardie, diocese of Amiens, son of Claude Cantrelle and Marguerite Eurquin and widower of Marguerite Françoise Minquetze, deceased at the Natchez (massacre) and Marie Marguerite Larmisiau, native of Rennes in Hénaut, daughter of Jean Bte. Larmusiau and Catherine Hetterniso and widow of Pierre Houx, deceased at the Natchez, were married on April 16, 1730 by Father Hyacinthe, Capuchin, Apostolic Missionary at New Orleans. Witnesses:

Manadé, Rossard, Michel, Jean Louis. Signed also: Cantrelle and Fr. Hyacinthe.

#### FOOTNOTES

1. To improve the appetite some children were given a weak toddy daily and to increase their weight some were given raw eggs in sherry.
2. Les trois guêpes de Tante Telle-et-Telle — The three wasps of Aunt So-and-So — denoting very hot tempered women.
3. Pigeon volle — Pigeon flies.
4. Mam — Mam and Pape are used by Acadians for Father and Mother. Jai faim — I am hungry.
5. Manges une main et gardes l'autre pour demain. — Eat one hand and keep the other for tomorrow.
6. Busts — used here for break.

## XXVI

## IN CONCLUSION

Items of great interest in this parish are the early records of the church and the government, which date back to the founding of the parish. They are written almost entirely in French, but there are a few in Spanish — especially the communications of the Louisiana governors under Spanish domination. These records tell the story of the heroism and the hardships of the first colonists and the opulence and good living of a later period. Here we find the pathos and the grandeur of a day long past.

The spirited bidding in early succession sales shows the scarcity of all kinds of goods. In the plenty of today we wonder why thére were bidders for such articles as "des petites chaudières de differentes grandeures,[1] un pannier vide, deux cochons maigres, trois morceaux de savon, une corde pour amarrer un boeuf." Any article regardless of its condition or value found a buyer. Some buyers came from Des Allemands and Galveztown. They paid in gourdes, réaux, and picaillons.[2]

Inconsequential things today were grave matters yesterday. When Henri Rémy moved to the parish in 1810, his family came in a carriage, stopping for rest and sleep and food at the plantations along the way. His household effects were transported in a chalon[3] in care of his slaves. It rained all the way, his butin[4] was soaked, and his slaves sneaked across the river one night in search of amusement. While they were gone his chalon was robbed. Next morning all his chickens were gone. Rémi's protestations show how important mere chickens could be.

At a later period when the sugar dynasties had been founded, the records reflect the success and the prosperity that had come to the parish. There was animated bidding for a thousand acres of land and a lot of two hundred slaves. Sales of five hundred thousand dollars were recorded. There were no longer pittances and cabins. Instead were listed imported objets d'art, fine furniture, "l'argenteries, des bijoux, et des tapis."[5]

The succession sale was always held on the plantation involved, but early land sales were held in front of the church on a Sunday morning after mass. Bidding for land had to be carried on for three successive Sundays before the sale became final.

We find in the records the story of a freed-slave entreating the commandante for a small grant of land for herself and her child. It is written in a beautiful script, correct French, and choice vocabulary, but with the obeisance and the pathos of a woman who had long been held in bondage and because of this, expected little of life and less of government. One wonders who wrote her humble petition.

There are many letters; irate letters of protest; simple letters of deep gratitude; notes seeking mercy, or pardon, or favors, or permission to marry. And always there are the signatures: bold, trembling, illegible, precise; the pitiful little crosses of some of the Acadian illiterates and the inimitable flourishes of the educated Creoles.

Then there are the records of the War and the Reconstruction (The War was always the Civil War). Bills paid in script which sank lower and lower in value; articles begun in one penmanship and finished in another, because offices changed so often. Sometime the record stops abruptly in the middle of a word and the remaining page is blank.

In thousands of pages these old records tell the story of the stoic Acadian, the individualistic Creole, the slave, the *caboteur*,[6] the humble and the mighty — an endless procession of nearly two hundred years of people: their wills and weddings, their dowries and deaths, their births and bethrothals; their lives and loves — the building of a French section of the American nation.

"Let them sleep in tranquil slumber
They, who toiled, this place to conquer;
Like Jacques Cantrelle they passed the test,
Well have they earned their peaceful rest!"

### FOOTNOTES

1. Des petites chaudières de differentes grandeures — little pots of different sizes.
    Un pannier vide — an empty basket.
    Deux cochons maigres — two thin hogs.
    Trois morceaux de savon — three pieces of soap.
    Une corde pour amarrer un boeuf — a rope to tie a bull.
2. Gourdes, reaux, et picaillons — money in use at that time.
3. Chalon — here used for flatboat — the correct French word is chaland.
4. Butin — This is a French word meaning plunder. It is frequently used here to denote household goods.
5. Lárgenteries, des bijoux, et des tapis — silverware, jewels, and carpets.
6. Caboteur — one engaged in coasting trade — a river peddler.

# APPENDIX

## MILITIA — VERRETT'S COMPANY — CABAHANNOCER[1]

List of the inhabitants of the Coast of Cabahannocer in Verrett's Company on April 8, 1766. The names are listed in the same order as they appear on the original document. In some cases the present day spelling has been substituted and marked thus: *

Verrett — Captain
Olivier Landry
Joseph Landry
Pierre Bourg
Baptiste Cormie & father
Jean Cormie (Cormier)*
Joseph Richard
Jean Richard
Jean Poirrier (Poirier)*
André LeBlanc
Jean Seuny (Saunier)*
François Hebert
Joseph Dupuis
Joseph Poirié (Poirier)*
Laimable Blanchard
Joseph Blanchard
Victor Blanchard
Pierre Blanchard
Pierre Blánchard (son)
Pierre Doiron
Pierre Lambert
Pierre Lambert (son)
Pierre Thibodo
Joseph Bernabé
Joseph Robicho
Pierre Michel
Jean Azostegui
Pierre Azostegui

..... Vallée
Joseph Boudreau
Pierre Berteau
Jean Lavoier (Louviere)*
Jean Jaunic
Joseph Bourg
Paul Doucet
Joseph Forete
Jean Legeure
Jean Bourgeois
Baptiste Bourgeois
Michel Bourgeois
Joseph Tério
Pierre Godet
Salvador Mouton
Jean Bellefontaine
Ambroise Bernabé
Louis Mouton
Jean Mouton
Joseph Godet
Claude Godet
Jacques Dubain
Jean Milleu (Millet)*
Pierre Charpentier & son
Jean Dugas
Pierre Lanoux
Paul Bernabé

FOOTNOTES
1. Archive General de Indias — Santo Domingo, 2595, 181-182.

# CENSUS OF 1766

List of inhabitants established on the right bank of the Mississippi River from the habitation of Jacques Cantrelle to Bayou Lafourche (approximately from the present-day St. James Railway Station to the town of Donaldsonville.)

| Name | Age | Slaves | Land (Arpents) | Cattle | Sheep | Hogs | Arms (Guns) |
|---|---|---|---|---|---|---|---|
| Jacques Cantrelle | 66 | 5 | 28 | 0 | 0 | 20 | 1 |
| | | | | | | | |
| For the parish | ..... | ..... | 4 | 6 | 0 | 0 | 0 |
| Louis Judice | 36 | 11 | 24 | 8 | 0 | 20 | 3 |
| Jeanne Cantrelle, his wife | 30 | | | | | | |
| Louis, his son | 13 | | | | | | |
| Michel, son | 7 | | | | | | |
| | | | | | | | |
| Pierre Arsenaux | 36 | 0 | 4 | 0 | 0 | 0 | 1 |
| Anne Bergeron, his wife | 26 | | | | | | |
| Rosalie, daughter | 2 | | | | | | |
| Widow Bergeron, his mother-in-law | 63 | | | | | | |
| Widow Bergeron, his sister-in-law | 23 | | | | | | |
| Widow Bernard, his sister | 40 | | | | | | |
| Firmin Arsenaud, orphan | 13 | | | | | | |
| | | | | | | | |
| Làudry (Landry), fallow land | | | 20 | | | | |
| | | | | | | | |
| Bigeou, called la Violette, fallow land | | | 20 | | | | |
| | | | | | | | |
| Pierre Arsenaud | 31 | 0 | 6 | 0 | 0 | 5 | 1 |
| Marie Licourt, his wife | 22 | | | | | | |
| Usebe, his son | 4 | | | | | | |
| Pierre, son | 1 | | | | | | |
| | | | | | | | |
| Josephe Hébert | 31 | 0 | 6 | 0 | 0 | 2 | 2 |
| Widow, Dugas, sister-in-law | 23 | | | | | | |
| Joseph Dugas, son | 15 | | | | | | |
| Cecile, daughter | 13 | | | | | | |
| Magdelaine, daughter | 12 | | | | | | |
| | | | | | | | |
| Joseph Laudry (Landry) | 26 | 0 | 6 | 0 | 0 | 0 | 1 |
| Joseph, son | 3 | | | | | | |
| Pierre, son | 2 | | | | | | |

| | Age | | | | | | |
|---|---|---|---|---|---|---|---|
| Bonaventure Bellefontaine | 51 | 0 | 6 | 1 | 0 | 2 | 1 |
| Marguerite Bergeron, his wife | 43 | | | | | | |
| Bonaventure, son | 13 | | | | | | |
| Michel, son | 10 | | | | | | |
| Theotiste, daughter | 17 | | | | | | |
| Marie, daughter | 15 | | | | | | |
| | | | | | | | |
| Charles Bergeron | 38 | 0 | 6 | 0 | 0 | 1 | 1 |
| Isabelle Arsenaud, wife | 3 | | | | | | |
| Simon, son | 13 | | | | | | |
| Jean Théodore, son | 4 | | | | | | |
| Marguerite, daughter | 3 | | | | | | |
| | | | | 6 (for a family expected soon) | | | |
| Widow Melançon | 35 | 0 | 6 | 0 | 0 | 4 | 0 |
| Jean Baptiste, son | 11 | | | | | | |
| Jean, son | 4 | | | | | | |
| Marie, daughter | 13 | | | | | | |
| Nastasie, daughter | 7 | | | | | | |
| | | | | | | | |
| Jean Baptiste Bergeron | 44 | 0 | 6 | 0 | 0 | 5 | 2 |
| Marguerite Bernard, his wife | 36 | | | | | | |
| Jean Baptiste, son | 16 | | | | | | |
| Marin, son | 12 | | | | | | |
| Mathurin, son | 10 | | | | | | |
| Marie, daughter | 14 | | | | | | |
| Theotiste Thibodau, widow Godin | 26 | | | | | | |
| Barbé, her daughter | 5 | | | | | | |
| | | | | | | | |
| Ducros    (fallow land) | | | 30 | | | | |
| | | | | | | | |
| Gerome Gaudet | 26 | 0 | 6 | 0 | 0 | 0 | 1 |
| | | | | | | | |
| Charles Gaudet | 36 | 0 | 6 | 0 | 0 | 1 | 1 |
| Widow Gaudet, his mother | 63 | | | | | | |
| Rosalie, sister | 27 | | | | | | |
| | | | | | | | |
| Anathase Braud | 31 | 0 | 6 | 0 | 0 | 0 | 1 |
| Marie le Blanc, his wife | 22 | | | | | | |
| Joseph, son | 3 | | | | | | |
| Nastasie, daughter | 1 | | | | | | |

| Name | Age | | | | | | |
|---|---|---|---|---|---|---|---|
| Josephe le Blanc | 48 | 0 | 6 | 5 | 0 | 8 | 2 |
| Isabelle Gaudet, his wife | 47 | | | | | | |
| Josephe, son | 16 | 0 | 4 | 0 | 0 | 0 | 1 |
| Gilles, son | 9 | 0 | 2 | 0 | 0 | 0 | 0 |
| Anne, daughter | 18 | | | | | | |
| Isabelle, daughter | 13 | | | | | | |
| | | | | | | | |
| Simon Gautrod | 28 | 0 | 6 | 9 | 0 | 3 | 1 |
| Magdelaine Braud, wife | 23 | | | | | | |
| Louis, son | 2 mo. | | | | | | |
| | | | | | | | |
| Marcel le Blanc | 32 | 0 | 6 | 0 | 0 | 2 | 1 |
| Marie, wife | 29 | | | | | | |
| Marguerite, daughter | 3 | | | | | | |
| | | | 6 | (family momentarily due) | | | |
| Michel Verret (fallow land) | | | 10 | | | | |
| François Verret (fallow land) | | | 10 | | | | |
| Joseph Wiltz (fallow land) | | | 10 | | | | |
| Popolus (fallow land) | | | 20 | | | | |
| | | | | | | | |
| Bazille Préjen | 22 | 0 | 6 | 0 | 0 | 0 | 1 |
| | | | | | | | |
| Amand Préjen | 42 | 0 | 6 | 0 | 0 | 1 | 1 |
| Magdelaine Martin, wife | 38 | | | | | | |
| Marin, son | 16 | 0 | 4 | 0 | 0 | 0 | 1 |
| Joseph, son | 6 | | | | | | |
| André, son | 1 | | | | | | |
| Nastasie, daughter | 15 | | | | | | |
| Anne, daughter | 14 | | | | | | |
| | | | | | | | |
| Joseph Prejen | 34 | 0 | 6 | 0 | 0 | 1 | 1 |
| Marguerite Borel, wife | 24 | | | | | | |
| Jean Baptiste, son | 1 | | | | | | |
| Victorie, daughter | 6 | | | | | | |
| | | | | | | | |
| Charles Préjen | 30 | 0 | 6 | 0 | 0 | 0 | 1 |
| Marguerite Richard, wife | 21 | | | | | | |
| | | | | | | | |
| Joseph Richard | 50 | 0 | 6 | 0 | 0 | 3 | 1 |
| Anne Blanchard, wife | 40 | | | | | | |
| Marie, daughter | 6 | | | | | | |
| Rosalie, daughter | 3 | | | | | | |
| Anne, daughter | 10 mos. | | | | | | |
| | | | | | | | |
| Charles Claude Duyon | 30 | 0 | 6 | 0 | 0 | 2 | 1 |
| Marie Préjen, wife | 26 | | | | | | |
| Jean Baptiste, son | 6 | | | | | | |
| Marguerite, daughter | 2 | | | | | | |

| | | | | | | | |
|---|---|---|---|---|---|---|---|
| Claude Duyon | 28 | 0 | 6 | 0 | 0 | 1 | 2 |
| Marie Vincent, wife | 27 | | | | | | |
| Paul Duyon, orphan | 12 | | | | | | |
| | | | | | | | |
| Jean Sonné (Saunier) | 20 | 0 | 5 | 0 | 0 | 0 | 1 |
| | | | | | | | |
| Honoré Duyon | 50 | 0 | 6 | 0 | 0 | 0 | 2 |
| Marie Vincent, wife | 53 | | | | | | |
| Jean Duyon, son | 19 | 0 | 4 | 0 | 0 | 0 | 1 |
| François, son | 17 | | | | | | |
| Perpetué, daughter | 21 | | | | | | |
| | | | | | | | |
| Estienne leBlanc | 43 | 0 | 6 | 0 | 0 | 0 | 2 |
| Elizabeth Boudreau, wife | 45 | | | | | | |
| Simon, son | 22 | 0 | 4 | 0 | 0 | 0 | 1 |
| Estienne, son | 15 | | | | | | |
| Mathurin, son | 12 | | | | | | |
| Joseph, son | 5 | | | | | | |
| Marguerite, daughter | 19 | | | | | | |
| Magdelaine, daughter | 8 | | | | | | |
| Marie, daughter | 1 | | | | | | |
| | | | | | | | |
| Bruno Robichaud | 41 | 0 | 6 | 0 | 0 | 0 | 1 |
| Anne Broussart, wife | 34 | | | | | | |
| Firmin, son | 15 | 0 | 4 | 0 | 0 | 0 | 1 |
| Bruno, son | 2 | | | | | | |
| | | | | | | | |
| Charles Forest | 40 | 0 | 6 | 0 | 0 | 0 | 1 |
| Marguerite Saunier, wife | | | | | | | |
| Paul, son | 20 | 0 | 6 | 0 | 0 | 0 | 1 |
| Anselme, son | 15 | 0 | 4 | 0 | 0 | 0 | 1 |
| Charles, son | 2 | | | | | | |
| Marie, daughter | 6 | | | | | | |
| Marguerite, daughter | 4 | | | | | | |
| Marguerite, niece | 20 | | | | | | |
| | | | | | | | |
| Marc Maulet | 29 | 0 | 6 | 0 | 0 | 0 | 1 |
| | | | | | | | |
| Joseph Marant | 37 | 0 | 6 | 0 | 0 | 0 | 1 |
| Angelique Dugas, wife | 30 | | | | | | |
| Joseph Aurion, nephew | 18 | | | | | | |
| Marguerite Aurion, niece | 17 | | | | | | |
| | | | | | | | |
| Pierre Bidau | 34 | 0 | 8 | 0 | 0 | 0 | 1 |
| | | | | | | | |
| Joseph Barthêlemy | 33 | 0 | 8 | 0 | 0 | 0 | 1 |
| | | | | | | | |
| François Dugas | 26 | 0 | 6 | 0 | 0 | 1 | 1 |
| Charles Dugas, nephew | 16 | 0 | 5 | 0 | 0 | 0 | 1 |

| | | | | | | | |
|---|---|---|---|---|---|---|---|
| Michel Dugas, nephew | 14 | 0 | 5 | 0 | 0 | 0 | 0 |
| Anasthase Dugas, nephew | 13 | 0 | 5 | 0 | 0 | 0 | 1 |
| Théodore Dugas, nephew | 8 | | | | | | |
| Rose Dugas, sister | 17 | | | | | | |
| | | | | | | | |
| Nastasie Dugas, widow Robichaud | 27 | 0 | 6 | 0 | 0 | 1 | 1 |
| Héry, son | 6 | | | | | | |
| Jean Baptiste, son | 4 | | | | | | |
| Marie, daughter | 2 | | | | | | |
| | | | | | | | |
| Mathurin L'audry (Landry) | 29 | 0 | 6 | 0 | 0 | 0 | 1 |
| Catherine Quessy, widow Bergeron | 30 | 0 | 4 | 0 | 0 | 1 | 1 |
| Jean Baptiste, son | 12 | | | | | | |
| Charles, son | 10 | | | | | | |
| Magdelaine, daughter | 16 | | | | | | |
| Ositte, daughter | 14 | | | | | | |
| Josephe Quessy, brother | 21 | | | | | | |

List of the inhabitants on the left bank of the river from the habitation of Joseph Hebert to the village of the Alibamon Indians.

| | | | | | | | |
|---|---|---|---|---|---|---|---|
| Joseph Hébert | 26 | 0 | 6 | 0 | 0 | 1 | 1 |
| Françoise Hébert, wife | 21 | | | | | | |
| Louis, son | 2 | | | | | | |
| Jean Charles, orphan | 15 | | | | | | |
| | | | | | | | |
| Claire Robichaud, widow Hebert | 52 | 0 | 4 | 0 | 0 | 1 | 0 |
| Mathurin, son | 12 | 0 | 0 | 0 | 0 | 0 | 1 |
| Marie, daughter | 16 | | | | | | |
| Théotiste, daughter | 13 | | | | | | |
| Jean Louis Hebert, grandson | 3 | | | | | | |
| Agnes Hebert, widow Bourgeois | 24 | | | | | | |
| | | | | | | | |
| Antoine la Bauve | 40 | 0 | 6 | 0 | 0 | 1 | 1 |
| Anne Vincent, wife | 28 | | | | | | |
| Marin, son | 7 | | | | | | |
| Baptiste, nephew | 8 | | | | | | |
| | | | | | | | |
| Francois Spître, orphan | 3 | | | | | | |
| | | | | | | | |
| Pierre Vincent | 21 | 0 | 6 | 0 | 0 | 0 | 1 |

| | | | | | | | |
|---|---|---|---|---|---|---|---|
| Joseph Savoye | 37 | 0 | 6 | 0 | 0 | 1 | 1 |
| Anne Prejen, wife | 38 | | | | | | |
| | | | | | | | |
| Marguerite, daughter | 7 | | | | | | |
| Charles Savoye | 44 | 0 | 6 | 0 | 0 | 0 | 1 |
| Judith Arsenaud, wife | 30 | | | | | | |
| Jean, son | 3 | | | | | | |
| Basile des Roches, orphan | 12 | | | | | | |
| | | | | | | | |
| Pierre Bourgeois | 20 | 0 | 6 | 0 | 0 | 0 | 1 |
| | | | | | | | |
| Michel Bourgeois | 25 | 0 | 6 | 0 | 0 | 0 | 1 |
| | | | | | | | |
| Josephe Bourgeois | 30 | 0 | 6 | 1 | 0 | 0 | 1 |
| Marie Giroir, wife | 28 | | | | | | |
| Marie, daughter | 14 | | | | | | |
| | | | | | | | |
| Paul Bourgeois | 34 | 0 | 6 | 1 | 0 | 0 | 1 |
| Rosalie le Blanc, wife | 21 | | | | | | |
| | | | | | | | |
| Joseph Guilbaud | 35 | 0 | 6 | 0 | 0 | 0 | 1 |
| | | | | | | | |
| Michel Poirier | 28 | 0 | 6 | 0 | 0 | 0 | 1 |
| Marie Cormier, wife | 20 | | | | | | |
| | | | | | | | |
| Simon Mire | 22 | 0 | 6 | 0 | 0 | 0 | 1 |
| Magdelaine Cormier, wife | 22 | | | | | | |
| | | | | | | | |
| Bellony Mire | 30 | 0 | 6 | 0 | 0 | 0 | 1 |
| François Parre, orphan | 14 | | | | | | |
| | | | | | | | |
| Joseph Parre (Part) | 28 | 0 | 5 | 0 | 0 | 0 | 1 |
| Pierre Parre | 16 | 0 | 3 | 0 | 0 | 0 | 1 |
| Marie Parre, sister | 15 | | | | | | |
| | | | | | | | |
| Barthelemy Bellefontaine | 31 | 0 | 5 | 0 | 0 | 0 | 1 |
| Marie Martin, wife | 32 | | | | | | |
| | | | | | | | |
| Olivier Parre | 20 | 0 | 5 | 0 | 0 | 0 | 1 |
| | | | | | | | |
| Pierre Hebert | 29 | 0 | 5 | 0 | 0 | 0 | 1 |
| | | | | | | | |
| Pierre Bernard | 35 | 0 | 4 | 0 | 0 | 0 | 1 |
| Marguerite Arsenaud, wife | 31 | | | | | | |
| Jean Baptiste, son | 12 | | | | | | |
| Marie, daughter | 6 | | | | | | |
| Pierre, son | 8 | | | | | | |

| Name | Age | | | | | | |
|---|---|---|---|---|---|---|---|
| Joseph Bellefontaine | 26 | 0 | 5 | 0 | 0 | 0 | 1 |
| Marie Forest, wife | 18 | | | | | | |
| | | | | | | | |
| Firmin Giroir | 17 | 0 | 3 | 0 | 0 | 0 | 1 |
| | | | | | | | |
| Jean Arsenaud | 38 | 0 | 3 | 0 | 0 | 1 | 1 |
| Judithe Bergeron, wife | 32 | | | | | | |
| Jean Charles, son | 14 | | | | | | |
| Joseph, son | 12 | | | | | | |
| Guillame, son | 8 | | | | | | |
| Paul, son | 4 | | | | | | |
| | | | | | | | |
| Jacques Bellefontaine | 26 | 0 | 4 | 0 | 0 | 0 | 1 |
| | | | | | | | |
| Baptiste Bellefontaine | 20 | 0 | 4 | 0 | 0 | 0 | 1 |
| | | | | | | | |
| Pierre Brioud | | | 6 | (absent) | | | |
| | | | | | | | |
| Pierre Forest | 27 | 0 | 6 | 0 | 0 | 0 | 1 |
| Anne Dupuy, wife | 25 | | | | | | |
| | | | | | | | |
| Pierre Chiasson | 37 | 0 | 6 | 0 | 0 | 0 | 1 |
| Ositte L'audry, wife | 32 | | | | | | |
| Michel, son | 7 | | | | | | |
| Marie, daughter | 1 | | | | | | |
| Jean Baptiste, nephew | 4 | | | | | | |
| | | | | | | | |
| Paul Chiasson | 20 | 0 | 6 | 0 | 0 | 0 | 1 |
| | | | 6 | (for a family who will arrive soon) | | | |
| Joseph Arsenaud | 26 | 0 | 4 | 0 | 0 | 0 | 1 |
| Marie Bergeron, wife | 21 | | | | | | |
| | | | | | | | |
| Germain Bergeron | 23 | 0 | 4 | 0 | 0 | 1 | 2 |
| | | | | | | | |
| Genevieve Bergeron, widow d'Amour | 36 | 0 | 4 | 0 | 0 | 1 | 1 |
| Charles, son | 15 | 0 | 4 | 0 | 0 | 0 | 1 |
| | | | | | | | |
| Baptiste, son | 12 | | | | | | |
| François, son | 7 | | | | | | |
| Ysidore, son | 3 | | | | | | |
| Nastasie, daughter | 8 | | | | | | |
| Suzanne, daughter | 1 | | | | | | |
| Marie Dugas, widow Bergeron | 55 | | | | | | |
| Anne, her daughter | 17 | | | | | | |

| | | | | | | | |
|---|---|---|---|---|---|---|---|
| Françoise Mellenson, widow Terriot | 57 | 0 | 4 | 0 | 0 | 0 | 0 |
| Thomas Terriot, son | 21 | 0 | 5 | 0 | 0 | 0 | 1 |
| Ambroise Terriot, son | 18 | 0 | 4 | 0 | 0 | 0 | 1 |
| Paul Terriot, son | 15 | 0 | 0 | 0 | 0 | 0 | 1 |
| Exavier Terriot, son | 12 | 0 | 0 | 0 | 0 | 0 | 1 |
| L'augebourg | 17 | 0 | 4 | 0 | 0 | 0 | 1 |
| Joseph Bourg | 26 | 0 | 5 | 0 | 0 | 0 | 1 |
| Magdelaine, his cousin | 20 | | | | | | |
| Marie, cousin | 12 | | | | | | |
| Joseph | 13 | | | | | | |
| Ollivier Boudrau | 29 | 0 | 5 | 0 | 0 | 0 | 1 |
| Simon, son | 13 | 0 | 0 | 0 | 0 | 0 | 1 |
| Joseph Saunier | 27 | 0 | 5 | 0 | 0 | 0 | 1 |
| Anne, wid. Babin, sister | 25 | | | | | | |
| Lize Babin, her daughter | 3 | | | | | | |
| Marie, daughter | 2 | | | | | | |
| Jean Baptiste Thibaudot | 23 | 0 | 6 | 0 | 0 | 0 | 1 |
| Anne Dupuy, widow of the? | 41 | 0 | 4 | 0 | 0 | 1 | 0 |
| Marie, her daughter | 15 | | | | | | |
| Monique, daughter | 12 | | | | | | |
| Joseph Dupuy, her nephew | 15 | | | | | | |
| Abraham Roy | 35 | 0 | 6 | 0 | 0 | 2 | 1 |
| Sauveur, son | 7 | | | | | | |
| Marie, daughter | 11 | | | | | | |
| Catherine, widow Lafaye | 40 | | | | | | |
| Marie Marquis, her niece | 16 | | | | | | |
| Joseph Melançon | 15 | 0 | 4 | 0 | 0 | 0 | 1 |
| Firmin Arsenaud | 13 | 0 | 4 | 0 | 0 | 0 | 0 |

Inhabitants established above the village of the Houma Indians (above Burnside).

| | | | | | | | |
|---|---|---|---|---|---|---|---|
| Saturnin Bruno | 26 | 0 | 6 | 0 | 0 | 0 | 0 |
| Felix Pax | 40 | 0 | 6 | 0 | 0 | 0 | 0 |

François Andro          18    0    6    0    0    0    0

## RECAPITULATION

| | | | |
|---|---|---|---|
| Men | 43 | Slaves | 16 |
| Women (wives) | 43 | Arpents of land | 687 |
| Boys above 15 | 55 | Hogs | 95 |
| Boys under 15 | 56 | Arms (guns) | 97 |
| Widows | 17 | Dated: | April 9, 1766 |
| Girls above 15 | 17 | Place: Kabannoces | |
| Girls under 15 | 35 | Signed: Louis Judice | |

Archive General de Indies Papeles de Cuba, 187A

### FOOTNOTES

The names are spelled as given on the original copy. The writer is of the opinion that the name listed as Laudry, or L'audry, should be spelled Landry. The present day spelling of many of the names is different; Broussart is now Broussard; Mellenson is now Melançon; Prejen is now Prejean, etc.

Many interesting observations can be made from this census. Since it was dated April 9, 1766, it lists the first Acadians who came to the Cabahannocer section of the Acadian Coast . . . St. James and Ascension Parishes. There were many broken families. Probably they had been separated in the expulsion, or perhaps many were unable to survive the hardships of thier wanderings. Several very young boys are listed . . . some as young as thirteen . . . with no family, but with a land grant and a gun. The Acadians were poor and had no slaves. Only the Cantrelles and Judices had slaves. Almost all the grants were for six acres fronting the river, but extending forty arpents back. There were many widows. The same Christian names predominate. Some lands were being held for expected families. There were no horses. There were two Indian tribes or villages. Almost every household had a gun. Cantrelle's family is not listed. Perhaps he had not yet moved them to Cabahannoccer.

## LIST OF THE ACADIANS MARRIED SINCE THE ESTABLISHMENT OF KABAHANNOSSÉ (CABAHANNOCER)

| MALE | FEMALE | DATE |
|---|---|---|
| Simon Mire | Madelaine Cormier | March 31, 1766 |
| Michel Poirier | Marie Cormier | March 31, 1766 |
| Joseph Godin | Marie Forret | April 10, 1766 |
| Pierre Lambert | Marguerite Doiron | May 5, 1766 |
| Pierre Berto | Rose Savoy | August 25, 1766 |
| Philippe Lachaussé | Rose Bourgeois | October 5, 1766 |
| François Savoy | Anne Thibaudos | October 5, 1766 |
| Josephe Ricard | Agnes Hebert | November 24, 1766 |
| Charles Babin | Elizabeth Babin | March 2, 1767 |
| Joseph Bourg | Marie le Blanc | March 2, 1767 |
| Joseph Guedry | Elizabeth Commeaux | May 19, 1767 |
| Pierre Hebert | Anne Bergeron | July 16, 1767 |
| Josephe Guillebeaux | Catherine Commeaux | October 2, 1767 |
| Olivier Beaudros | Anne Gaudet | October 2, 1767 |
| Simon Landry | Marguerite Babin | October 12, 1767 |
| Pierre Landry | Marie Landry | November 5, 1767 |
| Joseph Saunier | Marie Landry | November 6, 1767 |
| Simon le Blanc | Anne Arseneaux | November 6, 1767 |
| Pierre Bourgeois | Marie Bergeron | November 6, 1767 |
| Jean Richard | Rosalie Bourgeois | November 7, 1767 |
| Joseph Hebert | Anne Prejean (wid. Savoy) | December 22, 1767 |
| Joseph Commeaux | Marie Babin | January 8, 1768 |
| Jean Bourgeois | Ludivine Grangé | January 30, 1768 |
| Charles Melançon | Magdelaine le Blanc | February 7, 1768 |
| Isaac le Blanc | Marie Laudry (Landry) | February 7, 1768 |
| Joseph Babin | Marie Laudrie (Landry) | February 7, 1768 |
| Jacques Lachauseé | Marie Marthe le Blanc | February 7, 1768 |

### MARRIED IN NEW ORLEANS

| | | |
|---|---|---|
| Mathurin Laudry (Landry) | Anne Landry | Presumbaly 1768 |
| Michel Bourgeois | Ositte Gotros Gauthreaux | No date given |
| Pierre Forrest | Marie Laudrie | No date given |
| Étienne Bujol | Marguerite Forrest | No date given |
| Salvatorre Mouton | Anne Forrest | No date given |
| Joseph Bourg | Marie Dugas | No date given |

### MARRIED SINCE EASTER 1768

| | | |
|---|---|---|
| Joseph Grangé | Genevieve Babin | April 11, 1768 |
| Pierre Vincent | Marguerite Cormié | April 11, 1768 |
| Simon Broussard | Marguerite Blanchard | April 11, 1768 |
| Saturin Brinois (Bruno) | Collet Leger | April 11, 1768 |
| Jean Baptiste Melançon | Ozitte Dupuis | May 2, 1768 |

| | | |
|---|---|---|
| François Landry | Marie Rose LeBlanc | May 2, 1768 |
| Michel Bourgeois | Anne Laudrie | May 2, 1768 |
| Germain Bergeron | Marguerite le Blanc | May 3, 1768 |
| Charles Godet | Blanche Braud | May 16, 1768 |
| Abraham Roy | Marie Dousset | June 6, 1768 |
| François Dugas | Marguerite Babin | June 28, 1768 |
| Joachim Mirre | Marguerite Broussard | June 9, 1768 |

Archivo General de Indias

Papeless de Cuba 178A

N.B. Many marriages occurred on the same date because there was no resident pastor and when a priest visited the community, he performed many marriages and baptisms.

## CENSUS OF ACADIAN COAST — 1769

Archivo General de Indias
Papeles de Cuba, 187 A

September 14, 1769 — State of the Acadian inhabitants established on both banks of the Mississippi River from the habitation of Jacques Cantrelle and that of Joseph Hebert to the environs of — "l'isle aux mases."

### RIGHT BANK

| | NAME | AGE |
|---|---|---|
| # 1 | Jacques Cantrelle | 72 |
| | Marguerite Larmusieux, w | 59 |
| # 2 | Michel Cantrelle, s | 20 |
| # 3 | Jacques Cantrelle II | 19 |
| # 4 | Land belong to St. James Parish | |
| # 5 | Louis Judice | 38 |
| | Jeanne Cantrelle, w | 33 |
| | Louis, s | 17 |
| | Michel Judice, s | 11 |
| | Joseph Bouchard, tutor | 43 |
| # 6 | Pierre Arcenaux | 37 |
| | Anne Bergeron, w | 28 |
| | Rozalie, d | 5 |
| | Marie Jeanne, d | 3 |
| | Françoise, d (mos.) | 10 |
| | Firmin Arcenaux, o | 15 |
| | Charles Bergeron, o | 11 |
| # 7 | Sieur Andry (land presently occupied by Taensa Indians) | |
| # 8 | Jean Baptiste Adams | 33 |
| # 9 | Simon Leblanc | 28 |
| | Anne Arseneaux, w | 25 |
| | Marie Anne, d | 1 |
| | Margueritte Bergeron, o | 6 |
| # 10 | Joseph Hebert | 34 |
| | Anne Prejean, w | 38 |
| | Paul, s (mos.) | 8 |
| | Joseph Savoy, stepson | 3 |
| | Margueritte, sd | 9 |
| # 11 | Jacques Godain | 27 |

| | NAME | AGE |
|---|---|---|
| # 12 | Bonnaventure Godain | 46 |
| | Margueritte Bergeron, w | 46 |
| | Bonnaventure, s | 14 |
| | Michel, s | 12 |
| | Théotiste, d | 19 |
| | Marie, d | 17 |
| | Jean Baptiste Bergeron, n | 13 |
| # 13 | Philippe Lachaussée, surgeon | 41 |
| | Roze Bergeron, w | 37 |
| | Louise, d | 14 |
| | Paul Gravois, ss | 18 |
| | Joseph Gravois, ss | 16 |
| | Jean Gravois, ss | 14 |
| # 14 | Anne Bergeron, widow Godain | 39 |
| | Victor, s | 16 |
| | Pierre Paul, s | 12 |
| | Marie, d | 17 |
| | Marie Louiza, d | 9 |
| # 15 | Marie Braud, widow Melançon | 37 |
| | Joseph Melançon, s | 17 |
| | Baptiste, s | 13 |
| | Dominique, s | 7 |
| | Marie, d | 16 |
| | Nastazie, d | 10 |
| # 16 | Jean Baptiste Bergeron | 47 |
| | Margueritte Bernard, w | 40 |
| | Mathurain, s | 15 |
| | Mazain, s | 13 |
| | Marie Bergeron, d | 17 |
| | Rozalie, d (mos.) | 9 |
| # 17 | Jean Baptiste Bergeron | 19 |

| # 18 | Fallow land | |
|---|---|---|
| # 19 | Alexis Breau | 46 |
| | Magdelaine Trohan, w | 48 |
| | Honoré, s | 23 |
| | Joseph, s | 18 |
| | Charles, s | 16 |
| | Alexis, s | 4 |
| | Marie, d | 12 |
| | Nastazie, d | 7 |
| # 20 | Charles Godet | 36 |
| | Cecile Broa, w | 30 |
| | Joseph Cloatre, ss | 9 |
| | Charles, ss | 4 |
| | Magdelaine, sd | 7 |
| # 21 | Gerome Godet | 27 |
| | Marie Broust, m | 67 |
| | Roze, s | 30 |
| # 22 | Athanaze Broa | 35 |
| | Marie Leblanc | 26 |
| | Joseph, s | 6 |
| | Nastazie, d | 4 |
| | Marie, d | 1 |
| # 23 | Joseph Leblanc | 50 |
| | Izabelle Godet, w | 50 |
| | Gille, s | 11 |
| | Anne, d | 20 |
| | Izabelle, d | 14 |
| # 24 | Joseph Leblanc | 19 |
| # 25 | Simon Gauthorot | 23 |
| | Magdelaine Broa, w | 27 |
| | Louis, s | 3 |
| | Jean Baptiste, s (mos.) | 18 |
| # 26 | Marcel Leblanc | 37 |
| | Margueritte, d | 6 |
| | Marie Breau, w | 33 |
| | Marie, d | 3 |
| | Ozitte, d (mos.) | 7 |
| # 27 | Jacques Leblanc | 61 |
| | Catherine Forest, w | 59 |
| | Catherine, d | 19 |
| | Ozitte, d | 17 |
| # 28 | Michel Verret | 32 |
| | François Verret | 25 |
| | Baptiste Verret | 23 |
| # 29 | Fallow land | |
| # 30 | Jean Gagnard | ? |
| # 31 | Bazille Prejean | 24 |
| | Marie Lincourt, w | 25 |
| | Uzebe Arseneaux, ss | 7 |
| | Pierre, ss | 5 |

| # 32 | Marie Leblanc, | |
|---|---|---|
| | widow Lachause | 20 |
| # 33 | Amant Prejean | 40 |
| | Magdelaine Martin, w | 41 |
| | Joseph Prejean, s | 10 |
| | André, s | 4 |
| | Nastazie, d | 18 |
| | Marianne, d | 16 |
| | Marie Magdelaine, d | 1 |
| # 34 | Mazain Prejean | 19 |
| # 35 | Joseph Prejean | 34 |
| | Margueritte Durel, w | 32 |
| | Baptiste, s | 4 |
| | Bazille, s | 1 |
| | Victoire, d | 9 |
| # 36 | Charles Prejean | 32 |
| | Margueritte Richard, w | 24 |
| | Aimable, s (mos.) | 7 |
| # 37 | Joseph Richard | 53 |
| | Anne Blanchard, w | 45 |
| | Marie, d | 10 |
| | Pelagie, d (mos.) | 4 |
| | Joseph Richard, n | 7 |
| # 38 | Charles Duan | 35 |
| | Marie Prejean, w | 33 |
| | Jean Baptiste, s | 9 |
| | Michel, s (mos.) | 10 |
| | Margueritte, d | 5 |
| # 39 | Claude Duan | 32 |
| | Marie Joseph Vincent, w | 38 |
| | Paul Jeantonne, o | 14 |
| # 40 | Honoré Duan | 54 |
| | Marie Vincent, w | 56 |
| | Perpetue, d | 24 |
| # 41 | Jean Duan | 23 |
| # 42 | Izabelle Boudreau, | |
| | widow Leblanc | 45 |
| | Estienne Leblanc, s | 17 |
| | Mathurain, s | 13 |
| | Margueritte, d | 19 |
| | Magdelaine, d | 11 |
| | Marthe, d | 5 |
| # 43 | Simon Leblanc | 24 |
| # 44 | Euselnie Soust | 17 |
| # 45 | Charles Forest | 47 |
| | Margueritte Sounier, w | 44 |
| | Charles, s | 5 |
| | Marie, d | 10 |
| | Margueritte, d | 8 |

| # 46 | Paul Forest | 24 |
|---|---|---|
| | Margueritte Orsillon, w | 19 |
| | Margueritte, d (mos.) | 3 |
| # 47 | Seaul Chiason | 24 |
| # 48 | Marc Malet | 28 |
| # 49 | Joseph Marant | 40 |
| | Angelique Hugard, w | 34 |
| # 50 | Joseph Orillout | 21 |
| # 51 | Sathurnain Bruno | 27 |
| | Colastie Legeo, w | 24 |
| | Joseph Bruno, s (mos.) | 8 |
| # 52 | Joseph Roget, called Query | 23 |
| # 53 | Atanaze Hugas (Dugas) | 18 |
| # 54 | François Hugas (Dugas) | 28 |
| | Margueritte Babain, w | 20 |
| # 55 | Charles Hugas (Dugas) | 19 |
| | Michel Hugas, b | 12 |
| | Theodore Hugas, b | 9 |
| | Roze Hugas, | 20 |
| # 56 | Nastazie Hugas, widow Robichaud | 31 |
| | Henry Robichaud, s | 8 |
| | Jean Baptiste, s | 6 |
| | Louis Uzebe, s | 2 |
| # 57 | Mathurain Landry | 35 |
| | Anne Landry, w | 33 |
| | Marie, d (mos.) | 8 |
| # 58 | Joseph Landry | 30 |
| | Marie Grangé, w | 26 |
| | Joseph, s | 7 |
| | Pierre, s | 5 |
| # 59 | Abraham Landry | 59 |
| | Joseph, s | 12 |
| | Margueritte, d | 18 |
| | Magdelaine, d | 10 |
| # 60 | Pierre Landry | 17 |
| # 61 | Ten arpents not granted Above Bayou Lafourche | |
| # 62 | Mr. Sain, storekeeper at Natchitoches | |
| # 63 | Charles Lincour fallow land | |
| # 64 | Thomas Commer fallow land | |
| # 65 | Lionnois fallow land | |
| # 66 | Joseph Lincourt | 29 |
| | Geneviève Landry, w | 25 |
| | Rozalie, d | 2 |
| # 67 | Barthelemy Gilion | 36 |
| | Margueritte Blanchard, w | 36 |
| | Magdelaine Blanchard, n | 9 |
| # 68 | Morice Roch | 40 |
| # 69 | Augustin Berteau | 20 |
| # 70 | Cristopher Chalsmiste | 40 |
| | Marie Louise Detroit, w | 26 |
| | Marie Therese, d (mos.) | 4 |
| # 71 | Laurent Piltmane | 43 |
| # 72 | Gerome Leblanc | 20 |
| # 73 | Deziré Leblanc | 52 |
| | Marie Landry, w | 46 |
| | Deziré, s | 16 |
| | Binjamain, s | 9 |
| | Enselme, s | 6 |
| | Grégoire, s (mos.) | 5 |
| | Izabelle, d | 18 |
| | Marine, d | 14 |
| | Ozitte, d | 11 |
| | Augustin Broussard, n | 20 |
| # 74 | Joseph Bujeux | 46 |
| | Anne Leblanc, w | 36 |
| | Augustin, s | 16 |
| | Joseph, s (mos.) | 3 |
| | Margueritte, d | 18 |
| | Perpetue, d | 14 |
| | Anne, d | 12 |
| | Marie, d | 8 |
| | Joseph Landry, uncle | 65 |
| # 75 | Estienne Bujeau | 45 |
| | Anne Forest, w | 40 |
| | Pierre Bujeau, s | 14 |
| | Jean, s | 1 |
| | Magdelaine, d | 8 |
| | Marie Bujeau, d | 8 |
| | Joseph Babain, ss | 14 |
| | Charles, ss | 9 |
| # 76 | Mathurain Bujeau | 17 |
| # 77 | Silvain Leblanc | 28 |
| | Marie Babain, w | 22 |
| | Simon Leblanc, s | 5 |
| # 78 | Jozette Bourg | 56 |
| | Anne Gertrude, d | 18 |
| # 79 | Joseph Landry | 17 |
| # 80 | Estienne Landry | 35 |
| | Marie, w | 35 |
| | Jean Baptiste, s | 2 |
| | Ygnace, d (mos.) | 3 |
| | Nastazie, d | 12 |
| | Izabelle Landry, si-l | 3 |

| # 81 | Joseph Babain | | 21 |
|---|---|---|---|
| | Ursule Landry Babin, m | | 45 |
| | Marie Joseph Babain, s | | 19 |
| | Margueritte, s | | 17 |
| # 82 | Vincent Landry | | 42 |
| | Suzanne Godon, w | | 32 |
| | Charles Caliste, s | | 3 |
| | Félicité, d | (mos.) | 9 |
| | Brigitte Trahou, o | | 12 |
| # 83 | Amant Gautherot | | 39 |
| | Marie Landry | | 31 |
| | Anne, d | | 4 |
| | Margueritte, d | (mos.) | 9 |
| | Magdelaine, o | | 14 |
| # 84 | Pierre Landry | | 37 |
| | Marie Landry, w | | 25 |
| | Joseph, s | | 13 |
| | Pierre, s | | 7 |
| | Fabien, s | | 5 |
| | Anne, d | | 10 |
| | Marie, d | | 1 |
| # 85 | Amant Landry | | 23 |
| | Margueritte Melancon, w | | 22 |
| # 86 | Firmain Breau | | 20 |
| | Margueritte, w | | 22 |

### LEFT BANK, MISSISSIPPI RIVER

| | NAME | | AGE |
|---|---|---|---|
| # 87 | Joseph Hébert | | 32 |
| | Françoise, w | | 23 |
| | Louis, s | | 5 |
| | Joseph, s | (mos.) | 2 |
| # 88 | Mathurain Hébert | | 16 |
| | Claire Robichaud, m | | 56 |
| | Jean Louis, b | | 8 |
| | Marie, si | | 19 |
| | Theotiste, si | | 16 |
| # 89 | Pierre Vincent | | 25 |
| | Margueritte Cormier, w | | 25 |
| | Jean Vincent, s | (mos.) | 3 |
| # 90 | Antoine Labauve | | 4 |
| | Anne Vincent, w | | 35 |
| | Mazain, s | | 10 |
| | Jean, s | | 6 |
| | Pierre, s | | 2 |
| | Françoise Spitre, o | | 6 |
| # 91 | Philippe Vibert | | 36 |
| | Pelagie Semidon, w | | 39 |
| | Jacques Loisette, friend | | 35 |
| # 92 | Charles Savoy | | 46 |
| | Judique Arseneaux, w | | 32 |
| | Jean Baptiste, s | | 6 |
| | Pierre Savoy, s | (mos.) | 2 |
| | Jean, s | (mos.) | 2 |
| | Bazille Deroche, o | | 14 |
| # 93 | Pierre Darzoin | | 36 |
| | Marie Bourgeois, w | | 35 |
| | Ollivier, s | | 5 |

| | NAME | | AGE |
|---|---|---|---|
| # 94 | Pierre Bourgeois | | 29 |
| | Marie Bergeron, w | | 19 |
| | Pierre, s | (mo.) | 1 |
| # 95 | Michel Bourgeois | | 23 |
| | Ozitte Landry, w | | 26 |
| # 96 | Joseph Bourgeois | | 33 |
| | Marie Tiroize, w | | 32 |
| | Marie Broussard, o | | 2 |
| # 97 | Paul Bourgeois | | 38 |
| | Rozalie Leblanc, w | | 25 |
| | Magdelaine, d | | 2 |
| # 98 | Joseph Guilbeau | | 38 |
| | Catherine Coumeau, w | | 41 |
| # 99 | Michel Poirier | | 31 |
| | Marie Cormier, w | | 24 |
| | Pierre Poirier, s | | 3 |
| | Joseph, s | (mos.) | 8 |
| | Marie, o | | 16 |
| # 100 | Simon Mirre | | 25 |
| | Magdelaine Cormier, w | | 25 |
| | Joseph, s | (mos.) | 8 |
| | Marie, d | | 2 |
| # 101 | Belhonny Mirre | | 33 |
| | Magdelaine Melancon, w | | 25 |
| | Collastie, d | (mos.) | 3 |
| | François Part, b.l. | | 16 |
| | Margueritte Broussard, widow Melancon, m.l. | | 50 |
| | Izabelle Melancon, s.l. | | 23 |
| | Margueritte, s.l. | | 21 |
| # 102 | Joseph Part | | 28 |
| # 103 | Pierre Part | | 21 |

| # | Name | Value |
|---|---|---|
| # 104 | Barthelemy Godain, | |
| | called Belfontaine | 32 |
| | Marie Martin, w | 34 |
| | Louis, s | 2 |
| | Barthelemy, s (mos.) | 7 |
| # 105 | Ollivier Part | 23 |
| # 106 | Pierre Hebert | 30 |
| | Marie Bergeron, w | 22 |
| | Francois, s | 1 |
| | Marie Dugas, | |
| | widow Bergeron, m.l. | 59 |
| | Izidore Damons, n | 7 |
| # 107 | Pierre Bernard | 36 |
| | Jean Baptiste, s | 15 |
| | Pierre, s | 12 |
| # 108 | Joseph Arseneaux | 29 |
| | Marie Bergeron, w | 25 |
| | Françoise, d | 3 |
| | Margueritte, d (mos.) | 7 |
| | Theodore, nephew | 7 |
| #109 | Firmain Giroire | 20 |
| # 110 | Cecile Dugas, | |
| | widow Bergeron | 32 |
| | Joseph, s | 14 |
| | Nicolas Lahure (mos.) | 8 |
| | Cecile, d | 12 |
| | Marie Magdelaine, d | 10 |
| # 111 | Baptiste Godain | 24 |
| | Magdelaine Melancon, w | 19 |
| # 112 | Jean Arseneaux | 40 |
| | Judique Bergeron, w | 34 |
| | Jean Charles, s | 16 |
| | Joseph, s | 12 |
| | Guillaume, s | 8 |
| | Anne, d (mos.) | 7 |
| # 113 | Pierre Forest | 32 |
| | Marie Joseph Landry, w | 31 |
| # 114 | Pierre Chiason | 41 |
| | Ozitte Landry, w | 38 |
| | Michel Chiason, s | 10 |
| | Bazille, s | 11 |
| # 115 | Pierre Leblanc | 42 |
| | Ozitte Melancon, w | 39 |
| | Izaac, s | 9 |
| | Josime, s | 7 |
| | Simon, s | 2 |
| | Helaine, d | 5 |
| | Magdelaine Leblanc, m | 57 |
| # 116 | François Landry | 28 |
| # 117 | Baptiste Melançon | 28 |
| | Ozitte Dupuis, w | 24 |
| | Uzebe, s (mos.) | 4 |
| # 118 | Germain Bergeron | 25 |
| | Margueritte Leblanc, w | 18 |
| | Baptiste Damour, n | 14 |
| | François, n | 10 |
| # 119 | Charles Louviere | 20 |
| # 120 | Ambroise Theriot | 21 |
| # 121 | Thomas Theriot | 25 |
| | Paul Theriot, b | 18 |
| | François Theriot, b | 16 |
| # 122 | Ozitte Hebert, | |
| | widow Melancon | 39 |
| | Pierre, s | 19 |
| | Joseph, s | 15 |
| | Etienne, s | 13 |
| | Paul, s | 7 |
| | Charles, s (mos.) | 17 |
| # 123 | Joseph Bourg | 34 |
| | Marie Leblanc, w | 35 |
| | Margueritte Richard, s.d | 10 |
| # 124 | Ollivier Boudreau | 43 |
| | Anne Gaudet, w | 44 |
| | Simon, s | 14 |
| | Marie Dupuis, s.d. | 17 |
| | Monique, s.d. | 14 |
| | Joseph Dupuis, n | 18 |
| # 125 | Joseph Sonnier | 34 |
| | Marie Landry, w | 40 |
| | Margueritte, d | 1 |
| | Magdelaine Grangé, s.d. | 12 |
| | Agnaise Daigle, cousin | 17 |
| # 126 | Anne Gaudet, wife of | |
| | Olivier Boudreau, | |
| | fallow land | |
| # 127 | Abraham Roy fallow land | |
| # 128 | Paul Leblanc | 26 |
| | Anne Babain, w | 26 |
| | Marcel, s | 3 |
| | Marie Roze, d (mos.) | 7 |
| # 129 | François Simon | 41 |
| | Marie Corpron, w | 34 |
| | Joseph, s | 9 |
| | René, s | 7 |
| | Alexis, s | 3 |
| | Morize, s (mos.) | 6 |
| | Margueritte, d | 5 |
| # 130 | Pierre Lanoue | 22 |

| # 131 | Joseph Malançon | 18 |
| # 132 | Joseph Mire | 27 |
| # 133 | Joseph Lanoue | 23 |
| # 134 | Pierre Blanchard | 20 |
| | Land occupied by Alibamu Indians | |
| | Land occupied by Houma Indians | |
| # 135 | Jean Sonné | 23 |
| # 136 | François Douan | 21 |
| # 137 | François Andro | 21 |
| | Genevieve Hébert, w | 23 |
| | Jeanne, d (mos.) | 10 |
| | Land not granted | |
| # 138 | Ollivier Landry | 17 |
| # 139 | Mazain Landry | 20 |
| # 140 | René Landry | 53 |
| | Anne Landry, w | 37 |
| | Joseph, s | 12 |
| | Firmain, s | 9 |
| # 141 | Anne Landry, widow Melançon | 29 |
| | Ollivier Melançon, s | 9 |
| | Simon, s (mos.) | 16 |
| | Margueritte, d | 7 |
| # 142 | Charles Melançon | 26 |
| | Felicité Landry, w | 19 |
| | Magdelaine Leblanc, m | 52 |
| # 143 | Paul Melançon | 39 |
| | Marie Theriot, w | 33 |
| | Jean Baptiste, s | 10 |
| | Philippe, s | 19 |
| | Magdelaine, d | 13 |
| | Marie, d | 8 |
| | Bazille Landry, b.l. | 19 |
| # 144 | Isaac Leblanc | 23 |
| | Marie Melançon, w | 24 |
| # 145 | Joseph Grangé | 24 |
| | Genevieve Babain, w | 21 |
| # 146 | Pierre Landry | 48 |
| | Froizine Gautherot, w | 45 |
| | Firmain, s | 10 |
| | Paul, s | 7 |
| | Ozitte, d | 16 |
| | Baptiste Grangé, s.l. | 16 |

| # 147 | Firmain Broussard | 17 |
| | Jean, b | 9 |
| # 148 | Jean Landry | 15 |
| # 149 | Baptiste Landry | 14 |
| # 150 | Abandoned grant | |
| # 151 | Paul Bros | 24 |
| # 152 | Baptiste Breau | 45 |
| | Marie Landry, w | 39 |
| | Jean, s | 18 |
| | Magdelaine, d | 20 |
| | Anne, d | 15 |
| | Ester, d | 10 |
| # 153 | Armant Breau | 16 |
| # 154 | Estienne Landry | 27 |
| # 155 | Simon Landry | 25 |
| | Margueritte Babain, w | 30 |
| | Margueritte, d | 1 |
| | Marie Babain, s.l. | 16 |
| # 156 | Pierre Leblanc | 38 |
| | Anne Landry, w | 32 |
| | Anne, d | 10 |
| | Marie Leblanc, o | 16 |
| # 157 | Amant Babain | 27 |
| | Nastazie Landry, w | 22 |
| | Paul, s (mos.) | 15 |
| | Izabelle Landry, s.l. | 15 |
| # 158 | Joseph Babain | 24 |
| | Marie Babain, w | 20 |
| | Anne Thèriot, widow Babain, m | 48 |
| # 159 | Charles Babain | 27 |
| | Magdelaine Babain, w | 24 |
| | Joseph, s (mos.) | 4 |
| # 160 | Efraine Babain | 24 |
| | Margueritte Leblanc, w | 22 |
| | Magdelaine, d (mos.) | 8 |
| | Bergitte, si | 19 |
| # 161 | Jacques Landry | 26 |
| | Françoise Blanchart, w | 22 |
| | Victore Landry, s | 1 |
| | Joseph Landry, b | 18 |
| # 162 | Charles Landry | 31 |
| | Marie Landry, w | 22 |
| | Pelagie, si | 20 |
| # 163 | Jacques Babain | 22 |

## RECAPITULATION

| | | | |
|---|---|---|---|
| Men bearing arms | 163 | Horses | 50 |
| Women | 103 | Hogs | 1867 |
| Boys under 15 yrs. | 120 | Sheep | 16 |
| Girls — 1 to 20 yrs. | 115 | Guns | 164 |
| Land granted (arpents) | 1148 | Total population—slave | |
| Slaves | 36 | exclusive | 501 |
| Cattle | 512 | | |

Dated: September 14, 1769      Signed: Louis Judice

### FOOTNOTES

Abbreviations designate:

w — wife
s — son
d — daughter
m — mother
s.l. — son-in-law
d.l. — daughter-in-law
b — brother
si — sister
m.l. — mother-in-law

b.l. — brother-in-law
si.l. — sister-in-law
wd. — widow
o — orphan
engager — hired help
ss. — stepson
sd. — stepdaughter
n — nephew

N.B. — According to the heading on this census, it is supposed to be the census of the Acadians, but several listed are not Acadian: Cantrelle, Judice, etc. This census covers St. James and Ascension Parishes ... then called La Cote d'Acadie. Many of the names are spelled differently from other census given.

## MILITIA OF THE FIRST ACADIAN COAST
### January 23, 1770
### OFFICERS

Don Nicholas Verret — Captain
Don Michel Cantrelle — Lieutenant
Don Jacques Cantrelle, Jr. — Second Lieutenant

### RIGHT BANK
#### FROM SIEUR PIROTEAU'S TO SIEUR DUCROIX'S
#### SOLDIERS

| NAME | AGE | NATIONALITY | STATE |
| --- | --- | --- | --- |
| Jean Baptiste Adam | 33 | Louisianian | Single |
| Baptiste Bergeron | 19 | Acadian | Single |
| Laimable Blanchard | 28 | Acadian | Married |
| Joseph Blanchard | 31 | Acadian | Married |
| Paul Gravois | 18 | Acadian | Single |
| Joseph Gravois | 16 | Acadian | Single |
| Jacques Gaudain | 27 | Acadian | Married |
| Victor Gaudain | 16 | Acadian | Single |
| Joseph Hébert | 34 | Acadian | Married |
| Pierre Lambert | 21 | Acadian | Single |
| Joseph Landry | 21 | Acadian | Married |
| Simon LeBlanc | 28 | Acadian | Married |
| Joseph Melançon | 17 | Acadian | Single |
| Jean Richard | 25 | Acadian | Married |
| Auguste Verret | 15 | New Orleanian | Single |
| Jacques Verret | 16 | New Orleanian | Single |

### LEFT BANK
#### FROM SIEUR DUPART'S TO GERMAIN BERGERON'S

| NAME | AGE | NATIONALITY | STATE |
| --- | --- | --- | --- |
| Jean Arcenaux | 41 | Acadian | Married |
| Pierre Arcenaux | 39 | Acadian | Married |
| Joseph Arcenaux | 29 | Acadian | Married |
| Jean Bellefontaine | 25 | Acadian | Single |
| Michel Bourgeois | 34 | Acadian | Married |
| Baptiste Bourgeois | 37 | Acadian | Married |
| Joseph Bourgeois | 33 | Acadian | Married |
| Pierre Bourgeois | 23 | Acadian | Married |
| Paul Bourgeois | 39 | Acadian | Married |
| Joseph Bourg | 32 | Acadian | Married |
| Pierre Bourg | 18 | Acadian | Married |
| Jean Baptiste Bernard | 15 | Acadian | Single |
| Germain Bergeron | 25 | Acadian | Married |
| Pierre Barrios | 40 | Acadian | Married |
| Pierre Bertaud | 29 | Acadian | Married |
| Pierre Bernard | 38 | Acadian | Married |
| Charles Coruseau | 19 | Acadian | Single |
| Jean Baptiste Cormier | 32 | Acadian | Married |

Sugar Harvest in Louisiana — Harper's Weekly Oct. 30, 1875. (Courtesy Leonard V. Huber)

At left—Building a Bonfire on the levee for Christmas celebration.

Coming from Church on Bayou Lafourche — near Donaldsonville. Harper's Weekly Jan. 19, 1867. (Courtesy Leonard V. Huber)

# SIGNATURES OF FAMOUS MEN OF ST. JAMES

(Governor of Louisiana)

(Acadian exile)

(First Spanish Commandante)

(First parish judge)

(Negro sheriff – Reconstruction)

(The orthographic puzzle)

| | | | |
|---|---|---|---|
| Pierre Chiasson | 41 | Acadian | Married |
| Joseph Comeaux | 30 | Acadian | Married |
| Paul Doucet | 26 | Acadian | Single |
| Jean Baptiste Damour | 15 | Acadian | Single |
| Charles Damour | 20 | Acadian | Married |
| Joseph Faures | 41 | Acadian | Married |
| Pierre Forest | 32 | Acadian | Married |
| Charles Gaudet | 22 | Acadian | Single |
| Firmain Girior | 20 | Acadian | Single |
| Joseph Gillebeau | 29 | Acadian | Married |
| Joseph Guedry | 37 | Acadian | Married |
| Jean Baptiste Gaudain | 24 | Acadian | Married |
| Joseph Gaudet | 32 | Acadian | Married |
| Joseph Hebert | 32 | Acadian | Married |
| Prosper Hebert | 22 | Acadian | Single |
| Mathurin Hebert | 16 | Acadian | Single |
| Pierre Hebert | 30 | Acadian | Married |
| François Hebert | 28 | Acadian | Single |
| Jean Pierre Leblanc | 42 | Acadian | Married |
| François Landry | 28 | Acadian | Married |
| Louis Mouton | 28 | Acadian | Married |
| Ambroise Martin | 35 | Acadian | Married |
| Salvador Mouton | 35 | Acadian | Married |
| Pierre Michel | 32 | Acadian | Married |
| Joseph Martin | 33 | Acadian | Married |
| Jean Baptiste Melançon | 28 | Acadian | Married |
| Simon Mire | 25 | Acadian | Married |
| Belhouny Mire | 33 | Acadian | Married |
| Charles Mouton | 28 | Acadian | Married |
| Joseph Poirier | 28 | Acadian | Married |
| Michel Poirier | 31 | Acadian | Married |
| François Part | 16 | Acadian | Single |
| Joseph Part | 28 | Acadian | Single |
| Olivier Part | 24 | Acadian | Single |
| Pierre Part | 21 | Acadian | Single |
| Abraham Roy | 40 | Acadian | Single |
| Jean Roger | 18 | Acadian | Single |
| Joseph Richard | 31 | Acadian | Married |
| Jean Saunier | 21 | Acadian | Single |
| Jean Savoie | 19 | Acadian | Single |
| Joseph Solet (Sauley) | 34 | French | Married |
| François Savoie | 38 | Acadian | Married |
| Joseph Theriot | 32 | Acadian | Married |
| Baptiste Thibodeau | 28 | Acadian | Single |
| Charles Thibodeau | 24 | Acadian | Married |
| Pierre Vincent | 25 | Acadian | Married |

N.B. — This list of the Militia of St. James Parish of 1770 is taken from: Papeles Procedentes de Cuba, 161, General Archives of the Indies, Seville, Spain.

The militia of July 1770 had the following additional soldiers:

| NAME | AGE | NATIONALITY | STATE |
|---|---|---|---|
| Honoré Breau | 23 | Acadian | Single |
| Charles Breau | 18 | Acadian | Single |
| Jean Bourgeois | 29 | Acadian | Married |
| Pierre Blanchard | 19 | Acadian | Single |
| Jean Baptiste Dambaises | 20 | Acadian | Single |
| Joseph Dupuis | 26 | Acadian | Single |
| Joseph Dupuis | 18 | Acadian | Single |
| Paul Dario | 17 | Acadian | Single |
| Simon Gautheraux | 33 | Acadian | Married |
| Jean Gisclare | 35 | French | Married |
| Joseph LeBlanc | 20 | Acadian | Single |
| Marcelle Leblanc | 38 | Acadian | Married |
| Joseph Lanaux | 24 | Acadian | Married |
| Paul Leblanc | 27 | Acadian | Married |
| Charles Louviere | 20 | Acadian | Single |
| Jacques Melançon | 19 | Acadian | Single |
| Joseph Mire | 26 | Acadian | Single |
| Jean Poirier | 37 | Acadian | Married |
| Bazille Prejean | 24 | Acadian | Married |
| Louis Pacquet | 30 | Canadian | Single |
| Thomas Theriot | 25 | Acadian | Single |
| Jean Baptiste Verret | 24 | Louisianian | Single |

CENSUS OF ACADIAN COAST — 1777

Archivo General de Indias
Papeles de Cuba, 190

January 1, 1777 . . . General Census of the inhabitants who are established in the environs of the Parish of St. James at Cabahannocer on both sides of the river. . . .

## RIGHT BANK

| | Age |
|---|---|
| Sieur Jacques Cantrelle, former Captain | 80 |
| Marguerite de Larmuzieaux, wife | 65 |
| Michel Cantrelle, son, Lieutenant Commandante | 27 |
| Jacques Cantrelle, son, Second Lieutenant | 25 |
| Marie Cantrelle, widow Verret (of former Commandante) | 44 |
| Nicholas Verret, son | 26 |
| Jacques Verret, son | 24 |
| Auguste Verret, son | 23 |
| Philippe Verret, son | 19 |
| Louis Verret, son | 17 |
| Marie Verret, daughter | 27 |
| Marguerite Verret, daughter | 20 |
| | |
| Jean Gisclare, beadle of the parish | 44 |
| Marguerite Eustache, wife | 25 |
| Jean Louis, son | 11 |
| Nicholas, son | 9 |
| Catherine, daughter | 5 |
| Felicité, daughter | 3 |
| Marguerite, daughter | 2 |
| | |
| Rev. Father Prospert, Curé | 78 |
| François Croizet former inhabitant of Pointe Coupée | 54 |
| Marianne Trepages, wife | 35 |
| François, son | 24 |
| Marie, daughter | 16 |
| Manette, daughter | 14 |
| Jeanne, daughter | 12 |
| Henriette, daughter | 10 |
| Elizabeth, daughter | 8 |

| | |
|---|---|
| Helaine, daughter | 6 |
| Suzanne, daughter | 3 |
| Émilie, daughter (mos.) | 6 |
| | |
| Pierre Arcenaux, Acadian inhabitant | 45 |
| Anne Bergeron, wife | 34 |
| Louis, son | 7 |
| Pierre, son | 5 |
| Rozalie, daughter | 13 |
| Marie, daughter | 10 |
| Françoise, daughter | 4 |
| Charles Arcenaux, orphan | 19 |
| | |
| Charles Arsenaux | 22 |
| Marie Josephe Babin, wife | 15 |
| | |
| Pierre Arcenaux | 28 |
| Marie Bergeron, wife | 22 |
| Pierre, son | 7 |
| Joseph, son | 5 |
| Marianne, daughter of the so-called Pierre Bourgeois | 3 |
| Louise, daughter of the so-called Pierre Bourgeois | 2 |
| (probably these two little ones were separated from their parents and could not be identified properly.) | |
| | |
| Pierre Darrios (Barrios) | 40 |
| Marie Bourgeois, wife | 42 |
| | |
| Simon Leblanc | 35 |
| Anne Bergeron, wife | 31 |
| Alexandre, son | 7 |
| Edouard, son | 5 |
| Constance, daughter | 3 |
| Jean Roger | 20 |
| Guianne (Guillame) engager (hired help) | 34 |

— 183 —

| | |
|---|---|
| Joseph Hébert | 45 |
| Anne Prejean, wife | 42 |
| Joseph, son | 9 |
| Paul, son | 7 |
| Jean, son | 5 |
| Marguerite, daughter | 17 |
| | |
| Bonnaventure Gaudin | 56 |
| | |
| Marguerite Bergerson, wife | 57 |
| Bonnaventure, son | 20 |
| Michel, son | 18 |
| Theotiste, daughter | 26 |
| Marie, daughter | 22 |
| | |
| Lachaussay, surgeon | 50 |
| Marie Bourgeois, wife | 46 |
| Philippe, son | 5 |
| Louise, daughter | 22 |
| Rozalie, daughter | 7 |
| Joseph Gravois, son-in-law | 24 |
| Jean, son-in-law | 22 |
| | |
| Jean Baptiste Damboiser | 45 |
| Marguerite Bergeron, wife | 57 |
| Marin, son | 22 |
| Mathurin, son | 20 |
| Rozallie, daughter | 8 |
| Victoire, daughter | 5 |
| | |
| Jean Baptiste Bergeron | 26 |
| Marie Faurest (Foret), wife | 22 |
| Michel, son | 1 |
| | |
| Joseph Blanchart (Blanchard) | 29 |
| Marie Dupuis, wife | 25 |
| Rozallie, daughter | 3 |
| Anastasie, daughter | 2 |
| Elizabeth, orphan | 8 |
| | |
| François Morreaux | 32 |
| Marie Melanson, wife | 40 |
| Louis, son | 2 |
| Jean Baptiste, step-son | 20 |
| Dominique, stepson | 17 |
| Ozitte, stepdaughter | 19 |

| | |
|---|---|
| Honoré Breau | 28 |
| Magdelaine, wife | 26 |
| Marie, daughter | 3 |
| | |
| Alexis Breau | 52 |
| Magdelaine Trahaut (Trahan) wife | 54 |
| Charles, son | 24 |
| Alexis, son | 11 |
| Anastasie, daughter | 14 |
| Charles Trouhaut (Trahan) orphan | 11 |
| | |
| Charles Gaudet | 48 |
| Cecile Breaux, wife | 39 |
| Joseph Cloitre, son | 15 |
| Charles, son | 12 |
| Michel, son | 4 |
| Jerome, son | 2 |
| Magdelaine Cloitre, orphan | 14 |
| (probably the Joseph Cloitre above mentioned was Magdelaine's brother and an orphan also.) | |
| | |
| Gerome Gaudet | 33 |
| Marie Doucet, wife | |
| | |
| Anasthase Breau | 45 |
| Marie Leblanc, wife | 34 |
| Joseph, son | 13 |
| Paul, son | 2 |
| Anastazie, daughter | 12 |
| Marie, daughter | 7 |
| Anne, daughter | 5 |
| | |
| Joseph Leblanc | 57 |
| Elizabeth Gaudet, wife | 57 |
| Gille, son | 17 |
| Grégoire, son | 15 |
| | |
| Joseph Leblanc | 25 |
| Marguerite Leblanc, wife | 28 |
| Simon, son | 3 |
| Rozallie, daughter | 5 |
| Magdelaine, daughter | 1 |

| | | | | |
|---|---|---|---|---|
| Simon Gautherau | 41 | Ozitte Barbé, daughter | | 8 |
| Magdelaine Breau, wife | 35 | Angelique, daughter | | 5 |
| Louis, son | 11 | | | |
| Jean Baptiste, son | 9 | Joseph Babin | | 30 |
| Charles, son | 7 | Marie Landry, wife | | 27 |
| Simon, son | 5 | Louis, son | | 14 |
| Marie Magdelaine, daughter | 3 | Elizabeth, daughter | | 6 |
| | | Marguerite, daughter | | 4 |
| Jacques Leblanc | 68 | Joseph Breau | | 25 |
| Catherine Faurest, wife | 67 | Marie Melanson, wife | | 20 |
| | | Hilaire, son | | 2 |
| Marcelle Leblanc | 45 | | | |
| Marie Breau, wife | 41 | Jacques Babin | | 27 |
| Silvain, son | 7 | Marguerite Landry, wife | | 25 |
| Paul, son | 1 | Donatte, son | | 3 |
| Marguerite, daughter | 14 | Paul, son | (mos.) | 4 |
| Marie Joseph, daughter | 11 | Pelagie, daughter | | 5 |

LEFT BANK OF THE MISSISSIPPI RIVER

| | | | | |
|---|---|---|---|---|
| Michelle Chiasson | | 20 | Joseph Saunier | 45 |
| | | | Marguerite, daughter | 8 |
| Bazitte Claire | | 28 | Magdelaine Grangé, daughter-in-law | 19 |
| Joseph Melanson | | 23 | Marie Babin, orphan | 14 |
| Joseph Dupuis | | 24 | Ollivier Boudreau | 49 |
| Marie Poirier, wife | | 21 | Anne Gaudet, wife | 51 |
| Marie, daughter | | 2 | | |
| Monique, daughter | (mos.) | 5 | Simon Boudreau | 21 |
| | | | Monique Dupuis, wife | 21 |
| Pierre Lanoue | | 30 | Marie, daughter | 1 |
| Catherine Leblanc, wife | | 25 | | |
| Simon, son | | 6 | François Antailla | 40 |
| Michelle, son | | 4 | Marie Leblanc, wife | 42 |
| Marianne, daughter | | 1½ | Jean Baptiste, son | 7 |
| | | | Maddes, son | 5 |
| Paul Leblanc | | 33 | Besson, son | 3 |
| Anne Babin, wife | | 33 | | |
| Marcelle, son | | 11 | Joseph Fayant | 40 |
| Jacques, son | | 6 | Marguerite Richard, wif | 17 |
| Paul, son | | 4 | Ozitte Hébert | 45 |
| Marie, daughter | | 8 | | |
| Pollone, daughter | (mos.) | 9 | Joseph Melanson, son | 22 |
| | | | Estienne, son | 20 |
| Jacques Melanson | | 24 | Paul, son | 14 |
| Elizabeth Landry, wife | | 21 | Charles, son | 9 |
| Joseph, son | | 2 | Williame, engager (hired hand) | 37 |
| Paul, son | (mos.) | 3 | Charles, engager (hired hand) | 29 |

| | | | | |
|---|---|---|---|---|
| Thomas Theriot | | 32 | Charles Louviere | 26 |
| Anne Daigle, wife | | 25 | Elizabeth, wife | 30 |
| Cezar, son | | 5 | Louis, son (mos.) | 6 |
| Hubert, son | | 3 | Anne, daughter | 6 |
| François, son | (mos.) | 10 | Felicitée, daughter | 4 |
| | | | Genevieve, daughter | 2 |
| Xavier Theriot | | 19 | Jacques Lhabit (no status given) | 14 |
| Ambroise Theriot | | 27 | Pierre Bernard | 44 |
| | | | Cecile Bergeron, wife | 42 |
| Jean Baptiste Adam | | 36 | Joseph Dugas, son | 22 |
| | | | Pierre Bernard, son | 18 |
| Jean Baptiste Melanson | | 36 | Nicholas Lahure (no status given) | 8 |
| Ozitte Dupuis, wife | | 33 | Louis Bernard, son | 3 |
| Eusebe, son | | 8 | Delaide, daughter | 5 |
| Marie, daughter | | 5 | Joseph Arcenaux | 35 |
| Genevieve, (no status given) | | 5 | Marie Bergeron, wife | 31 |
| Pierre Breaux | | 37 | Jean Charles, son | 3 |
| Brigitte Faurest, wife | | 24 | Françoise, daughter | 10 |
| Marie Charlotte, daughter (mos.) | | 4 | Marianne, daughter | 8 |
| Jean Roger (no status given) | | 22 | Collastie, daughter | 5 |
| | | | Theodore Bergeron, orphan | 14 |
| Pierre Chiasson | | 48 | | |
| Ozitte Landry, wife | | 44 | François Part | 26 |
| Jean Baptiste, son | | 8 | Anne Bergeron, wife | 27 |
| Bazille, son | | 6 | Rozalie, daughter | 6 |
| Simon, son | | 3 | Izidore Damour, orphan | 13 |
| Monique Ustache, orphan | | 18 | | |
| | | | Joseph Richard | 41 |
| Marie Josephe Faurest | | 38 | Marie Martin, wife | 41 |
| Theotiste, daughter | | 6 | Louis, son | 10 |
| Marie, daughter | | 4 | Pierre, son | 3 |
| Rabar, engager (hired hand) | | 40 | Simon, son | 2 |
| | | | Marie, daughter | 10 |
| Jean Arcenaux | | 47 | Roze, daughter | 7 |
| Judice Bergeron, wife | | 44 | Françoise, daughter | 7 |
| Joseph, son | | 20 | Angelique, daughter | 5 |
| Guillame, son | | 18 | | |
| Paul, son | | 15 | Pierre Part | 28 |
| François, son | | 6 | Marguerite Melanson, wife | 30 |
| Laurent, son | | 4 | François, son | 4 |
| Manon, daughter | | 8 | Joseph, son | 3 |
| | | | François Damour, orphan | 17 |
| Jean Baptiste Gaudin | | 28 | Marguerite Brounard | |
| Jean Baptiste, son | | 7 | (Broussard), mother | 57 |
| Marguerite, daughter | | 5 | Ollivier Part, brother | 30 |
| Françoise, daughter | | 2 | | |
| Rozalie, daughter | | 8 | | |

| | |
|---|---|
| Belhonny Mirre | 43 |
| Magdelaine Melanson, wife | 33 |
| Benjamin, son | 5 |
| Jean Baptiste, son | 1 |
| Scolastie, daughter | 8 |
| Marie, daughter | 7 |
| Felicité, daughter | 7 |
| Rozalie, daughter | 4 |
| Joseph Mirre, brother | 34 |
| | |
| Simon Mirre | 33 |
| Magdelaine Cormier, wife | 36 |
| Joseph, son | 8 |
| Pierre, son | 6 |
| Simon, son | 4 |
| Marianne, daughter | 10 |
| Pelagie, daughter | 2 |
| | |
| Marie Cormier | 32 |
| Pierre Poirier, son | 10 |
| Joseph, son | 8 |
| Marguerite, daughter | 6 |
| Rozalie, daughter | 3 |
| | |
| Jean Baptiste Bernard | 22 |
| Magdelaine Bergeron, wife | 18 |
| | |
| Joseph Bourgeois | 41 |
| Marie Giroir, wife | 40 |
| Scolastie, daughter | 7 |
| Celeste, daughter | 2 |
| | |
| Marie Broussard, orphan | 10 |
| Jean Rabier, orphan | 13 |
| | |
| Michel Bourgeois | 36 |
| Anne Landry, wife | 33 |
| Jean Baptiste, son | 2 |
| Soffie, daughter | 7 |
| Angelique, daughter | 5 |
| Victoire, daughter | 4 |
| | |
| Pierre Blanchard | 25 |
| | |
| François Landry | 35 |
| Rozalie Dugas, wife | 27 |
| Edouard, son | 2 |
| Marguerite, daughter | 6 |

| | | |
|---|---|---|
| Marie Rose, daughter | | 4 |
| Jean Mixe, engager (hired hand) | | 28 |
| | | |
| Charles Savoy | | 51 |
| Judice Arcenaux, wife | | 40 |
| Jean Baptiste, son | | 14 |
| Joseph, son | | 8 |
| Emédée, son | | 8 |
| | | |
| Daniel Normant | | 25 |
| Françoise, wife | | 22 |
| Daniel, son | | 3 |
| Joseph, son | | 1 |
| | | |
| Antoine La Bauve | | 50 |
| Anne Vincent, wife | | 40 |
| Marain, son | | 18 |
| Jean, son | | 18 |
| Pierre, son | | 9 |
| Izidorre, son | | 5 |
| Paul, son | (mos.) | 5 |
| Adelayde, daughter | | 7 |
| Ludivine, daughter | | 3 |
| Modeste, daughter | ( mos.) | 5 |
| | | |
| Jean Baptiste Picone | | 31 |
| Marie Lorotte, wife | | 19 |
| Marie Louise, daughter | | 3 |
| | | |
| Madame Dufresne | | 66 |
| Madame Morrice | | 20 |
| Jacques Bouvillain | | 47 |
| Charlotte Sintire, wife | | 36 |
| Jacques, son | | 13 |
| Jean Baptiste, son | | 3 |
| Marianne, daughter | | 17 |
| Genevieve, daughter | | 15 |
| Charlotte, daughter | | 8 |
| Felicité, daughter | | 6 |
| Pierre, son | | 2 |
| | | |
| Charles Scellier | | 56 |
| Marie Roze (no status given) | | 52 |
| Michel Tourel, engager (hired hand) | | 46 |

| | | | |
|---|---|---|---|
| Joseph Martin | 38 | Pierre Michel | 39 |
| Marguerite Pitre, wife | 37 | Marie Leger, wife | 33 |
| Joseph, son | 12 | François, son | 9 |
| Michel (no status given) | 4 | Joseph, son | 4 |
| Marguerite, daughter | 8 | Marie, daughter | 7 |
| Marie, daughter | 6 | Anastasie Dugas, daughter | 5 |
| Pelagie, daughter | 2 | Colasty, daughter | 1 |
| | | | |
| Joseph Guedry | 42 | Paul Martin | 28 |
| Elizabeth Coumeau, wife | 36 | Paul Leger, engager | |
| Donat, son | 8 | (hired hand) | 19 |
| Joseph, son | 7 | | |
| Alexandre, son | 5 | Ambroise Martin | 42 |
| Felicité, daughter | 3 | Magdelaine Gaudin, wife | 39 |
| Judice, daughter | 1 | Paul, son | 2 |
| | | Helainne, daughter | 16 |
| Pierre Lambert | 51 | Elizabeth, daughter | 12 |
| Marie Deron, wife | 40 | Marguerite, daughter | 7 |
| Michelle (no status given) | 8 | Rozalie, daughter | 5 |
| Joseph, son | 4 | Jean Gaudin, brother-in-law | 30 |
| Felix, son | 3 | | |
| Paul, son | 1 | Germain Bergeron | 31 |
| Anne, daughter | 10 | Marguerite LeBlanc, wife | 25 |
| Pelagie, daughter | 6 | Jean Louis, son | 5 |
| Pierre ( no status given) | 26 | Elizabeth, daughter | 7 |
| | | Marie, daughter | 3 |
| Andrée Ouvre | 45 | | |
| Marie Bouvillain, wife | 44 | Louis Pacquet | 48 |
| François, son | 7 | Marie Leblanc, wife | 24 |
| Pierre, son | 3 | Jean Lambroumont, orphan | 8 |
| Binjamin, son | 2 | Charles Gaudet, son | 25 |
| Françoise, daughter | 15 | | |
| Charlotte, daughter | 13 | Michel David | 58 |
| Bazil Derroche, engager | | Genevieve Hebert, wife | 50 |
| (hired hand) | 20 | Jean, son | 18 |
| | | Claude, son | 16 |
| Pierre Vincent | 34 | Pierre David, son | 6 |
| Marguerite Cormier, wife | 34 | Angelique, daughter | 12 |
| Joseph, son | 7 | Rozalie, daughter | 5 |
| Charles, son | 5 | Marie, daughter | 3 |
| Felix, son | 4 | | |
| Rozallie, daughter | 1 | Paul David | 23 |
| | | Pelagie Oubre, wife | 18 |
| François Savoy | 37 | Marie, daughter | 1 |
| Marie Martin, wife | 31 | | |
| François son | 13 | Charles Coumeau | 55 |
| Pierre, son | 10 | Marguerite Babin, wife | 49 |
| Jean, son | 7 | François, son | 8 |
| Marie, daughter | 6 | Anne, daughter | 14 |

| | |
|---|---|
| Arneaux Sceville | 38 |
| Agnes, wife | 19 |

| | |
|---|---|
| Jean Bourgeois | 38 |
| Ludivine Granger, wife | 27 |
| Dominique (no status given) | 7 |
| Jean Louis (no status given) | 2 |
| Felicité, daughter | 5 |

| | |
|---|---|
| Baptiste Bourgeois | 44 |
| Ozitte Melanson, wife | 45 |
| Jean Baptiste, son | 16 |
| Joseph, son | 12 |
| Pierre, son | 8 |
| Tadée, son | 6 |
| Paul, son | 2 |
| Izaac Leblanc, stepson | 16 |
| Jozime Leblanc, stepson | 14 |
| Simon Leblanc, stepson | 9 |
| Helaine Leblanc, stepdaughter | 11 |
| Marie, daughter | 5 |
| Marguerite, daughter | 4 |

| | |
|---|---|
| Joseph Poirier | 37 |
| Marie Bourgeois, wife | 27 |
| Pierre, son | 10 |
| Louis, son | 8 |
| Marie, daughter | 6 |
| Marguerite, daughter | 4 |

| | |
|---|---|
| Michel Bourgeois | 42 |
| Ozitte Gauthrerau, wife | 42 |
| Paul, son | 8 |
| Marguerite, daughter | 2 |
| Magdelaine, daughter | 2 |

| | |
|---|---|
| Joseph Theriot | 46 |
| Magdelaine Bourgeois, wife | 37 |
| Pierre, son | 10 |
| Joseph, son | 8 |
| Jean, son | 4 |
| Rozallie, daughter | 18 |
| Marie, daughter | 13 |
| Magdelaine, daughter | 1 |
| Paul Doucet, engager (hired hand) | 33 |

| | |
|---|---|
| Abraham Roy | 47 |
| Madelaine Doucet, wife | 41 |
| Pierre, son | 17 |
| Charles, son | 14 |
| Sauveur, son | 17 |
| Joseph, son | 6 |
| Marguerite, daughter | 12 |

| | |
|---|---|
| Andrée Bourgeois | 57 |
| Andrée, son | 24 |
| Marie, daughter | 12 |

| | |
|---|---|
| Jean Sonnier | 25 |
| Marie Roy, wife | 17 |
| Jean Baptiste, son | 4 |
| Rozallie, daughter | 3 |

| | |
|---|---|
| Pierre Laperine | 51 |
| Marie Bourgeois, wife | 52 |
| Nicholas, son | 16 |
| Jean, son | 14 |

| | |
|---|---|
| Jean Baptiste Correaux | 50 |
| Marie Thérese Assays, wife | 40 |
| Joseph Sincire, son | 13 |
| Grégoire, son | 13 |
| George, son | 10 |
| Baptiste, son | 19 |
| Catherine, daughter | 9 |

| | |
|---|---|
| Pierre Charpentier | 57 |
| Jeanne Moutarne, wife | 45 |
| Jean Baptiste, son | 7 |
| Victoire, daughter | 17 |
| Perine, daughter | 14 |
| Marguerite, daughter | 9 |
| Marie, daughter | 7 |
| Louise, daughter | 3 |

| | |
|---|---|
| Jacques Lhabet | 45 |
| Thérese Goreau, wife | 35 |

| | |
|---|---|
| Marie François Lagrange | 40 |
| Pierre Fonteneau, son | 26 |
| Louis, son | 24 |
| Morice, son | 18 |
| Augustin, son | 14 |
| François, son | 2 |

| | | | |
|---|---|---|---|
| Arriée, son | 18 | Antoine Chauf | 26 |
| Elizabeth, daughter | 20 | Marie David, wife | 21 |
| Jacques Irlandois, engager | 32 | Louis, son | 1 |
| | | | |
| Pierre Brignac | 50 | François Dufresne | 30 |
| Marie Louise Fonteneau, wife | 36 | Françoise Poitier, wife | 25 |
| Mathieu, son | 20 | François, son | 5 |
| Alexandre, son | 14 | Joseph, son | 3 |
| Marie Louise, daughter | 18 | Charles Dufresne, brother | 27 |
| | | | |
| Saveur Lacombe | 62 | | |
| Anne Lacombe, daughter | 17 | Edmond Rousseaux | 29 |
| Francois Colombe, son-in-law | 26 | | |
| Marie Colombe, wife | 25 | Etienne Toup | 37 |
| Froisine, daughter of Francois (mos.) | 11 | Délery | ? |
| | | Mathias Frederick | 40 |
| Jean Marcotte | 37 | Marie Bernard, wife | 40 |
| Marguerite Traigle, wife | 24 | Mathias, son | 13 |
| François, son | 5 | Jean Pierre, son | 12 |
| Gennevieve, daughter | 1 | Antoine, son | 9 |
| | | François, son | 7 |
| Bastianne Illme | 25 | Marie Magdelaine, daughter | 22 |
| Gennevieve Badouin, wife | 21 | Catherine, daughter | 20 |
| André Hedlemaire, foster son | 1 | Marianne, daughter | 18 |
| Charlotte, daughter | 6 | Aniesse, daughter | 5 |
| | | Charlotte, daughter | 3 |
| Jean Baptiste Lagrange | 22 | | |
| Marie Louise Dubier, wife | 20 | Louis Mouton | 40 |
| Jean Baptiste, son | 1 | Marie Barastarache, wife | 44 |
| Marie Louise, daughter | 2 | David, son | 7 |
| Nicolas Troclay (no status given) | 24 | Anne, daughter | 12 |
| | | Elizabeth, daughter | 3 |
| Thomas Dervain | 35 | | |
| Catherine Maderne, wife | 40 | Charles Mouton | 56 |
| Marguerite, daughter | 12 | Anne Coumeau, wife | 55 |
| Jean Baptiste Eustache, orphan | 12 | George, son | 21 |
| Marie Dervain, daughter | 9 | Marie Mouton, niece | 12 |
| | | | |
| Jacques Troclay | 21 | Pierre Berteau | 38 |
| Marie Baudoin, wife | 18 | Roze Savoy, wife | 36 |
| François Lembert, orphan | 14 | Charles, son | 9 |
| | | Joseph, son | 5 |
| Louis Josome | 36 | Françoise, daughter | 10 |
| Magdelaine David, wife | 20 | Marie, daughter | 4 |
| Louis (no surname given), orphan | 7 | Marguerite, daughter | 3 |
| | | Elizabeth, daughter | 1 |

| | |
|---|---|
| Michel Goudain | 26 |
| Magdelaine Delony | 27 |
| Marie, daughter | 7 |
| Anne, daughter | 5 |
| | |
| Saturnain Bruneau | 34 |
| Colastie Leger, wife | 30 |
| Pierre, son | 8 |
| Joseph, son | 3 |
| Adelahide, daughter | 5 |
| Marguerite, daughter | 1 |
| | |
| Pierre Le Baut | 28 |
| Magdelaine Illme, wife | 16 |
| | |
| Joseph Gaudet | 38 |
| Marguerite Bourgeois, wife | 33 |
| Jean, son | 10 |
| Joseph, son | 2 |
| Rozalie, daughter | 13 |
| Marie, daughter | 5 |
| | |
| Joseph Bourg | 43 |
| Marguerite Durel, wife | 42 |
| Joseph, son | 14 |
| Jean Baptiste, son | 11 |
| Bazille, son | 8 |
| Victoire, daughter | 16 |
| Roze, daughter | 15 |
| Marie Roze, daughter | 7 |
| Anne, daughter | 6 |
| Pelagie, daughter | 3 |
| | |
| Joseph Blanchard | 38 |
| Ester Bourgeois, wife | 26 |
| Morice, son | 3 |
| Joseph, son | 2 |
| Frederick, son | 1 |
| Felicité, daughter | 6 |
| | |
| François Hebert | 42 |
| Magdelaine Trahout, wife | 44 |
| Honnorée, son | 10 |
| Charles, son | 5 |
| Joseph, son | 1 |
| Elizabeth, daughter | 12 |

| | |
|---|---|
| Jean Leger | 55 |
| Cecile Poirier, wife | 52 |
| Widow Faurest | 56 |
| Jean Baptiste Faurest, orphan | 4 |
| Rozalie, orphan | 7 |
| Marguerite, orphan | 3 |
| Pierre Poirier, orphan | 13 |
| | |
| Charles Thibodeau | 36 |
| Marie Landry, wife | 25 |
| Jean Charles, son | 2 |
| Marguerite, daughter | 7 |
| Magdelaine, daughter | 5 |
| Marie, daughter (mos.) | 7 |
| | |
| Jean Richard | 57 |
| Catherine Cormier, wife | 56 |
| Rozalie, daughter | 21 |
| | |
| Jean Poirier | 40 |
| Magdelaine Richard, wife | 35 |
| Jean, son | 17 |
| François, son | 12 |
| Michel, son | 3 |
| Marie, daughter | 10 |
| | |
| Jean Richard | 32 |
| Rozalie Bourgeois, wife | 26 |
| Pierre, son | 8 |
| Paul, son | 6 |
| Michel, son | 1 |
| Pellagie, daughter | 4 |
| | |
| Jean Baptiste Cormier | 68 |
| Marie Richard, wife | 51 |
| Pierre Bourg, son-in-law | 24 |
| Anastasie Cormier, wife | 24 |
| Marguerite, daughter | 2 |
| Rozalie, daughter | 2 |
| Felicité, daughter | 5 |
| Charles Bourg, orphan | 15 |
| | |
| Firmin Giroire | 26 |
| Marguerite Cormier, wife | 25 |
| Simon, son | 5 |
| Jacques, son | 4 |
| Pierre, son (mos.) | 5 |

| | | | |
|---|---|---|---|
| Joseph Landry | 27 | Pierre Savant | 21 |
| Anne Cormier, wife | 30 | Françoise Manuel, wife | 19 |
| Joseph, son | 7 | | |
| | | Pierre, son | 2 |
| | | Charlotte, daughter | 3 |
| Laimable Blanchard | 34 | | |
| Anastasie Giroire, wife | 32 | Joseph Ouvre | 20 |
| Marrain, son | 12 | Marie Manuel, wife | 22 |
| Nastazie, daughter | 9 | | |
| Pierre, son | 7 | Joseph Canadien | 30 |
| Marguerite, daughter | 3 | Marienne Lambert, wife | 18 |

|  |  |
|---|---|
| Total land owned | 1020 arpents |
| Slaves | 172 |
| Cattle | 2204 |
| Horses | 388 |

Signed: Michel Cantrelle, Lieutenant Commandante of the King at the Post of Cabahan-noces

Dated: April 15, 1777

---

## THE FIRST GRAND JURY IMPANELED IN ST. JAMES — JULY 8, 1805 — WAS COMPOSED OF:

| | |
|---|---|
| J. M. Armant | Joseph Landry |
| Jacques Roman | Olivier Theriot |
| P. Uriell | J. W. Scott |
| G. Roulier | Christophe Colomb |
| Pierre Richard | Daniel Blouin |
| A. D. Tureaud | Antoine Palau |
| Paul Ebert | Pierre Theriot, alias Perret |
| Politte Babin | Jean Berry |
| Charles Frederic | Jean Charles Arcenaux |
| Pierre Carmouche | Etienne Reynes |
| Joseph Comes | Joseph Landry, Fils. |

Taken from the records of the St. James Parish Courthouse archives.

LIST OF FAMILIES IN ST. JAMES ON EAST BANK IN 1807, taken from René de Sennegy, "Une Paroisse Louisianaise."

Abraham Arcenaux
Charles Arcenaux
Jean Arcenaux
Laurent Arcenaux
Simon Arcenaux
Major Beaulier
Étienne Dugas
Jean Dugas, dit Cadet
Joseph Dugas
Vve. Dumaine
Vve. Honoré Duriz
Joseph Gaudet
Joseph Michel
Pierre Michel
Benjamin Mirre
Joseph Mirre
Paul Mirre
Pierre Mirre
Theodore Bergeron
Vve. André Bernard
Baptiste Bernard
Michel Bernard
Louis Gaudin
Luc Gaudin
Bonaventure Gaudin
Louis Gaubert
Donat Guidry
Jacques Grabert
Paul Hébert
Charles Berteau
Jean Bery
Charleville Blouin
Baptiste Bouillon
Baptiste Bourgeois P.
Vve. Joseph Bourgeois
Vve. Paul Bourgeois
Jh. Paul Bourgeois
Simon Paul Bourgeois
Pierre Bourgeois
Joseph Caillouet
Jacques Cantrelle II
Jean Cable
Jean Baptiste Charpiot
A. Chapdu
Jean Baptiste Chiasson
J. Chauvin
Coussot
Jean Décareau
J. Dicharry
Martin Dubourg
Vve. Jean Baptiste Gaudin
M. Myet (Millet)
Pierre Oubre
Régile Oubre
Jh. Part
Pierre Part
Regis Part
J. L. Part
Baptiste de Louvière
Pierre Lanaux
Robert Lavigne
Joseph Landry
Joseph Larosa
Eudré LeBlanc
Jacques LeBlanc
Donat Landry
Vve. Isaac Leblanc
Pierre LeBourgeois
Noel Matherne
Alexandre Melançon
Ant. Melançon
Henry Melançon
Hippolite Melançon
Oliv. Melançon
Vve. Michel Migan
Paul Pertuis
Jean Peytavin
Ethelder Picou
Joseph Poirier
François Poché
Jacob Poché
Louis Rodic
Alexis Rome
Pierre Richard
Christofle Roussel
Georges St. Cyre
Nicholas Saurage
Sexnayder
Joseph Theriot
Basile Thibodeaux
Charles Thibodeaux
François Tircuit
Jean Baptiste Vickner

# LIST OF OFFICERS OF THE MILITIA OF 1808 — SIXTH REGIMENT
## (ST. JAMES PARISH)

Taken from the files of *Le Diamant*, Vol 1   No. 21

| | |
|---|---|
| Colonel: | Jean Baptiste Armant. |
| Captains: | J. B. Cantrelle, P. Perret, J. Reynaud, J. Gomes, O. Theriot, J. W. Scott, J. Benois, P. Theriot. |
| Lieutenants: | V. Roman, J. Cantrelle, L. Keller, F. Landry, J. Perret, L. Landry. |
| Second Lieutenants: | C. Cantrelle, R. Breaux, J. Bujeau, M. Breaux, B. Mire, J. Michel. |
| Adjutants: | P. Hebert, J. Landry. |
| Standard Bearers: | L. Cantrelle, J. Conway. |

## TAXPAYERS OF ST. JAMES — 1808

List of taxpayers of the Coast of Cabahannocer (St. James Parish) dated October 15, 1808. . . . Taken from: "Archives of the Spanish Government of West Florida," Vol. III, pp. 414-419.

French terms used herein:
Père — father or senior
Fils — son or junior
Vieux — old
veuve — widow
Et — and
Mineurs de — minors of
Frères — brothers
Dit — called or alias
Sa mère — his or her mother
négociânt — merchant

The names are spelled and arranged (in the order) as they appeared in the document.

Autin, George
Arcenaux, L.
Arcenaux, Michel
Arcenaux, François
Arcenaux, Jean
Arcenaux, Gabriel
Arcenaux, Jh. (probably Joseph)
Arcenaux, Jh., fils
Berthelot, Henri
Bery, A.
Bodouin, Jean
Bon Amy, Alexis C.
Bringier, D.

Bourg, Jh. (vieux Jo)
Braux, Armant
Babin, Benjamin
Bourgeois, Baptiste
Bourgeois, Veuve Amant
Bourgeois, Paul
Braux, Honoré
Bernard, André
Bernard, Baptiste
Blouin, Daniel
Boudro, Simonet, fils
Bourgeois, Pierre
Bourg, Jh.

Bourgeois, Jn. L.
Bourgeois, Edouard
Blanchard, Frederick
Braux, Manuel
Blanchard, Pierre
Babin, Polite
Bello, William
Breaux, Alexis
Bergeron, Theodore
Breau, Hypolite
Breau, Constance,
    veuve de Simond Breau
Berthaud, Charles
Bourgeois, Simon, fils
Bourgeois, Jh.
Bringier, Douradou Ml.
Caillouet, Jh.
Chisnaeldre, Adam
Cornu, Marcely
Cloatre, Joseph
Clairo, Antoine
Cailler, Jh.
Cormier, Anastasie,
    veuve de Pierre Bourg
Coxe, John
Chiasson, Jean Baptiste
Dumaine, Jean
Duhon, François
Dugas, Gregoire
Dugas, Jh.
Dupuy, Pierre
Darosa, Jh.
Dugas, Jh., père
Dugas, Jh., fils
Éber, Jn. P.
Fabre, Jh. L.
Frederic, Pierre
Frederic, les mineurs
Frederic, Antoine
Frederic, François
Frederic, Catherine,
    veuve de Nas. Troxcler
Frederic, Charles
Falgoults, Ls.
Fowler, Richard
Gisclar, Noel
Gaudin, Bonnaventure
Guedry, Jh., père
Guedry, Donat
Guedry, Pierre

Guedry, Alexandre
Gravois, Auguste
Godet Michel
Godet, Auguste
Grégoire, Ls., dit Maltais
Granger, Ludivine,
    veuve Jn. Bourgeois
Garcie, Antoine
Godet, Jh.
Graber, Jacques
Gaudin, Luc
Gaudin, Bonnaventure, fils
Guerlain, L. H.
Houvre, Pierre
Hymel, Ls.
Hymel, André
Hebert, Paul
Houvre, Henry
Joseph, Michel
Keller, Nas. (Nicholas)
Luquet, Baptiste
Loup, Pierre
Leblanc, Giles
Landry, Jh., fils
Levert, Jh.
Lanoue, Michel
Lanoue, Simon
Lasseigne, Noel
Ledoux, Antoine
Leblanc, Helene,
    veuve Jh. Bourgeois
Landry, Jh., père
Landry, Jh., fils
Leblanc, Jean Baptiste
Leblanc, Donat
Leblanc, Olivier
Lalande, Edouard
Leblanc, Isaac
Leblanc, Dque. (Dominique)
Landry, Valentin
Leblanc, Benjamin
Lanoix, Pierre
Landry, Jh. A.
Michel, François
Michel, Jh.
Myr, Pierre
Millet, Alexis
Melançon, Henry
Melançon, Eusebe
Melançon, Jh.

Momet (?) Baptiste de Lignac
Materne, Noel
Myr, Benjamin
Mouton, George
Melançon, Baptiste
Myr, Jean Baptiste
Malarcher, Chevalier
Olivier, Pierre
Pocher, François
Poirié, Jh
Dart, Pierre
Pauché, Jacques
Part, Jn. Ls. (Jean Louis?)
Pierre à Michel, fils
Picou, Etelder
Perret, Alexis
Priestley, William
Paul, David
Pertuit, Paul
Perret, Pujol & Alphonse, frères
Poirier, Marguerite,
   veuve Charles Hebert
Rome, Jean
Reyne, Marguerite
Richard, Simon
Rom, David
Rémy Hubert
Roussel, Cristophe

Roman, Jacques
Rom, Alexis (?)
Reine, Étienne
Rom, Abraz.
Sionaux, dit Dumoulin, Pierre
Saint-Cyr, George
Sechnedre, Jn. Paul
Tassin, Me. Jeanne, veuve Curo
Terril, Justin
Troscler, Auguste
Tomelet, Jh.
Theriot, Jh.
Thibodeau, père et fils,
   Charles & Olivier
Troxler, Cristophe
Toups, Étienne
Tregre, Antoine
Thibodeau, Jean Charles, fils
Tureaud, A. D.
Thomeé, Charles
Terrio, Charles & Etienne
Terrio, Olivier
Vioner, Jean Baptiste
Vebre, Jn.
Vickner, Jean Baptiste
Vincent, Felix & Charles, frères
Villiarasse, Evariste, négociant
   de sa mère, Rosalie Andry.

This is not a complete list of all the taxpayers of St. James Parish in 1808. They were the taxpayers who owed taxes at that time. The amount of taxes due was $1097 . . . an average of $6.31 . . . no wonder we hear so much about the *good old days*.

# LIST OF PLANTATION OWNERS IN ST. JAMES PARISH IN 1845-56*

| WEST BANK | MILES FROM NEW ORLEANS |
|---|---|
| Mrs. Joseph Melançon | 73 |
| Onézime LeBlanc | 72 |
| Mrs. Jos. Gautreau & Co. | 71 |
| Nicholas & Bell | 71 |
| Évariste Mire | 71 |
| Évariste Blouin | 70 |
| B. Winchester | 70 |
| Valery Gaudet | 70 |
| Michel Bergeron | 69 |
| François Gannier & Co. | 69 |
| Poirier Brothers | 67 |
| P. M. Lapice | 65 |
| E. J. Forstall | 64 |
| M. B. Cantrelle | 63 |
| Estate Mrs. Webre | 63 |
| J. X. Cantrelle | 62 |
| A. B. Roman | 62 |
| Choppin & Roman | 61 |
| David & Robin | 60 |
| Mrs. V. Roman & Co. | 59 |
| T. S. Roman | 58 |
| Valcour Aime Refinery | 57 |
| J. Armant | 56 |
| Locoul & Dupare | 55 |
| Sosthene Roman | 54 |
| L. Saxon & Co.* | 53 |
| J. S. Armant | 53 |
| Évariste Champagne | 52 |

*Name almost illegible

| EAST BANK | MILES FROM NEW ORLEANS |
|---|---|
| Mrs. Tureaud & Co. | 71 |
| Mrs. James Conway | 71 |
| Aristide Landry | 70 |
| Mrs. Donat Landry & Co. | 69 |
| J. B. Penny & Co. | 68 |
| Mrs. Alexandre Melançon | ...... |
| Jean Chardon | 67 |
| Joseph Hébert | ...... |
| Noel Jourdan & Gaudin | 66 |
| Ed. Jacob & Co. | ...... |
| P. & O. Colomb | ...... |
| Adolphe Malarcher | 65 |
| Vasseur Webre | ...... |
| Amant Bourgeois | ...... |
| Mrs. Malarcher & Sons | 64 |
| François Duhon | ...... |
| J. B. Boucry & Co. | 63 |
| Samuel Fagot | ...... |
| Arnaud LeBourgeois | 61 |
| W. Welham | ...... |
| Donat Guidry | 59 |
| Pierre Theriot | 58 |
| J. B. Caillouet | ...... |
| Welham & Godberry | 57 |
| Mrs. L. leBourgeois | ...... |
| Mrs. Mather & Co. | 56 |
| A. Terry & Co. | 55 |
| Eugene Bourgeois | 54 |
| C. & D. Bourgeois | ...... |
| Edouard Bourgeois | .... |
| J. L. Délatte | 53 |
| J. B. Parent & Co. | ...... |
| Livain Bourgeois & Co. | ...... |
| Jean Laiche | 52 |
| Dr. A. Humphreys | ...... |
| François Reine | ...... |
| Gervais Gaiennie | 51 |
| Moses Shepherd | 50 |
| Armant Duplantier | 49 |

*This is taken from P. A. Champomier, A statement of the sugar crop made in Louisiana, 1846.

## ST. JAMES SOLDIERS IN THE CIVIL WAR

A complete file of the St. Jamesians who fought in the Civil War is not now available, but a partial list follows:

Colonel Léopold Armant
Evariste Bergeron
Michel Bergeron
Aristide Berthaut
J. Bingay
A. Blouin
Camille Blouin
Al. Bourgeois
C. Bourgeois
Theodore Bourgeois
Adelard Braud
E. Braud
Numa Braud
Louis Chauvin
Pierre Chauvin
S. Choppin (Surgeon)
Livingston Clouatre
Alfred Colomb
Camille Comes
Juste Comes
Auguste Damaré
F. Damaré
F. Dicharry
David Donaldson
Capt. Henry Doyle
Capt. Jules Druilhet
Hippolite Dubourg
Placide Dubourg
Joseph Dufresne
Louis Dugas
Capt. Alb. Ferry
George Ferry
Justin Fontenaux
Louis Fortier
Michel Fortier
Clement Frederick
M. B. Gainie
Aristide Gaudin
Emile Gaudin
Leon Gaudin
Simon Gaudin
J. A. Gaudet
Leonard Gaudet
O. Gaudet
T. Gaudet
Rosemond Gaudet
Capt. Jos. Gonzales
Jean Granier
Constant Gravois
Donat Gravois
Charles Green
Camille Hebert
Théophile Himel
Thoédore Huguet
Lieut. Emile Jacob
Jules Jacob
Octave Jacob
Valsin Jacob
Adelard Jourdan
Augustin Keller
Aristide Keller
Auguste Lambert
Eusebe Lambert
Felicien Lambert
Aristide Landry
Donat Landry
Donat Lanoux
Landry Lanoux
Alexandre Leblanc
Eloi Leblanc
Elphege Leblanc
Euphemon Leblanc
Gregoire Leblanc
Emile Lebréton
Emile Letulle
V. Letulle
E. Laiche
Jos. Louque
Onésiphore Melançon
Camille Mire
Cleophas Mire
Leon Mire
Ozémé Mire
Theodule Mire
Prudent Mire
Edgard Naquin
Edouard Nicolle
Tekelet Nicolle

Telismar Nicolle
C. L. Ory
F. Ory
A. Oubre
Ludger Peytavin
............... Phelt
Capt. Felix Poché
Octave Poché
Pierre Poché
Leivin de Poorter
Caesar Porta
J. Pourcine
Amilcar Reine
Optimé Richard
Telesphor Richard
Hughes Reider
Colonel Alfred Roman
Victor Rome
Auguste Roussel
Alfred Roussel
Charles Roussel
Joseph Roussel
Marcelin Roussel
Ovide Roussel
Pierre Roussel
Auguste Sarazin
Lucien Schexnaildre
Cleophas Schexnaildre
Xavier Sarazin

Eugene St. Cyr
Numa St. Pierre
Sauveur Subra
Antoine Sobral
Alph. Sexchnaidre
E. Schexnaidre
Et. Schexnaidre
Leno. Tetrau
Bob. Triche
Belisaire Tomassi
Brigadier-General Trudeau
Louis Trudeau
E. Thibodeau
Arthur Theriot
Felix Waguespack
Joseph Walsh
Adolphe Webre
Alfred Webre
Charles Webre
Emile Webre
Ernest Webre
Melphor Webre
Septime Webre
Vasseur Webre
Dick Winchester
Capt. Felix Winchester
Edmond Zeringue
Fortuné Zeringue

Taken from Sennegy, René de: Une Paroisse Louisianaise and the List of Pensioners, Board of Pension Commissioners, 1916.

A few of the above listed may be from Ascension instead of St. James. It was exceedingly difficult to differentiate between the two. It is quite possible that Sennegy did not list all who served. His list is not official.

## LIST OF ST. JAMESIANS WHO PARTICIPATED IN THE SPANISH-AMERICAN WAR

| NAME | RATING | COMPANY | PERIOD OF SERVICE |
|---|---|---|---|
| McPherson, J. A. | Sergeant | B — 2d La. Vl. Inf. | May 2, 1898 to April 8, 1 |
| Meyer, E. A. | Corp. | B — 2d La. Vl. Inf. | May 2, 1898 to April 8, 1 |
| Nettles, J. B. | Pvt. | B — 2d La. Vl. Inf. | May 2, 1898 to April 8, 1 |
| Lafosse, P. A. | Pvt. | B — 2d La. Vl. Inf. | May 2, 1898 to Jan. 7, 189 |
| Prescott, L. D. | Pvt. | B — 2d La. Vl. Inf. | May 2, 1898 to Dec. 31, 18 |
| Colomb, E. | Pvt. | Batt. B La. Lt. Art. | June 21, 1898 to Nov. 22, 1 |
| Plaisance, G. | Sergeant | Batt. B La. Lt. Art. | June 21, 1898 to Nov. 22, 1 |
| Guidry, J. | Ferrier | Batt. B La. Lt. Art. | June 21, 1898 to Nov. 22, 1 |
| Levert, F. A. | Ferrier | Batt. B La. Lt. Art. | June 21, 1898 to Nov. 22, 1 |
| Folse, R. J. | Pvt. | Batt. B La. Lt. Art. | June 21, 1898 to Nov. 22, 1 |
| Erwin, T. | Pvt. | Batt. B La. Lt. Art. | June 21, 1898 to Nov. 22, 1 |
| Rutledge, J. R. | Pvt. | Batt. B La. Lt. Art. | June 21, 1898 to Nov. 22, 1 |
| Bourgeois, E. S. | Pvt. | CO. L 2d La. Vl. Inf. | |
| Copponex, Emile P. | | | |

The above list is taken from the report of the Adjutant General of the state of Louisiana for the year ending December 31, 1900.

## EXECUTIVE OFFICERS OF ST. JAMES PARISH FROM ITS FOUNDING TO THE PRESENT TIME

| | | |
|---|---|---|
| Jacques Cantrelle | French Commander | *1765 - 1768 |
| Nicholas Verret | Spanish Commandante | 1768 - 1775 |
| Michel Cantrelle | Spanish Commandante | 1776 - 1805 |
| Michel Cantrelle | American Territorial Judge | 1805 - 1812 |
| Antoine Maurin | Sheriff | 1815 - 1817 |
| Charles André Cérisay | Sheriff | 1817 - 1833 |
| Arnaud LeBourgeois | Sheriff | 1833 - 1843 |
| Eugene Ory | Sheriff | 1843 - 1855 |
| John B. Ory | Sheriff | 1856 - 1859 |
| Sosthene Theriot | Sheriff | 1860 - 1871 |
| J. Celestin Olivier** | Sheriff | 1871 - 1872 |
| William H. Hagins* | Sheriff | 1872 - 1875 |
| Victor Miles** | Sheriff | 1875 - 1880 |
| A. Livain Bourgeois | Sheriff | 1880 - 1896 |
| Louis Le Bourgeois | Sheriff | 1896 - 1912 |
| Joseph B. Dornier | Sheriff | 1912 - 1948 |
| Gaston Brignac | Sheriff | 1948 - 1956 |
| Gordon Martin | | 1956 - |

*Approximate date
**Negro Sheriffs

List taken from the St. James Parish Courthouse Archives.

## JUDGES OF THE DISTRICT COURT

| | |
|---|---|
| Michel Cantrelle | 1805 - 1812 |
| Augustin D. Tureaud | 1812 - 1826 |
| André Bienvenu Roman | 1826 - 1828 |
| William Fabre | 1828 - 1830 |
| Lewis M. Taney | 1830 - 1839 |
| Jean Jacques Roman | 1839 - 1846 |
| Thomas C. Nicholls | 1846 - 1847 |
| Robert Wellman Nicholls | 1847 - 1849 |
| Albert Duffel | 1849 - 1859 |
| William C. Lawes | 1860 - 1861 |
| St. M. Berault | 1861 - 1862 |
| Raphael L. Beauvais | 1864 - 1872 |
| O. J. Flagg | 1873 - 1876 |
| Morris Marks | 1876 - 1877 |
| Henry L. Duffel | 1878 - 1879 |
| John A. Cheevers | 1880 - 1884 |
| Henry L. Duffel | 1884 - 1892 |
| Walter Guion | 1892- -1900 |
| Paul Leche | 1900 - 1912 |
| Charles Wortham | 1912- -1916 |
| Philip H. Gilbert | 1916 - 1920 |
| Sam A. LeBlanc | 1920 - 1929 |
| Philip H. Gilbert | 1930 - 1932 |
| Henry L. Himel | 1932 - 1950 |
| Clyde V. St. Amant | 1950 - |

Listed in the St. James Parish Courthouse Archives.

## PASTORS OF ST. MICHEL DE CANTRELLE

| | |
|---|---|
| 1809 - 1812 | No resident pastor |
| 1812 (October) | Rev. Gabriel Chambon de la Tour |
| 1813 | Rev. Ligúe de L'Espinasse |
| 1818 | Rev. Charles Mariani |
| 1820 | Rev. Anselin |
| 1822 | Rev. Charles Mariani |
| 1822 | Rev. Martin |
| 1823 | Rev. Charles de la Croix |
| 1834 | Rev. Boué |
| 1840 | Rev. Pierre Ladavière, S.J. |
| 1849 | Rev. G. F. Abbadie, S.J. |
| 1853 | Rev. L. Dufour |
| 1853 | Rev. I. Benoit |
| 1854 | Rev. Tholomier |
| 1857 | Rev. E. Vigonnet |
| 1863 | Rev. Henri Bellanger, S.M. |
| 1869 | Rev. Onézime Renaudier, S.M. |
| 1885 | Rev. Felix Coppin, S.M. |

| | |
|---|---|
| 1887 | Rev. Jean Baptiste Descreux, S.M. |
| 1898 | Rev. Francis Morcel, S.M. |
| 1899 | Rev. Jean Marie Le Grand, S.M. |
| 1908 | Rev. Joseph Delahaye, S.M. |
| 1931 | Rev. Francis Georgelyn, S.M. |
| 1937 | Rev. Aime Ratté, S.M. |
| 1938 | Rev. Ernest Pfleger, S.M. |
| 1944 | Rev. Constantin Chauve, S.M. |
| 1950 | Rev. Paul Rietsch, S.M. |
| 1950 | Rev. Constantin Chauve, S.M. |

This list does not include acting pastors and assistants. List taken from the St. Michael's Church Records.

## VARIOUS ENUMERATIONS OF THE POPULATION

| Date | White People | Slaves | Arpents Of Land | Cattle | Hogs | Guns | Horses |
|---|---|---|---|---|---|---|---|
| April 9, 1766 | 266 | 16 | 687 | 15 | 95 | 97 | 0 |
| Sept. 14, 1769 | 501 | 36 | 1148 | 512 | 1867 | 163 | 50 |
| Jan. 1, 1777 | 699 | 172 | ............ | 2204 | ............ | ............ | 50 |
| 1785 | 1332 | | | | | | |
| 1788 | 1559 | | | | | | |
| 1803 | 2200 | | | | | | |
| 1830 | 2254 | 5027 Free persons of color 60 Foreigners 26 | | | | | |

## CENSUS OF 1830-1840

| | |
|---|---|
| Whites | 2762 |
| Slaves | 5711 |
| Free Negroes | 75 |
| Students at the college and the convent | 545 |
| Cattle | 4762 |
| Hogs | 3290 |
| Sheep | 5107 |
| Corn | 155,790 bu. |
| Cotton | 1,032,950 lbs. |
| Sugar | 15,157,000 lbs. |
| Manufactured goods | $246,000 |
| Stores | 10 |

## CENSUS OF THE PARISH 1850

| | |
|---|---|
| Whites | 3285 |
| Slaves | 7751 |
| Free persons of color | 62 |
| Foreigners | 8 |

## OFFICIALS OF THE PARISH OF ST. JAMES — 1957

| | | |
|---|---|---|
| Gordon J. Martin | Convent, La. | Sheriff |
| Laurie J. Roussel | Hester, La. | Representative |
| A. J. Nobile, M.D. | Lutcher, La. | Coroner |
| Andre Abadie | Vacherie, La. | Assessor |
| Lawrence J. Babin | Convent, La. | Clerk of Court |

### POLICE JURORS

| | | |
|---|---|---|
| Louis Martin | Paulina, La. | 1st Ward Member |
| Ernest Roussel | Hester, La. | 2nd Ward Member |
| James I. Hymel | Rt. 1, Convent, President | 3rd Ward Member |
| Willy J. Boudreaux | Rt. 1, Convent, La. | 4th Ward Member |
| Wilfred Poirrier | Welcome, La. | 5th Ward Member |
| Guy J. Caire | St. James, La. | 6th Ward Member |
| Francis Waguespack | Vacherie, La. | 7th Ward Member |
| A. D. Constant | Vacherie, La. | 8th Ward Member |
| Lawrence Vicknair | Gramercy, La. | 9th Ward Member |
| G. C. Boucvalt | Lutcher, La., Vice-President | 10th Ward Member |
| E. J. Roussel | Hymel, La. | Secretary |
| Alvyn Woods | Lutcher, La. | Treasurer |
| Sidney A. Gaudet | Vacherie, La. | Registrar of Voters |

### SCHOOL BOARD MEMBERS

| | | |
|---|---|---|
| Louis Brady, Jr. | Paulina, La. | 1st Ward |
| Marks Poche | Hester, La. | 2nd Ward |
| Edward Rome | Rt. 1, Convent, La. | 3rd Ward |
| Winnie T. Keller | Rt. 1, Convent, La. | 4th Ward |
| Sidney E. Wood | Welcome, La. | 5th Ward |
| Cyril Waguespack | St. James, La. | 6th Ward |
| J. Paul Gravois | Vacherie, La. | 7th Ward |
| Joseph Waguespack | Vacherie, La. | 8th Ward |
| O'Neil Weber | Gramercy, La. | 9th Ward |
| Thomas J. Foret | Lutcher, La., President | 10th Ward |
| E. L. Roussel | Lutcher, La., Superintendent | |

### DISTRICT OFFICERS

| | |
|---|---|
| Judge of the Twenty-Third District | Clyde V. St. Amant |
| District Attorney | Aubert D. Talbot, Jr. |
| Senator . . . Eleventh District | Farrell Blanchard |

St. James Parish is part of the twenty-third judicial district and the second Congressional district.

## ST. JAMES TODAY

LOCATION: On either side of the Mississippi River, approximately midway between New Orleans and Baton Rouge.

BOUNDARIES: N. Ascension — E. St. John — Lafourche — W. Assumption.

**AREA:** 219,520 acres.

**SURFACE:** Level.

**SOIL:** Very fertile, mostly alluvial.

**AVERAGE TEMPERATURE:** Winter 54° — Summer 82°.

**AVERAGE RAINFALL:** 57 to 60 inches.

**ELEVATION:** At Convent 18 ft.

**POPULATION:** 15,351.

**NUMBER OF FARMS:** 446.

**OCCUPATIONS:** Farming, trapping, manufacturing, trade, mining.

**PRODUCTS:** Sugar, corn, rice, truck, potatoes, oats, hay, tobacco, fruit, Pecans, moss, oil, gas, furs, cattle, poultry, eggs, swine, game, fish, sheep, etc.

**TRANSPORTATION FACILITIES:** Rail, deep water, motor.

**HIGH SCHOOLS:** Lutcher, Romeville, St. James.

**TOWNS:** Lutcher, Gramercy, Vacherie.

**BANKS:** St. James Bank & Trust Company (Lutcher), Vacherie Bank (Vacherie).

**CHURCHES:** Catholic in every community. Protestant at Lutcher.

**NEWSPAPER:** News-Examiner, River Parishes Journal.

**POLITICAL DIVISION:** 10 wards.

**COUNTY SEAT:** Convent.

# BIBLIOGRAPHY

Aime, Valcour. *Plantation Diary of the late Mr. Valcour Aime.* New Orleans, Clark and Hofeline, 1878.
Alvord, Clarence Walworth. ed. *Kaskaskia Records, 1778-1790;* with introduction and notes. (Collections, U.S.; Virginia Series 2 v.) Illinois State Historical Library, Springfield, Ill., 1909.
Alvord, Clarence Walworth. *The Illinois Country, 1673-1818.* Illinois State Historical Library, Springfield, Ill., 1920.
................ *American State Papers, Public Lands,* Vol. II, Washington, D. C., 1834.
Baudier, Roger. *The Catholic Church in Louisiana.* New Orleans, Hyatt, 1939.
Biggar, H. P. *The Early Trading Companies of New France.* Toronto, Warwick Bros. & Rutter, 1901.
Billon, Frederick L. *Annals of St. Louis in Its Early Days under the French and Spanish Dominations, 1764-1804.* St. Louis, 1886.
................ *Biographical and Historical Memoirs of Louisiana,* Vol. II. Chicago, Goodspeed Publishing Co., 1892.
Booth, Andrew B. *Records of Louisiana Soldiers and Louisiana Confederate Commands.* Vols. I, II, III. New Orleans, 1920.
*Boucry Family Account Books, 1814-1884.* 1910.
Breaux, Joseph A. *Some Early Colleges and Schools of Louisiana.* New Orleans, Publication of the Louisiana Historical Society, Vol. VII, 1913-14.
Calhoun, Robert Dabney. *The Origin and Early Development of County-Parish Government in Louisiana.* New Orleans, The Louisiana Historical Quarterly. Vol. XVIII.
Callan, Louise. *The Society of the Sacred Heart in North America.* New York, Longmans, Green, & Co., 1937.
................ *Catholic Action of the South.* New Orleans, Vol. XI, No. 35, 1943.
Caughey, John Walton. *Bernardo De Galvez in Louisiana 1776-1783.* Berkeley, University of California Press. 1934.
Caulfield, Ruby Van Allen. *The French Literature of Louisiana.* New York, Institute of French Studies, Columbia University, 1929.
Chambers, Henry Edward. *A History of Louisiana.* Vol. I. Chicago and New York American Historical Society, 1925.
Champomier, P. A. *Statement of the Sugar Crop Made in Louisiana.* New Orleans, Magne and Weisse, 1846.
Chapin, Adele Le Bourgeois. *Their Trackless Way.* New York, Henry Holt & Co., 1932.
Deiler, John Hanno. *The Settlement of the German Coast of Louisiana and the Creoles of German Descent.* Philadelphia, Americana Germanica Press, 1909.
Delanglez, Jean. *The French Jesuits in Lower Louisiana, 1700-1763.* Baltimore, J. H. Furst Co., 1953.
Ditchy, Jay Karl. *Les Acadiens Louisianais et Leur Parler.* Baltimore, John Hopkins Press, 1932.
Dorman, Caroline. *Forest Tress of Louisiana and How to Know Them.*

New Orleans, Dept. of Conservation, Bulletin 15, 1928.

............... . *Early Voyages Up and Down the Mississippi by Cavelier, St. Cosme, Le Sueur, Gravier, Guignas with an Introduction, Notes, and an Index by John Dawson Gilmary Shea.* Munsell's Historical Series #8. Albany, Joel Munsell, 1861.

English, William Hayden. *Conquest of the Country Northwest of the Ohio.* 1778-1783, with biography of George Rogers Clark, 2 v., Bobbs.

Fortier, Alcée. *History of Louisiana,* Vol. III. Nazi-Joyant, 1904.

Fortier, Alcée. *Louisiana, Comprising Sketches of Counties, Towns, ........Events, etc.* Vol. I, II. Atlanta, Sou. His. Assn., 1901.

Fortier, Alcée. *Louisiana Folk Tales.* Boston and New York, Houghton Mifflin, 1895.

Fortier, Alcée. *Louisiana Studies.* New Orleans, F. F. Hansell & Bro. 1894.

Gayarré, Charles Etienne Arthur. *A History of Louisiana.* Vol. I, II, III. New Orleans, Hansell, 1903.

Hodge, Frederick Webb. *Handbook of American Indians North of Mexico.* Part I. Washington, Smithsonian Institution Bureau of American Ethnology, Bulletin 30, Government Printing Office, 1912.

King, Grace Elizabeth Edna. *Creole Families of New Orleans.* New York, the Macmillan Co., 1921.

Kniffen, Fred Bouerman. *The Indians of Louisiana.* Baton Rouge, Bureau of Educational Materials, Statistics and Research, Louisiana State University, 1945.

Lauvriere, Emile. *Histoire de la Louisiane Française 1673-1939.* University, Louisiana. Louisiana State University Press, 1940.

LeBlanc, Dudley J. *The True Story of the Acadians.* Lafayette, 1932.

Lindsey, Coleman. *The Government of Louisiana.* Baton Rouge, Louisiana Library Commission, 1937.

............... . *Louisiana, A Guide to the State Compiled by Workers of the Writers' Program of the Works Projects Administration in the State of Louisiana.* New York, Hastings House, 1941.

............... . *The Louisiana Historical Quarterly.* New Orleans, Louisiana Historical Society, Vol. I, No. 1 — Vol. XXVII, No. 4, 1917-1944.

Lowry, Richard P. *A History of the Public Schools of St. James Parish.* (Thesis presented to the faculty of Louisiana State University), 1928.

Marchand, Sidney Albert. *Acadian Exiles in the Golden Coast of Louisiana.* Donaldsonville, 1943.

Marchand, Sidney Albert. *The Flight of a Century in Ascension Parish, Louisiana.* Baton Rouge, Ortlieb, 1936.

Magruder, Harriet. *History of Louisiana.* Boston, D. C. Heath & Co., 1909.

Martin, Desirée. *Les Viellées d'une Soeur ou Le Destin d'un Brin de Mousse.* New Orleans, Imprimerie Cosmopolite, 1877.

Martin, François Xavier. *The History of Louisiana from the Earliest Period.* New Orleans, Lyman & Beardslee, 1827-1829.

McWilliams, Richebourg Gaillard. *Fleur de Lys and Calumet.* Baton Rouge, Louisiana State University Press, 1953.

Peytavin, John Ludger, Unpublished Memoirs.

Pittman, Captain Philip. *The Present State of the European Settlements on the Mississippi.* Cleveland, the Arthur H. Clark Company, 1906.
Procter, Albert. *The Acadian House.* Hammond, The Louisiana Progress, October 21, 1938.
Read, William Alexander. *Louisiana French.* Baton Rouge, Louisiana State University Press, 1931.
Read, William Alexander. *Louisiana Place Names of Indian Origin.* Baton Rouge, Louisiana State University Press, 1927.
Ripley, Eliza Moore McHatton. *Social Life in Old New Orleans.* New York and London, D. Appleton & Co., 1912.
Robertson, James Alexander. *Louisiana Under the Rule of Spain, France, and the United States, 1785-1807.* Vol. I, II. Cleveland, The Arthur H. Clark Co., 1911.
Saxon, Lyle. *Old Louisiana.* New York and London. Century, 1929.
Schlarman, Joseph H. *From Quebec to New Orleans; the story of the French in America, Fort de Chartres.* Buechler Publishing Company, Belleville, Ill., 1929.
Scroggs, William Oscar. *The Story of Louisiana.* Indianapolis, Bobbs-Merrill, 1924.
Seebold, Herman de Bachellé. *Old Louisiana Plantation Homes and Family Trees.* Vol. I, II. New Orleans, Pelican Press, 1941.
Sennegy, René de. *Une Paroisse Louisianaise, St. Michel du Comté d'Acadie.* New Orleans, Capo, 1877.
................ *Spain in the Mississippi Valley, 1765-94.* Annual report of the American Historical Association for the Year 1945, Vol. II. Washington, D. C., Government Printing Office.
Spratling, William P. and Scott, Natalie V. *Old Plantation Houses in Louisiana.* New York, Helburn, 1927.
Swanton, John Reed. *Indian Tribes of the Lower Mississippi Valley and the Adjacent Coast of the Gulf of Mexico.* Washington, Bureau of American Ethnology, Bulletin 43, Government Printing Office, 1911.
Tinker, Edward Laroque. *Bibliography of French Newspapers and Periodicals.* Worcester, American Antiquarian Society, 1933.
Wallace, Joseph. *The History of Illinois and Louisiana Under the French Rule.* Cincinnati, Robert Clarke & Co., 1893.
................ *Yearbook of the Louisiana Society, Sons of the American Revolution, 1919-1920-1921.*

## MISCELLANEOUS RECORDS

Ascension Parish Courthouse Archives — Donaldsonville, Louisiana.
The Illinois State Historical Library — Springfield, Illinois.
The Library of Congress — Washington, D. C.
The Louisiana State University Library — Baton Rouge, Louisiana.
The William Henry Smith Memorial Library — Indianapolis, Indiana.
The St. James Parish Courthouse Archives — Convent, Louisiana.
The St. Louis Cathedral Archives — New Orleans, Louisiana.
The St. Louis University Library — St. Louis, Missouri.
State Land Office Records — Baton Rouge, Louisiana.
St. Michael's Church Records — Convent, Louisiana.
The Spanish Archives — Seville, Spain.

## INTERVIEWS

Bourgeois, Louis S. — Convent, Louisiana.
Braud, Felisca — Convent, Louisiana.
Brignac, Gaston — Convent, Louisiana.
Chauvin, Charles — Union, Louisiana.
Copponex, Mrs. Euphrasie Bourgeois — New Orleans, Louisiana.
Dornier, Joseph B. — Convent, Louisiana.
Gravois, Ernest — Vacherie, Louisiana.
Huguet, George — Convent, Louisiana.
Laiche, Mrs. Mathilde Bourgeois — Convent, Louisiana.
Part, Marcel — Convent, Louisiana.
Pertuit, Mrs. Clara Bourgeois — Convent, Louisiana.
Platz, Mrs. Clothilde Bourgeois — Convent, Louisiana.
Poché, Louis Aristée — Convent, Louisiana.
Poché, Mrs. Lezima Keller — Hester, Louisiana.
Poché, Marks — Belmont, Louisiana.
Reulet, Victor — Vacherie, Louisiana.
Rome, Roger — Romeville, Louisiana.
Sobral, Jacintha — Convent, Louisiana.
Subra, Mrs. Agnes Bourgeois — Convent, Louisiana.
Woods, Duralde — Lutcher, Louisiana.

# INDEX

**A**

Acadians vs. Creoles—53
Aime, Valcour—26, 27, 31, 37, 48, 49, 60, 82, 97, 140, 147, 156
Alexis, Grand Duke, visits Belmont Plantation—141
Amelia Plantation—58
Anisette—151
Antailla, Francisco—19
Arceneau, Jean—13
Arceneau, Joseph—13
Arceneau, Pierre—13
Arcenaux, Francois—41
Armant Family—24
Armant, Col. Leopold L.—60
Armant, J. B.—60
Armant, Gen. Seraphim—60
Ashland Plantation—144
Aubry, Capt. Chas. P.—13
Audé, Mother Eugenie—42, 79
Audubon, John J. Visits St. James—139
Azaquequa, Father—38

**B**

Bagatille Plantation—34, 144
Balot Family—24
Baton Rouge, Capture of, 1779 —47
Baudry, Jr. Octave, Died World War I—50
Blanpin, Sieur Joseph—6
Bean, E. N.—101
Beauvais, Jean Baptiste St. Gem—24
Belanger, Father Henri—43
Belmont Indian Mount—3
Belmont Plantation—140, 141
Bentley, L. E.—122
Bergeron, Germain—14, 15
Bergeron, Jean Baptiste—13
Bertaut, Auguste—65
Bessie K. Plantation—35
Blouin, Daniel—24, 90
Blouin, Daniel, Jr.—41
Blouin, Leon—120
Bocage Plantation—144
Boisjolies Plantation—36
Boucry, Madame—145
Boucry, Jean Baptiste—36, 52, 71
Boudreaux, Rev. Mother—44
Bouchard, Jeseph, "Tutor"—78
Bourg, Ben—37
Bourgeois, Joseph—13, 17
Bourgeois, Lionel—98
Bourgeois, Livian—91
Bourgeois, Paul—41
Breaux, Mye—42, 105
Bovee, George E.—122
Brignac, Mr. & Mrs. Alexandre (Charivari)—102
Bringier, Betsy—29
Bringier, Fraincoise—44
Bringier, Michel Douradou—140
Bringier, Marius Pons—29, 34, 37, 39, 44, 139, 140, 144
Brioche—131, 137
Broiard, Etienne—16
Burr, Hudson E.—91
Burthe, Dr. F.—82
Butler, Gen. Benj., Occupies St. James—48, 49

**C**

Cabanocey Plantation—35
Caillouet's Plantation—41

Cantrelle, Jacques—2, 7, 9, 16, 17, 20, 38, 46, 47, 59, 80, 88, 157, 162
Cantrelle, Michel—9, 20, 35, 41, 46, 58, 59, 89, 90, 91, 92, 94, 139
Carite, Mme.—35
Catholic Churches in St. James —156
Census—(1766) 162; (1769) 173; (1777) 183; (1807) 193
Census Enumerations—202
Chambon, Rev. C. M.—144
Chambon de la Tour, Father Gabriel—41
Chapdu, Louise—19, 20
Chapin, Adele Le Bourgeois—140
Charbonier Family—35
Charivari—102
Charleville, Helene Chauvin—24
Charleville, Joseph Chauvin—24
Charpentier, Jean—41
Chauvin Family—24, 25, 30, 69,, 71, 142
Chauvin, Charles—142, 144
Chauvin, Jacques—142
Chauvin, Pierre—30
Chenet, Pierre—5, 41, 113
Chenette, Francois—16
Cherry Bounce—136
Chiason, Miguel—19
Cholera—145
Choppin, Jules—84
Chouquette—130
Cirillo, Bishop—17
Civil War Soldiers—198
Coffee—132, 150
Colomb, Christofle—23
Colomb, Christophe—44, 45, 90, 139
Colomb Park—35
Constant, Jeseph—71
Conway, Maurice—3
Conway, William—90, 91
Cormier, Jean Baptiste—13
Court House—90, 91
Cox, George—37
Creoles—53
Croizet, Francois—13, 71

**D**

Daigle, Marie Josephe—31
Dalferes Family—58
d'Anceny, Marquis—6
Daspit, Oscar—98
Dautreive, Antoine Bernard—13
Deaths and Funerals—107
de Bellevue, Chevalier Grand—19
Debuys, Gaspard—89, 94
de Charost, Duke—6
de la Croix, Father—42, 79
de LEpinet—6
de Nechere, Bishop—42, 43
de Seneguey, Rene—84
Delery Family—69
Dicharry, Florian B.—120
Donaldson, William—91, 94
Dornier Brothers—36
Dornier, Joseph B.—92, 94
Dornier, Mme. Jules—52
Dornier, Mrs. Marie—52
Dorr, J. W., visits St. James in 1860—151
Dubourg, Archbishop—140

Dubourg, Louise E. Aglai—140
Dubourg, Martin—41
Ducroix, Sieur—14
Dufau, Louis—120
Dufresne Family—24
Dugas, Jean—13
Duhon, Francois—41
Duhon, Pierre—45
Dupart, Sieur—14
Durand Family—24
Duverney, Joseph Paris—31

**E**

Education, 62, 79, 84, 85, 86, 87, 145
Education, Superintendents of —87

**F**

Fabre, Joseph Laurent—71
Fagot Family—138
Fagot, Mrs. D.—44
Fagot, Samuel—28
Family Names—69, 70, 73
Ferry, Alexis—37
Flagil, Mme.—97
Flagil, Monsieur; his wine—150
Fortier, Alcee—48, 84, 123
Fowler, Richard—71
Frederick, Matthias—7, 11, 12
French Language—63

**G**

Gallitizin, Madame—81
Gallup, J. R.—101
Galvez, Governor—47
Games of Children—152
Gaudin, Bonaventure—17, 41
Gauthreaux, Louis—41
Gauthier, Celeste Palmyre—37
Gentil, Jean—84
Gentil, J. J., newspaper editor—23, 121
Godberry, Mrs.—44
Godchaux's Store—119, 146
Gombo—116, 134, 136
Gonzales, Evalina—58
Gordon, Capt. Henry—14
Goudain, Jean—71
Gramercy—35
Grand Jury, first—193
Gravois Family—4
Gray, Dr. Charles—55, 101
Gregoire—20
"Gris-gris"—124
Guedry, Joseph—13
Guillebeau, Joseph—13

**H**

Hale, Edward Everett, visits St. James—141
Hardy, Mother Aloysius—80
Hayward, Campbell—144
Hebert Family—72
Hebert Louis—72
Helvetia Plantation—35
Hermitage Plantation—144
Henry, Mrs. Eugenie Cantrelle Himel—17
Himel, Aline Cantrelle—17
Home Place Plantation—34
Hubert, Joseph—17
Huget, George—102
Hunsaker, A. F.—122
Indian Medicine Stone—4
Indian Tribes—1

— 209 —

## J

Jackson, Andrew, visits St. James—139
Jackson, M. T.—122
Jacobs Family—138
Jambalaya—66
James, Francis H.—34
Jefferson College—36, 37, 50, 62, 81; during Civil War, 48, 83; names of students (1865), 155
Jourdan, J. J.—35
Judice, Louis—14, 20, 78

## K

Karlsdorf, Dr. and Mrs. E.—144
Keller, Leon—74
Kenner, Duncan—36
Kerlerec, Governor—11
Kleibert, Adrien, died in World War I—50
Korean War, deaths—52

## L

La Boucherie—137
La Buissonniere, Alphonse—71, 72
Lagardere, A.—119
Lagniappe—100
Lagraine, Marie—110
Lambremont, P. M.—93
Landry, Capt. Prosper of Donaldsonville Artillery—58, 
Landry, Francois—17
Landry, Joseph—80, 90, 91, 94
Landry, Lazzard L., died in World War I—50
Lapagenier, Capt. F. E.—50
Laplanche, Fillette—19
Lasseigne, Alcide C., died in World War I—50
La Touissaint—104
Le Blanc, Alexander—16
LeBlanc, Silvain—41
LeBlanc, Simon—13, 17
LeBourgeois Family—140
LeBourgeois, Mr. J.—44
LeBourgeois, Louis—42, 91
Loisel Family—24
Louis Phillipe, visits St. James—45
Lourdes Grotto—44
Louviere Family—24
Lusson, Father Charles—41

## M

Mansan, Rev. Patrick—17
Manuel Family—24
Marigny from New Orleans, La.—139
Marist Society—43, 44, 50
Marlarcher, Chevalier—23, 128
Malarcher, Louis—41
Marriages at Cabahannoce (1766-1768)—194
Martin, Ambroise—13, 17
Martin, Desirée—84
Martin, Gordon—94
Mary of Jefferson College—56
Mather, James—71
Mattingly, Dr. Walter—144
Maurin, Antoine—24, 91
Mazureau, Etienne—82
Melancon, Etienne—41
Menny, J. B., educator—79, 85
Menuet, Henri, School Teacher—78
Mercier Family—24
Mericq, Dr. Cazimir B.—37

Michel, Joseph—41
Michel, Pierre—41
Militia—Cabahanocer (1766), 161; First Acadian Coast, 180; Officers of (1808), 194
Millet, J. O.—151
Mimi Zelia—42, 43
Mire, Camille—101
Mollere, Louis—90
Montegut, Dr. Joseph—16
Morey, Charles—119
Moss—115
Mt. Airy Plantation—3, 35
Mouton, Jean—12
Mouton, Louis—12
Mouton, Salvador—11, 12

## N

Names of Families—69, 70, 73
Names of Plantations—75, 76
New Orleans, Battle of—47
Newspaper Publishers—122
New Year's Celebrations—154
Nicolle, Tecle—34
Nita Crevasse—96

## O

Oak Alley Plantation—31, 35, 58
Ockmann Family—67
Ockmann, Henry, War Hero—51
Official Directory of St. James—200, 203
O'Reilly, Gov., visits St. James—21

## P

Panherne, Marguerite—16
Pape Vert—35, 142, 143, 144
Part, Marcel—121
Peltier Family—24
Perique Tobacco—113
Pertuis Family—24
Petrimonet, Jean Baptiste—41
Peyroux de Rochemolive, Marie Jean G.—19
Peytavin, John L.—84
Physicians in St. James—156
Picou, Jean Baptiste—41
Pierre, in service of St. Michel—45
Piroteau, Sieur—14
Plantation Names—75
Plantation Owners (1845-1856)—197
Poché Family—71
Poché Anastasie—94
Poché, Felix P.—93, 101
Poché, Jacques—71
Poeyfarré, Jean Baptiste—71
Poirier, Michel—13
Potts, Dr. & Mrs. R. H.—144
Pralines—131, 135
Public Schools—84, 85, 86, 87

## Q

Quarante-Poules, Mme.—83

## R

Racing, Horse—151
Rapidan Plantation—36
Reconstruction Era in St. James—50, 92
Rémy, Henri—84, 159
Reine, Etienne—41
Rémy, Hubert—71
Rémy, L.—89
Reynes, Etienne—90
Richard, Denis—55, 101

Roman Family—31, 33
Roman, Alfred—48, 84
Roman, Gov. André B.—19, 31, 57, 82, 93
Roman, Jacques Telespore—31, 32
Roman, Louise—33
Rome Family—74
Roussel, Christofle—41, 118
Roussel, Christophe—118
Rouzan, Francois Meffre—71
Roy, Abraham—13
Ru, Father Paul—4

## S

Sacred Heart Convent—62, 79, 87, 145
Sagamité—134
St. Jacques de Cabahanocer—16, 38
St. James Parish, it's name—20
St. Joseph Plantation—35, 37
St. Michael's Convent—80
St. Michel de Cantrelle Church—24, 41, 146, 202
St. Michel de Cantrelle pastors—201
St. Rose Plantation—35
Sarrodet, Mrs. Atole—98
Saunier, Jean—13
Schexnaydre, A.—17
Schexnaydre Name Spellings—73
Scott, W. C.—90
Shannon, Mother of Sacred Heart—39, 48, 49
Sheppard, J. H.—82
Sibley, Dr. John—36
Simon Family—37
Slave, ad for run-a-way—128
Sobral, Antoine J.—58
Spanish-American War—200
Stein Family—67
Stewart, Mrs. Andrew—33
Superintendents of Education—87
Superstitions—126

## T

Taxpayers of Ct. James (1808)—194
Terrell, Justin—71
Tessier Family—24
Tete, B.—71
Tezcuco Plantation—144
Theriot, Pierre—41
Thibodaux, Mrs. Lillie Trust Gray—55
Thibodaux, Lucian—55
Tremoulet Family—35
Tureaud, Judge Augustin D.—23, 29, 89, 91, 140
Trudeau, Francois—71
Trudeau, Marie Théres—71
Trudeaux, Zenon—36, 37

## U

Uncle Sam Plantation—28, 138
Union Plantation—144
Uriell, Patrice—71

## V

Vacharie—67, 68
Valentin, Father—16
Vavaseur Family—36, 82
Verret, Marguerite—38
Verret, Nicholas—8, 14, 19, 20, 22, 86, 88, 89, 139, 161
Vetiver—117
Vigneries, Frank—55

— 210 —

## W

Waguespack, Felician—35
Waguespack, Stanislaus—37
War in Korea, deaths—52
Weather Record, old—147
Webre Family—4, 5, 74
Webre Brothers in Civil War—48
Webre, Joseph—67
Webre, Walter B., died in World War I—50
Webre, Vasseur—45
Wederstrand, Robert—89
Welham Plantation—35, 44, 74
White Hall Plantation—29, 37, 74, 140, 144
Wine—149
Woods, Mrs. Alwyn—116
World War I, deaths—50
World War II, deaths—51

## Y

Yellow Fever—145

## Z

Zelia, Mimi—42, 43
Zeller Family—67

www.ingramcontent.com/pod-product-compliance
Lightning Source LLC
Chambersburg PA
CBHW031139160426
43193CB00008B/191